The People, Press, and Politics of CROATIA

Stjepan Malović
and Gary W. Selnow

PRAEGER

Westport, Connecticut
London

Library of Congress Cataloging-in-Publication Data

Malović, Stjepan.
    The people, press, and politics of Croatia / Stjepan Malović and Gary W. Selnow.
      p. cm.
    Includes bibliographical references and index.
    ISBN 0–275–96543–0 (alk. paper)
    1. Mass media—Political aspects—Croatia. 2. Press and politics—Croatia. 3.
Croatia—Politics and government—1990– I. Selnow, Gary W. II. Title.
    P95.82.C87M35   2001
    302.23'094972—dc21   00–064946

British Library Cataloguing in Publication Data is available.

Library of Congress Catalog Card Number: 00–064946
ISBN: 0–275–96543–0

First published in 2001

Praeger Publishers, 88 Post Road West, Westport, CT 06881
An imprint of Greenwood Publishing Group, Inc.
www.praeger.com

Printed in the United States of America

The paper used in this book complies with the
Permanent Paper Standard issued by the National
Information Standards Organization (Z39.48–1984).

10 9 8 7 6 5 4 3 2 1

Contents

Part V: Public Input and Globalization in Croatia's Future

Abbreviations

ABA	American Bar Association
AED	Academy for Educational Development
CJA	Croatian Journalists' Association
CPJ	Committee to Protect Journalists
DTP	desktop publishing
EPH	Europress Holding Company
EU	European Union
GONG	"Gradani organizirano nadziru glasovanje" ("Citizens are monitoring the elections in an organized way")
HAK	Croatian Automobile Club
HDZ	a political party
HHO	Croatian Helsinki Committee for Human Rights
HINA	Croatian Informative News Agency
HIS	Croatian Information Service
HP	Croatian Post
HRTV	a television station
HSLS	Croatian Social Liberal Party
IBRD	World Bank
ICEJ	International Center for Education of Journalists
ICTY	International Criminal Tribunal for the Former Yugoslavia
IFEX	International Freedom of Expression Exchange

IFJ	International Federation of Journalists
IKA	Informative Catholic Agency
IPI	International Press Institute
IRC	International Rescue Commission
IREX	Independent Research Exchange Commission
IRI	International Republican Institute
ISP	Internet Service Provider
JNA	Yugoslav National (People's) Army
JRT	Yugoslav Radio and Television
MUP	a secret service agency
NDH	Independent Croatian State
NDI	National Democratic Institute
NGOs	nongovernmental organizations
OSCE	Organization for Security and Cooperation in Europe
OSI	Open Society Institute
OTV	Open Television
RAP	Return Assistance Program
RSF	Reporters sans Frontiers (the International Federation of Journalists)
SDP	Social Democrat Party
SO	strategic objective
SONS	a secret service agency
SSRN	Socialist Union of the Working People (Socijalistički savez radnog naroda)
ST	*Slobodni tjednik*
SZUP	a secret service organization
TASS	official news agency of the Soviet Union from 1925 to 1991
TI	Transparency Institute
UDBA	Yugoslav Secret Service Police
UNHCR	UN High Commissioner for Refugees
UNPA	UN protected areas
UNPROFOR	UN peacekeeping forces
USAID	United States Agency for International Development
USIS	United States Information Service
VONS	a secret service agency
WAN	World Association of Newspapers
WAZ	West Allgemaine Zeitung
WTN	Worldwide Television News

Introduction

A popular government, without popular information or the means of acquiring it, is but a Prologue to a Farce or a Tragedy; or perhaps both.

James Madison

Madison's theatrical reference to a people without a free press could have been written for Croatia. Both the tragedy and the farce have been played out over the recent past in that troubled land. Act I was the tragedy of iron censorship under Tito. Act II was the farce wherein censorship masqueraded as press freedom under Tuđman.

Happily, the first act ended with Tito's death, and the curtain came down on the second with Tuđman's demise in 2000. Today, the curtain is just rising on Act III, the birth of free expression and, with it, Madison's dream of a popular government, popular information, and the means of acquiring it. The pivotal word, however, is *dream*. From the actions backstage of the newly elected Parliament—a slim democratic majority over Tuđman's Croatian Democratic Union (HDZ) party—one senses a new politics. And from the landslide victory of independents in the presidential campaign—almost 70 percent of the people voted against the HDZ candidate in the primary—a new day of press freedom may be in the offing as well. Or—and this must be said during the "gestation" period for the prodemocracy forces—the dream could turn into a nightmare, because such has been the case in the past.

Before the trumpets of the new democratic Croatia sound, therefore, we should carefully scrutinize the conditions in the Balkan drama that led through the years to this hopeful era of more liberal journalism. Those press relationships began earlier in Tito's Yugoslavia, relaxed a bit during the troubled years of the Croatian republic, and hardened once again in the new nation emerging under strongman Tuđman after the horrific war of the early nineties. We always bear in mind, Americans especially, that Croatia lost 250,000 lives in a short war that spewed forth 2.5 million refugees. In such a climate of blood and fear, it is unseemly for outsiders to stand in judgment on the news professionals who often caved in to ominous threats. We can only admire the bravery of the few who put their careers, sometimes their lives, on the line.

If the new democracy is not to sink back into tragedy or farce, the warning signals of censorship must be heeded. The possibility that new leaders may merely rearrange the press furniture backstage and return to the old ways of state control or independent but impotent media has to be around the clock concern much like the nervousness of a householder as he sets the burglar alarm in a high crime area.

This book traces the ringing down of the curtains on both the Tito and Tuđman regimes as they sought to control the news and information carried by newspapers, magazines, radio, and television, while courageous and clever journalists resisted their censorship tooth and nail.[1] That legacy is appraised as it bears upon this freshly born, but fragile, democracy.

In Part I, we will describe the repressive tactics of Tuđman's HDZ party toward each segment of the media (chapter 1, "The Media Situation under Tuđman") and briefly review the election of a new parliament and president following the dictator's death (chapter 2, "Victory for Democracy: A Dream Fulfilled or a False Hope?").

In Part II, we look at the great divide between the idea of a free press (chapter 3) and a controlled one (chapter 4) and contrast the ideas of Locke, Madison, and others with the nationalistic mindset of the Tuđman era. Then in chapter 5, we describe the hangover of media control, the agonizing self-censorship foisted upon reporters.

In Part III, we will see how publishers and reporters threw off the shackles of state control, first in chapter 6, "Rise of the Press, the Fall of the Secret Services," and then in chapter 7, a case study, both ludicrous and revealing, of the forty-one days during which Tuđman was dying and a free press was being born.

Part IV examines the background of the Tito legacy, the brief period of the Croatian republic with a relatively free press (chapter 8), the effect of the war on reportage (chapter 9), and then the postwar censorship of the Tuđman era (chapter 10).

Part V concludes the book with an account of public attitudes as conditioned by the ethics of reporters, the international community, and, finally, the new technology built on the Internet. Chapter 11 details the conflicting values of reporters, editors, and journalists. Chapter 12 deals with the responsibility of the Croatian people themselves for their own destiny. Chapter 13 looks at the impact of the international community, and chapter 14 ventures into the great unknown, the new world of uncontrollable communication, the Internet, and how it has affected and will affect the press in Croatia and the Balkans at large. Predictably unpredictable, the Net will rain its blessings (and curses) on the just and the unjust, but it will undoubtedly bring volatility.

After only a brief run of the new democratic Croatia, it is impossible, at the time of this writing, to predict its stability and endurance. But, put simply, the free press of the new democratic Croatia of 2000 and beyond will be shaped in large part by the old realities: the tragedy under Tito, the farce under Tuđman, and the new democracy tied to a shaky economy, a shaky infrastructure, and a very shaky hold on the dynamics of free expression. Much depends upon the grit of the people themselves. Madison might have said the same thing about the fledgling nation he helped to launch.

NOTE

1. Often the name of a company and the name of a newspaper or journal are the same. To avoid confusion for the reader, the name of a company is set in roman type and the name of a newspaper or journal is set in italic type. For example, Novi list is the name of a company and *Novi list* is the name of a newspaper.

PART I

A WATERSHED IN CROATIAN POLITICS

The Media Situation under Tuđman

Franjo Tuđman's death, Stipe Mesić's rise to power, and the ascension of the opposition in Parliament all hold out the extraordinary promise of change in Croatia. Expectations within the country and among outside observers are that the new leadership will relax constraints on the press, abandon nationalistic philosophies, and embrace public input for a genuine democracy never before witnessed in this former Communist country.

During this short transition, at the end of 1999 and the beginning of 2000, the people were swept into a national euphoria heightened by the disbelief that such monumental changes could take place so quickly. The previous year had been one of the most repressive of the Tuđman era, and thus the contrasts during the transition were even more remarkable. But Croatians have been on such highs before: notably, after the fall of Communism in 1991, as they anticipated the national rebirth under Tuđman; then after the war in 1995, as they reveled in hopes of peace and rapid stabilization of national life.

None of that public euphoria proved to be warranted, however, and the future now is no more certain. The economy remains horribly crippled, international relations need substantial patch work, and public institutions, racked by decades of neglect and mismanagement, will take years to reclaim. In short, Croatia's recovery has been launched, but its long-term trajectory is not assured.

If this view appears overly pessimistic, you must set your "history channel" back to the period between the two "Ts"—Tito and Tuđman. Those were the critical years in which the present relationships among the press, the people, and the political system in Croatia took form. These three elements were mutually depressing and progressively destructive to the fabric of society. Political leaders restrained the press and the people. The press became a promotional extension of the government. The people, cowered by the government and ignored by the press, demanded little from either institution. It was negative synergy, a cycle of complacency, compliance, and control.

The key to democratic change may well have been Tuđman's departure and his party's decline, but whether that was sufficient for long-term change in the complex relationship among the people, the press, and politics is unknown. Those relationships prior to Tuđman's death, however, left deep scars and open wounds that must be healed, lest Croatia lapse into the repressive old ways that still fester in the Balkans and its neighbors.

THE MEDIA SITUATION UNDER TUĐMAN

From all outward signs, during the 1990s, the media in Croatia truly were free, and the flow of news and information genuinely was open. First-time visitors were impressed by the busy newsstands with an inventory of papers and magazines that rivaled many in the Western world, and they were wowed by the convincing lineup of radio and television news shows that dominated much of the programming day. The volume and variety of papers and programs of news and information, made a prima facie case that this former Communist country embraced an open media and fostered a robust marketplace of ideas.

In fact, that evidence was deceptive. With a wily touch, the state party controlled the press and broadcasting with an invisible hand. The ownership and editorial structures of the media in Croatia and the coercive laws and government strong-arm tactics told the true story.

The dominant newspaper *Večernji list*, was influenced strongly by the leading political party, the HDZ.[1] This large, daily paper shamelessly promoted the views of the HDZ while suppressing or attacking the policies of the Croatian opposition. Several other papers with significant press runs were tied one way or another to the party, and these, like *Večernji list*, peddled the government's line and told the government's version of news to the exclusion of other viewpoints.[2]

As bad as conditions were for print, for broadcast they were worse. Croatian law crippled independent broadcasters and sanctioned only one network (HRTV). Inasmuch as HRTV was run by, for, and about the leading party, it was hardly surprising that the staff, from top to bottom, adhered to a policy that no story, no point of view, no public figure made it onto the air unless it bolstered the party image, proclaimed the party virtues, set the party agenda.[3]

Public surveys revealed that 90 percent of the Croatian people obtained all or nearly all of their news from HRTV.[4] Naturally, HDZ took comfort in such statistics, because all its bases were covered: The commanding print and broadcast media were squarely in the government's pocket.

If these few powerful media stood as Croatia's only options, the stark media presence would quickly have exposed the truth about government control. In fact, the sheer profusion of papers and channels that operated so conspicuously throughout the land created the illusion of a free press, so it was ironic that the media themselves became part of the deception.

Newspapers

All independent newspapers were muzzled,[5] not by censors in the dark of night, whose machinations would have triggered the wrath of reporters everywhere, but through two subtle mechanisms: distribution controls and legal restraints.[6]

Distribution Controls

The government controlled the distribution channels from the printing plants to the street corners. Tisak, a centralized distributorship whose owner was a charter member of the leading party, operated the pipeline for newspapers and magazines.[7] If Tisak closed the tap, publishers withered, there being nowhere else to turn for another distributor. They had to fall in line or go out of business. That was the leverage, and Tisak was known to keep up the pressure on dissident publishers in a number of ways.

One of the company's mean-spirited tricks was to hide offending papers from public view. Editors or writers who transgressed against the party would find that their writing never had an audience because their papers were never sold.

Another ploy was the delivery of offending press runs to remote villages, a practice that, like hiding the papers, imposed a double penalty in that the papers failed to reach the audiences for whom they were intended, and the revenues for an entire day's production would be lost. For shoestring operations, like most independents in Croatia, the loss of a few days' revenue was bruising. Sooner or later, defiant publishers had to yield to the pressure of the bottom line or be driven out of business; either way, HDZ maintained its invisible grip on the country's publishers.

The variations on this sorry theme were endless. One was to withhold sales revenues. In these cases, Tisak, which collected money at the point of sale, simply failed to pay the publisher for papers sold. The unpaid publisher then had to go to court to complain about the shakedown, but sluggish courts made it impossible for quick redress of disputes, and as "little guys" everywhere know, justice postponed is justice denied. The paper was simply starved out of existence.

One of the most celebrated cases involved the *Feral Tribune*, which dared to ridicule the president, his family, and the ruling party. The government had long had it in for *Feral*, and this time it withheld more than half a million dollars (3.2 million kuna) of the paper's sales revenue. That would have been the knockout punch, but the party censors had not counted on *Feral*'s international visibility. Under considerable pressure from international free press organizations and foreign governments, Tisak settled part of the bill late in 1998 but still held back several hundred thousand dollars (1.5 million kuna). Other papers, not so visible in the public limelight, would have buckled from this financial assault.

Finally, if neither hiding, misdistribution, nor withholding revenue worked, Tisak could demand substantial distribution fees, usually in excess of 20 percent of revenue, to be paid up front. This meant that cash-strapped publishers had to budget not only for staff and publication costs, but also for prepaid distribution, all before the company sold its first paper. In effect, for many would-be publishers, the fee became an insurmountable threshold of entry.[8]

All of these censorious devices were practiced without outward restrictions so that the many papers stocking city newsstands subtly masked Tisak's coercions. The public, by and large, was unaware of the methods by which the state controlled free political expression. Who would have told them about the tactics on and off the streets and about the financial blackmail that ultimately forced the independents to toe the line? Sooner or later, the defiant ones yielded. Public outrage was prevented because public knowledge was denied. Were some paper to blow the whistle, who would believe it? After all, the constitution itself guaranteed a free press.

Legal Restraints

Articles 71 and 191 of the Croatian penal code made Croatia the only country in Europe where journalists could be locked up for "slander or insult to the character of the President [or of other officers[9]] of the republic." Reporters can be sued by officials for causing "mental anguish," and they can be jailed for the "spread of information liable to generate concern in the majority of the population."[10] "Insult," "mental anguish," and "concern" are low thresholds of offense by almost any definition of those terms. Void of fixed legal meanings, they become opportunistic weapons in the government's hands for harassing anyone they don't like.

Those laws were not mere withering vestiges of Communist rule. Most of the articles were enacted in 1996, after having been previously abolished in 1991. The "mental anguish" law took effect in 1998.

The administration of these rules had been vigorous. The U.S. government reported in 1999 that more than 300 criminal prosecutions and 600 civil proceedings were underway against the country's journalists.[11]

Should a journalist beat the rap in lower court, prosecutors had the right to appeal acquittals, thereby exposing litigants to double jeopardy. This was in direct contradiction to the laws and legal practices of nearly every Western nation. At the time of this writing, none of the restrictive laws have been repealed, although it is uncertain if they have been enforced since Stipe Mesić assumed the presidency.

No reporter can predict which words he writes will offend or who will be offended. Moreover, truth is no defense in such matters. Ironically, factually correct stories may be even more vulnerable to challenge, because truth, more than fiction, may insult the state and cause anguish and concern among party leaders. In most of the lawsuits against Croatian journalists, the *potential for harm* to officials was the measure of the offense, and the *validity of a story* offered no protection.

This standard turned journalism on its head: The government's most egregious offenses, which warranted the greatest public exposure, were the least likely to be reported, precisely because their public disclosure stood to create, in the offenders, the greatest discomfort.

By contrast, most Western countries long ago recognized the standard of truth in defense of journalistic reporting. Exceptions, when they exist, deal with state and military secrets and not with offenses against the sensitivities of public officials.

Worse, these sanctions against journalists who run afoul of the law are no mere slaps on the wrists. Punishments can include multimillion-dollar fines, closing of newspaper offices, and jail time. Such punitive actions destroy the foundation of a functioning democracy, which must have public access to information on which voters can make sound electoral decisions. This was a point made more than 200 years ago by James Madison and noted in a proceeding against *Feral Tribune* journalists Viktor Ivančić and Marinko Čulić:[12] "The power to prosecute libel of public officials ought to produce universal alarm, because it was leveled against the rights of freely examining public characters and measures, and of free communication of the people thereon, which has ever been justly deemed the only effectual guardian of every other right."[13]

Broadcast

In contrast to the Tuđman government's sometimes ham-fisted control of newspapers, its licensing lock on broadcasters was more elegant and decisive. Irrevocable rules, inequitably applied, determined who got licenses, how stations were run, and what programs were permitted to air. Licensing requirements firmly limited how Croatian broadcasters lined up their programming and covered the news. Inordinately high concession fees prevented many would-be broadcasters from entering the market.

Regarding this system, the U.S. State Department reports that broadcasters were held to strict taboos, which spelled out "topics that may not be discussed, persons [who] may not appear, voices [that] may not be heard, and persons and political moves that may not be criticized."[14]

Faultfinding of the president, his policies, or his person would have been foolish, for he was sacrosanct in the law. Even prominent coverage of the opposition during a political campaign, normal for Western media and vital to democracies, could have cost Croatian broadcasters their licenses, hardly a prescription for a level playing field.

Broadcast media are governed by the Public Information Act, the Croatian Radio and Television Act, and the Telecommunication Act. These laws direct stations to allocate 60 percent of their airtime to "Croatian programs." Under

Tuđman, with no guiding definition of a Croatian program, stations were not able to determine if, at some time, by some definition, their shows could get them in trouble. Further, the acts (changed under Mesić) prohibited the formation of independent radio or television networks. Under the previous party, this ensured that no broadcaster became too big or too powerful or even threatening to the absolute dominance of party-run HRTV. Isolated and controlled by state transmitters and relays, independent stations had no way to configure an integrated broadcasting system.

The coercive broadcast laws were administered at will by a nine-seat Telecommunications Council that allocated and revoked private radio and television concessions. HDZ party members occupied five of the nine seats—with that composition, there was rarely suspense over pending decisions.

One of the best-known cases of broadcast control was the government's repression of Radio 101, an independent radio station in Croatia. With an ownership and editorial board that was not afraid to criticize the party, the station found itself in hot water in November 1996. The Telecommunications Council had already rejected, for the third time, the station's application for a long-term operating license. Ordinarily, that might have been the end of the story, but bringing to mind the case of *Feral*, intense national and international pressures began to build after license denial. Perhaps to preserve the fiction of a free press, the council provisionally approved the license several months later. It wasn't about to cave in, however, and it stipulated that the station move its transmitter to a different location prescribed by the Ministry of Maritime Affairs. Broadcasting from this new site, it turns out, would have reduced Radio 101's coverage to 50 percent of its original Zagreb market. Nibbling away at freedom, the government's concession was not cost-free.

Bruising stories in the world press led to an unprecedented demonstration by 100,000 people in Zagreb's bana Jelačića Square. Finally, in the face of intense public pressure (an unprecedented event), Radio 101 was allowed to broadcast from its old transmitter. Sadly for free-media advocates and citizens of Zagreb, Radio 101 also ceded ground. The station switched to a bland mix of pop music and banal news, hardly the courageous journalism that initially provoked government irritation and galvanized public support.

The practical result of draconian licensing laws, of a stacked administrative council, and of extraordinary concession fees was the overwhelming dominance of HRTV, party-run radio and television. This government network—which pays no fees and receives two-thirds of its revenues from forced subscription charges[15]—blankets the country through three radio and television channels. Its governing board, which under Tuđman was packed with party operatives—no surprise there—oversaw every administrative and editorial decision, ensuring the party's absolute control.[16] To no one's wonder, the government, especially its president and senior cabinet officers and generals, enjoyed glowing coverage, while opposition parties and government critics remained hopelessly locked out. For their invisibility, political outsiders suffered public obscurity—out of sight was out of mind.

The biases of state-run broadcasting inflicted the greatest damage in the days and weeks preceding an election. This is the hallowed time before the vote when public attention fixes on political affairs and electoral decisions solidify. The faithful are reinforced and the undecided at long last choose up sides. In Croatia, where nine of ten people get their news from television and paid advertising is not yet possible, the anchor desk becomes a pulpit and the news story serves as gospel.

That makes the numbers even more ominous. Press Now reports that, in the days leading up to the (1997) presidential election, the main daily news show provided President Tuđman eight to twelve times more coverage than the other two candidates combined.[17] In one key period during that 1997 election, the Organization for Security and Cooperation in Europe (OSCE, 1997) reported that the evening news program gave Tuđman 300 times the coverage it gave to the second-place candidate.[18]

Peter Galbraith, former U.S. ambassador to Croatia, said that he raised this matter with the head of Croatian television, who argued that HRTV was more than generous, because it actually gave more airtime to the opposition's campaign than it gave to Tuđman's campaign. His claim was predicated on a deceptive definition of "campaigning." As government broadcasters saw it, Tuđman rarely campaigned, because his speeches, ribbon cuttings, banquets, and baby kissing were official presidential functions, whereas his opponents "campaigned" with every breath. By HRTV's ciphering, a prime-time hour of Tuđman's speeches was balanced by a fifteen second clip of the opposition aired at midnight.[19]

Faced with dirty tricks of this caliber, the OSCE final report declared the election "free, but not fair." In Croatia, independent news shows never mentioned this report. HRTV news quoted OSCE as saying the election was "free."[20] Somehow, they could not squeeze in the words "not fair."

Availability of News and Information

Control of the Croatian media was undeniable.[21] Outside observers and savvy insiders who had access to the facts, knowledge of the laws and information about the lawsuits, the jailings, the boarding up of print and broadcast facilities clearly saw that censorship masqueraded as freedom. For the Croatian public, though, the iron hand on information was invisible. That is always the problem with control of the media: The people can't know what they're missing.

The real trouble with Croatian media control was its reliance upon self-censorship. What stories had been dropped for fear of a press-run going to the dump? What news about political opponents got swept from cutting room floors because of threats to a license? What opinions had been sacrificed to avoid yet another lawsuit?

Self-censorship does the despot's job for him, then goes him one better, slicing a little deeper, stepping back from the line a little further, killing the spirit when journalists limit their own curiosities and curb their own interests, at first to elude the censor's wrath, but later to avoid facing their own culpability. Eventually, the spirit withers, the new, more timid standards calcify, and practitioners of self-censorship concede to the restrictions they themselves help set.

So under the Tuđman government, we end where we began, with the newsstands brimming with publications and the TV channels flush with programming. Such a façade. The conspiracy of abundance cloaked the truth. The destructive effects of so many publishers and broadcasters eager to put out a product concealed the blighted laws, the councils, the hooligans, the lawsuits, and a general climate that smothered free expression and shuttered an open society.

That, in a nutshell, was the state of media in the 1990s, and the flow of news and information in this former Communist country under the previous HDZ government. Media practices were set in force more than a decade ago by a government so unsure of its own legitimacy that it feared the very presence of a free press.[22] For their part, the media surrendered long ago; an occasional rebel arose to test the government's resolve, only to be slapped down again. Examples had to be made of them.

The final piece in this jigsaw puzzle of media control was the Croatian people. From one point of view, they were at the end of the whip, the hapless readers of empty newspapers, the clueless viewers of lopsided broadcasts. Yet, they were not mere victims, for they shared some of the guilt. With rare exceptions, like the Radio 101 protest, the people had not demanded a free press. They never cried out for media access to government affairs or for even-handed coverage of political campaigns.

Every day, the large majority of the population, without objection, laid down its cash for *Večernji list*, the state-influenced newspaper, then hurried home to watch HRTV, the state-run television network. Every day, the people willingly absorbed the government's version of the truth without demanding another point of view.

Was the hunger for free speech too much to have expected? After all, the people had no experience with an aggressive press, no knowledge of First Amendment guarantees, no robust models to guide them. For generations, their media had served dictatorships, not democracies. Where would they have obtained the notion that a free press and an open government need one another if such an idea wasn't in their history, their textbooks, or their consciousness? Only a small portion of the world's population has any heritage of press freedom, and it was unknown in this part of Europe.

Even if the people understood the co-dependency of media and government in functional democracies, how would they have understood their own role in such a system? Democracy and free media are attached to a rope that the people must pull for themselves. Pushing won't do. The success of an open society ultimately depends on the people. Without righteous anger, nothing can change. Supreme Court Justice Brandeis once wrote, "The greatest menace to freedom is an inert people."[23] Tyranny may be less a threat than indifference. Outside governments and well-meaning free-press organizations can train the journalists, coax the government, and hold forth promises of world fellowship, but in the end, it is the people who must pull the rope. They are the ones who must support the papers that probe and challenge and dissent. They are the ones who must choose the broadcasts that put official feet to the fire, and they are the ones who must elect a government that, at long last, lifts its thumb from the press's throat.

Tuđman's final year held three elements that may finally have pushed the people into demanding change. First, corruption of the HDZ, and the president specifically, had become a public spectacle. Oddly, it was a soccer scandal (see chapter 6 for details) that finally drew people's attention to the party's manipulations. The government's clumsy handling of the crisis finally gave the media an opportunity to break open the story and give people a window into the corruption that pervaded Croatian politics.

The uncharacteristic media aggression in coverage of this story provided the second element in the public demand for a new government. Although broadcasters remained mute on the subject, newspapers had a field day with government leaks and phone taps and other unethical and illegal practices. The fact that newspapers got away with such stories gave the people a sense that something new and liberating was afoot.

Finally, Tuđman's damaged character (he was caught personally involved in the scandal) and his failing health converged to weaken his own and his party's authority. The iron grasp loosened, the opposition found new strength, and the media joined merrily in the anticipation of a new leadership and new freedoms. We discuss this extraordinary period in chapter 7.

Where will Croatia go from here? It's anyone's guess. There is no precedent and no way of knowing how the government, installed in January 2000, is likely to steer the country. Sadly, Stipe Mesić and his parliamentary majority did not institute immediate provisions to ensure against the kind of control exercised by Tuđman and the HDZ. Many observers believe such revisions are necessary to ensure Croatia's economic, political, and social progress, but such wisdom is often lost on leaders in this region.

NOTES

1. *Večernji list* was owned by the Caritas Limited Fund, located in the Virgin Islands, although the owners of this company have not been identified and remain unknown. The Croatian Pension Fund, which owned over 50 percent of the shares of *Večernji list*, sold them in January 1998 to the unknown investors for 20 million deutsche marks. *Večernji list* remains the best-selling daily in Croatia, with an estimated 130,000 copies sold daily, although official data report 200,000 daily copies.

2. The other media companies included *Vjesnik, Slobodna Dalmacija, Nedjeljna Dalmacija, Glas Slavonije*, and *Hrvatski obzor* (newspaper).

3. Broadcasting laws are set forth in three acts: the Public Information Act, the Croatian Radio and Television Act, and the Telecommunication Act.

4. The survey company, Puls, reported that 90 percent of people questioned got their news from HRTV.

5. Media are considered to be independent if they are free of editorial influence by the state.

6. A number of independent observers have reported on government control of Croatia's press. The Organization for Security and Cooperation in Europe (OSCE) has been a particularly vocal critic. An example of OSCE's criticism can be seen in "OSCE slams muzzling of printed media in Croatia," November 20, 1998, posted on a Press Now website: <http://www.dds.nl/~pressnow/medial/kroatie/981120.html>.

7. Tisak was owned by Miroslav Kutle, a powerful member of the HDZ and a close personal friend of President Franjo Tuđman. In 1999, Kutle was caught in a scandal involving the Dubrovačka banka (see chapter 6, n.2), and the government had no choice but to remove him from ownership of Tisak.

8. The advance payment serves as an effective bond against journalistic practices offensive to the government, and from the purely business point of view, it's a tax-free loan to Tisak.

9. The other officers include: the prime minister, the president of Parliament, the president of the Constitutional Council and the president of the Supreme Court.

10. Information from Reporters sans Frontiers. February 1, 1999, on website: <http://www.ifex.org/alert/00004181.html>.

11. Bureau of Democracy, Human Rights, and Labor, U.S. Department of State. "Croatia Country Report on Human Rights Practices for 1998, on website: <http://www.state.gov/www.global/human_rights/1998_hrp_report/croatia.html>.

12. "Brief, Presented by James C. Goodale, from the Committee to Protect Journalists in Support of Defendants Viktor Ivančić and Marinko Čulić," presented to the Municipal Judge, Country Court in Zagreb, Croatia, regarding Indictment Proposal No. KT-8848/96. Document provided on website: <http://www.cph.org/attcks96/sreports/croatia.html>.

13. James Madison, "Mr. Madison's Report of 1799 on the Kentucky-Virginia Resolutions," presented to the General Assembly of Virginia, January 7, 1800. See website: <http://www.nidlink.com/~bobhard/madison.html>.

14. From Press Now excerpting "Human Rights Report for 1997," Bureau of Democracy, Human Rights, and Labor, U.S. Department of State, January 30, 1998.

15. Taxpayer subsidies account for two-thirds of HRTV's gross revenues. Reported in "Croatia Country Report on Human Rights Practices for 1998," Bureau of Democracy, Human Rights, and Labor, U.S. Department of State, February 26, 1999.

16. A (1997) law reducing the number of members of Parliament on the HRTV Council from fourteen of eighteen to ten of twenty-three did almost nothing to alter government control over the network, because Parliament retained the authority to nominate and confirm all other members on the council. Reported in "Croatia Country Report on Human Rights Practices for 1998," Bureau of Democracy, Human Rights, and Labor, U.S. Department of State, February 26, 1999.

17. Press Now, citing 1997 OSCE report.

18. Ibid.

19. Ambasssador Peter Galbraith in an interview with Gary Selnow on November 10, 1997:

I raised this with the head of Croatian television and radio, and he said, "Well, we were covering Tuđman as the president and, actually, if you look at the campaign coverage, the opposition got more coverage than Tuđman the candidate." But this coverage included 8.5 minutes of Tuđman opening a road. I tried to explain how we do it in the United States. For instance, in this last election, everyone in this last election thought President Clinton was going to win. Even so, the networks made a point of trying to give equal coverage to both candidates. And, if Clinton did something presidential, which after all was the oldest trick in the book if you're the incumbent, they'd still show Dole doing whatever he did on that day, or they would get a Republican reaction to whatever the presidential act was. All this was something they still have to learn.

20. Press Now, citing 1997 OSCE report.

21. The following measure of press freedom was a composite of four media-related characteristics. With a score of 63, the Croatian media environment falls into the category of "Not free." (From the Freedom House Survey of Press Freedom, 1997, released April 1997. See <www.freedomhouse.org/ratings>.)

	A	B	C	D
Broadcast	12	10	2	1
Print	12	12	9	5

Total: 63

Press Freedom Rating: Not Free

Scale: 1–15

A = Laws and regulations that influence media content

B = Political pressures and controls on media content

C = Economic influences over media content

D = Repressive actions (killing of journalists, physical violence against journalists or facilities, censorship, self-censorship, harassment, expulsion, etc.)

For Total Score:

Free = 0–30

Partly Free = 31–60

Not Free = 61–100

22. Croatia was nominally a democracy in that the selection of the president and legislators were put up for a popular vote. However, in the country's 1997 election, the U.S. government observed that the vote was "free, but not fair." Among other things, press coverage was overwhelmingly biased in favor of the HDZ as opposition candidates barely drew a few seconds of air time and a few column inches in the leading media. To sum up the U.S. view of the current government, the State Department, in its 1998 Human Rights Statement said, "The President's extensive powers, the HDZ's dominance, the government's influence over the judiciary, and its control of the media combine to make the country's nominally democratic system in reality authoritarian." U.S. Department of State, *Croatia Country Report on Human Rights Practices for 1998*, released by the Bureau of Democracy, Human Rights, and Labor, February 26, 1999. See <www.state.gov/www/global;/human_rights>.

23. Justice Brandeis concurring in *Whitney v. California*, 274 U.S. 357, 375–77 (1927).

2

Victory for Democracy: A Dream Fulfilled or a False Hope?

The end of the Tuđman era was a great relief for the average Croatian citizen. After ten years, the people had had enough of Tuđman's authoritarian governance, his twisted democracy, his handcuffed media, and governmental controls. He played the nationalist card too often, and his cries of "rally round the flag, boys" finally wore thin; the people realized what he was up to. In the end, Tuđman's accomplishments for the fledgling Croatian state were overwhelmed by his iron-fisted policies, which ruined the economy, increased social unrest, smothered personal freedoms, and isolated Croatia on the world stage.

Tuđman could never find in his character the capacity to yield a point or bow to a better idea. He was guided by a dream of an independent Croatia that, in the beginning, was shared by his countrymen. The people got behind Tuđman as Croatia established independence from Communist-controlled Yugoslavia, and they backed him in the war with Serbia and the mad man Milošević. But when Croatia was finally liberated in 1995 after five hard years of unbending support, the people expected the country to turn a new page. They envisioned democracy, free markets and a new economy, open media, integration into the West, and a richer, better life. That was to be their reward for enduring the despots and the devils who had taunted them for so long. They saw it as Croatia's destiny.

But it was not to be. Not yet. Rather than parcel out power to the people in the spirit of democracy, Tuđman tightened the reins and consolidated his controls. Without a strong external threat with which to fan the flames of nationalism, Tuđman turned his energies inward and assumed greater control of Parliament and the domestic economy, and that included stronger presidential management of information and the press. As a result, democracy withered, the economy concentrated in the hands of a privileged few, the press suffered greater constraints and indignities.

The cumulative effects of Tuđman's unyielding policies contributed to the creation of a new political environment at the end of the nineties. Opposition parties became stronger and united at least in their commitment to change, cries for a civil society became louder, international pressures increased, and independent media became bolder with the truth. Tuđman's illness and, finally, his death, accelerated the electoral losses of the HDZ, although that end would likely have been the same had Tuđman survived. The restrictive policies had simply run their course: The people reached their limit and wanted change.

In that sense, conditions at the end of the nineties paralleled conditions at the start of the nineties. Ten years earlier, electoral slogans read, "No to Communism," and that curtain came down. In 2000 they read, "No to the HDZ," and that curtain came down. The change at both times was significant, with the latter election allocating nearly two-thirds of the seats in Parliament to six opposition parties (divided into two main blocks) and causing a run-off for the presidency between two opposition candidates. In two months, the ruling HDZ party went from total control to near total collapse. It was a heady change for people who have not had much say about their own futures.

Several nongovernmental organizations (NGOs) played crucial roles during the electoral campaign, especially by monitoring the elections for fairness. The most influential was GONG (*Građani organizirano nadziru glasovanje*—which means "Citizens are monitoring the elections in an organized way"). Another group active during the election was "Glas 99" (Voice 99), actually an association of NGOs. The greatest contribution of these groups was helping Croatian citizens understand that voting was their democratic duty and that only through their active involvement could conditions change. Until this message was driven hard into the public consciousness, most people were afraid that a vote against the ruling party would be a vote against state independence. That was a gospel preached by Tuđman and the HDZ with obvious success, and not until the year before the election were the people told this was a lie. On election day, more than 5,000 volunteers, including students, pensioners, professors, and workers, monitored the polling places to prevent voting fraud.

The media's role was crucial during the political campaign. In the previous election, the OSCE berated the Croatian media for the bias of state-controlled organs and compliance of the independent press. Croatian Radio and Television were practically public relations mouthpieces for Tuđman and his party, and major newspapers almost always touted the HDZ line. Only a few independent media, such as *Novi list, Nacional, Globus*, Radio 101, and the *Feral Tribune*, remained reasonably impartial and maintained a diet of balanced news.

In the last few months of Tuđman's life—the time leading up to the parliamentary and presidential elections—the Croatian media experienced an enlightenment about their own capabilities to report political news and recognized their roles and responsibilities to the democratic process. Even many journalists in state-controlled media rejected their complicity in HDZ propaganda.

The Croatian Journalists' Association (CJA) contributed to the creation of the new media environment. In October 1999, at its annual "Days of the Croatian Journalism" meeting in Opatija,[1] the organization issued a statement on the role of the media in building a democratic society. It warned that the media should serve citizens, not politicians. Croatian TV, financed by taxpayers, should act as a public operation owned by all citizens. Regardless of each media's political preferences, the CJA maintained, reporting should be impartial and balanced. Journalists should use all reporting tools at their disposal, and they should confront the candidates directly and not reprint campaign handouts obediently.

In the best of all worlds, the CJA said, HRTV would give free airtime for each of the political parties, the time allocated according to their previous electoral success. Paid advertisements, often a chance for quick and easy profits, should not be seen as the last word in electoral information, but only as one part of the information spectrum. The Croatian Journalists' Association asked for legislation to enable small, independent broadcasters to participate equally in the media environment. The association also called on media owners to protect journalists from political and legal pressures during the electoral campaign. Finally, CJA called on the public to respond en masse to attempts of manipulation and media control.

To help promote its political reporting objectives, the CJA organized a series of training workshops that were attended by over 200 reporters.[2] Experienced international journalists and media experts worked with Croatian reporters on impartial, balanced, and fair reporting practices.

Why was the training so important? Media influence in Croatia was concentrated in HRTV, where an astounding 55 percent of the population watches prime-time news each day. About a quarter of the population listens to local radio stations, and only 8 percent regularly reads newspapers. During any given week, polls show, almost 84 percent of the Croatian population gets all its political news from HRTV. The station's population-wide influence is a fact well known to the ruling party and the driving reason that the party had for so long kept an iron grasp on its ownership and day-to-day operations.

Media coverage of the previous presidential election in 1997 was limited, biased, and very much in favor of Franjo Tuđman. In fact, HRTV's lopsided coverage largely accounted for the OSCE conclusion that media operations during that election were "free, but not fair." It was not unusual for HRTV to run ninety-minute segments on Tuđman's electoral campaign, less than eighteen minutes on Vlado Gotovac, and barely six minutes for the third candidate, Zdravko Tomac. Croatian radio typically offered similar proportions for the candidates. Taped messages of Tuđman were aired 112 times, of Vlado Gotovac 30 times, and of Zdravko Tomac 17 times. Such hugely distorted proportions were incredibly bold, particularly under the watchful eye of OSCE and other election observers. Consequently, with the previous election in mind, the CJA and other NGOs asked broadcasters for a more even-handed distribution of time and attention. Opposition parties, of course, supported this call.

Tuđman's illness played a significant part in the parliamentary elections in two ways. First, the president's condition potentially could effect the vote as people evaluated his chances for recovery and, thus, his continued influence on the political system. Voters also had to consider his possible death, a political element that would alter drastically the country's electoral chemistry. The HDZ, therefore, in control of the election date, had to weigh the likelihood of either outcome, the possible significance for voters, and, ultimately, the best timing for the vote in order to capitalize on public sympathies.

Public sympathies were the second significant matter related to Tuđman's illness. Tuđman the leader, Tuđman the "Father of Croatia," Tuđman the Moses who lead a nation from bondage was lying incapacitated in the hospital, and the HDZ used him until he drew his last breath. A vote for the HDZ, they said, was a vote for the ailing hero. In fact, they used him after his last breath. On the night when Tuđman died, the HDZ pasted in the streets jumbo posters bearing an image of the president holding a small child dressed in a national folk costume. The figure of Tuđman the Father could not have been bolder.

In the end, the parliamentary elections held little drama. A new electoral law provided for a proportional system in which parties confronted each other rather than individual candidates vying for seats. All together, a bewildering ninety-seven parties ran for Parliament, but less than ten won seats. Each party received the same amount of HRTV exposure, and most of them used the allotted time to drone on about programs of little public interest. Polls showed that public opinion was against the HDZ and in favor of two opposition coalitions: the coalition of Social Democrat Party (SDP) and the Croatian Social Liberal Party (HSLS). Another four-party coalition also stood against the HDZ, and together the leading coalitions comprised six parties.

Finally, on election day, January 3, 2000, these successful parties formed the majority in Parliament and created a coalition government. It is said among Croatian citizens that New Year's Day 2000 started on January 3. It was a great victory of democracy when, half an hour after midnight, HDZ leader Mate Granić announced that the HDZ had lost. Cheers went up as he congratulated the winners and street celebrations continued until dawn.

But, one more job remained: the presidential election. For reformers, it was important to end the rule of the HDZ, not only in Parliament but also in the presidency. This was particularly important because the slim opposition margin of victory in Parliament would require a supportive executive in order to carry out legislative reforms. HDZ candidate, Mate Granić, therefore, posed a signif-icant threat to real democratic changes because he could block initiatives. The presidential elections, therefore, held a particular suspense in this unfolding po-litical theater.

CASE STUDY: A RUN FOR THE PRESIDENCY, THE MEDIA MATURES

A look at several major newspapers demonstrates the significant development of a free media in Croatia. Nine candidates ran for the presidency; the two leading contenders were Mate Granić from the HDZ and Dražen Budiša from HSLS. On January 8, five days after the opposition's parliamentary victories, *Jutarnji list* ran a large, front-page headline with these poll results: "Budiša 37%: Granić 31 %." Stipe Mesić received fewer than 10 percent in this poll and was not featured in the story.[3] The headline was accompanied by photos of the two candidates. The seven other candidates, supported by less than 10 percent of the public, were pictured at the bottom of the page.

The next day, *Večernji list* published its polling results: "Granić 23.8%, Budiša 22.7% and Mesić 18.5%." A subtitle described how women supported Granić, men backed Budiša, and young people endorsed Mesić. Fully one-third remained undecided. Mesić's 18.5 percent was a small surprise, but it was not alarming.

The great surprise occurred a week later when, on January 15, *Jutarnji list* published the news that, according to their poll numbers, Mesić was now leading the race—due largely to voters in Istria, Rijeka, and Primorje. The poll results: Mesić 31.3 percent, Budiša 27.5 percent, and Granić 20.9 percent. The news shot through the public like an electric spark. How could Mesić be leading now when just last week he barely made it into the headlines?

The first impression was that *Jutarnji list* was wrong, but, hard on the heals of the *Jutarnji list* story, *Večernji list* published confirming poll numbers: Mesić 29.1 percent, Budiša 21.3 percent, Granić 16.0 percent. Evidently, something unexpected was afoot. Mesić explained it when he noted that when ratings start to grow, they're hard to stop. Budiša, sliding in the polls, said that he was waiting for results of the credible Puls survey. (Puls is a respected polling firm that emulates Gallup polling methods.) Granić, plagued with the HDZ's bad image, attempted to cultivate an independent image, but it was too late. His star quickly faded as he fell in among the second-string candidates.

The sensational polling results became a self-generating story in the media. The key question was, Had Mesić become a serious candidate, or was his apparent status simply a media-created fiction? *Vjesnik* (a daily newspaper),[4] analyzing the polling results, noted how remarkable Mesić's rise had been, particularly given his poor performance in the parliamentary elections, where he failed in his bid for Member of Parliament (MP) and his party (HNS) gained only two seats.

Nacional, the independent weekly, hit the streets with a large front-page picture of Mesić and the headline: "Stipe Mesić will be the President of Croatia." This prediction was based on *Nacional*'s poll, which found Mesić with 50.8 percent and Budiša with 30.6 percent. Fewer than 19 percent of likely voters were undecided.

The public was shocked, not just because of the rapid change in polling numbers, but also because voters were not used to the media playing such a role during electoral campaigns. Recall that media coverage historically consisted of reprinted press releases. Handicapping a political race was unheard of.

The political campaigns and their coverage were whipped up as election day neared. Ivica Račan, a candidate for prime minister (and coalition partner of Budiša), said he supported Budiša but that he did not want to unsettle his relationship with Mesić. Granić was so far down in the polls that, for all intents and purposes, he was out of the race. All other candidates were under 2 percent. Now, nearly one in four of the voters were undecided.

Meanwhile, as the electoral campaigns raged on, the government was handing over power to the newly elected officials, and HDZ leaders were not happy about it. Never before had they conceded authority, but now they had no choice. The media had a field day disclosing how the limousines, free credit cards, and cellular phones had to be pried from the hands of HDZ leaders and former VIPs who had come to believe that these privileges were their birthrights.

On January 21, 2000, the big Puls poll was published in *Globus*, a weekly magazine, and the numbers left no doubts: Mesić 31.1 percent, Budiša 23.0 percent, and Granić 14.3 percent. Mesić didn't hold half the votes as reported earlier, but he was clearly the leading candidate as even Budiša had to admit.

Finally, on Monday, January 24, the Croatian people voted, and the results of the vote tracked the polls: Mesić 41.6 percent, Budiša 28.0 percent, and Granić 21.7 percent. The outcome was favorable for many in the opposition because HDZ was out of the picture, and the second round would feature no hard-line candidates. Much, but not all, of the drama was squeezed from the campaigns as the two run-off candidates launched into the final phase of the presidential race.

Again, in the run-offs, the media ran polls, conducted serious interviews, analyses, and investigations. This time, however, the Croatian public did not remain passive in the election as it had in the past, but it adopted an active participatory role. It was as if the people realized, for the first time, their own importance in democratic governance.

Jutarnji list, as usual, was the first to publish polling results when it reported on January 25 that Mesić (50.4 %) was head and shoulders above Budiša (33.6 %). Understandably, Budiša did not like the outcome of the poll, although his angry reaction surprised some when he said, "Mesić represents a group which would like to stop the changes now evident in the Croatian government." Mesić came back with a non sequitur saying, "Budiša spent 1.3 million kuna on ads, while we spent only 460 thousand." The implication was that, with three times the ad budget, if people liked what they heard, they would have favored Budiša and his programs.

Both interviews were published next to each other on the front page of *Jutarnji list*. Such conspicuous, even-handed coverage of two candidates would have been impossible only a few months earlier. Something new was happening in the Croatian media, not the least of which was a charged activism in political coverage.

On January 29, *Novi list* published new polling results that showed a narrowing of the gap: Mesić received 36.8 percent and Budiša was neck and neck with him at 33.4 percent. Two days later, *Večernji list*'s poll results showed the gap widening again: Mesić with 40 percent and Budiša with 30 percent.

Budiša's headquarters desperately sought favorable promotion to reverse the momentum toward Mesić, and in their eagerness to do something dramatic, they did something foolish. Budiša invited two former candidates for the presidency, Granić and Letica, to become his personal advisors. By inviting the assistance of Granić, a representative of the HDZ, Budiša was seen by many voters to have given the fox a key to the hen house. HDZ had, at long last, been defeated at the polls, yet here was an opposition candidate welcoming it back for political gain. The people would have none of it, and overnight Budiša's party became a pariah.

As election day neared, Budiša's headquarters accused Mesić of using dirty money for his campaign. At the same time the newspaper *Slobodna Dalmacija* accused Mesić of being a collaborator in the former Yugoslavian Secret Service Police, the UDBA. This story surprised the public, but it also surprised *Slobodna Dalmacija* journalists, none of whom knew the author of the piece, which had been written anonymously. Over 100 journalists of *Slobodna Dalmacija* asked the editor in chief, Josip Jović, to explain who wrote the story and to prove it was accurate. Finally, Jović admitted that he was the writer and his source was the Croatian secret police.

Mesić's response was simple. He said that, as a political prisoner, he was ineligible for a passport. When his family went to France, he wished to visit them and regularly asked the government for a passport. To track his requests, the secret police routinely invited him to so-called "informative talks," for which he signed the logs at police headquarters. That was all, and it satisfied most people.

The race was in the last lap when *Jutarnji list* showed the margin closing once again. The paper reported that Mesić had 45 percent against Budiša's 40 percent, with the uncommitteds still holding the deciding votes. The homestretch of this first truly democratic round of elections in Croatia was a raucous affair. The HDZ tried to confuse the contest with false support of one candidate, then the other. Mesić and Budiša spent hours confronting each other on radio and television. Mesić would make bold claims saying that he would sell Franjo Tuđman's aircraft, and Budiša would come back with his own tough pronouncements about how he would liberate the state from the Mafia. *Jutarnji list* came through with another poll showing a statistical dead-heat: Mesić with 44.9 percent and Budiša with 41.3 percent.

After a final televised debate, a phone-in poll showed Budiša with a clear majority. Like many politicians at the wrong end of a poll, Mesić claimed that he trusted only the Puls polls and not these call-in surveys.[5] As it turns out, the call-in poll was wrong. No surprise.

On Monday, February 7, Croatian citizens went to the polls after the most exciting and democratic campaign in the country's recent history. Most people agree that the election this time was free AND fair, as the media covered all candidates fairly and parties ran honest campaigns void of the scandals and deceits so common in the past decade. At the end of the count, Stipe Mesić became the new Croatian president, the third in the last fifty-five years. The final results: Mesić had 56.4 percent and Budiša had 43.6 percent.

WHAT HAPPENED NEXT

This manuscript went to the publisher less than five months after the new government was installed in Zagreb. That's too short a time to assess major changes, but long enough to observe the first steps, and they are encouraging.

First, the government has announced a change of the Penalty Code, and although it may be largely symbolic, it is nonetheless significant. The Tuđman government protected five high-ranking officials: president of the republic, speaker of the Parliament, prime minister, and presidents of the Supreme Court and Constitutional Court. They were called "the untouchables" because they were beyond the laws. According to the new Article 204 of the Penalty Code, the state attorney could now prosecute each of these five.

Another law undergoing change was the law governing Croatian radio and television. The old law gave Parliament full authority to name the general manager and editor in chief, thus handing the ruling party complete control over HRTV. Parliament will no longer have such control.

The monopolistic distribution company, Tisak, which controlled the newspaper market and favored newspapers close to the HDZ, went bankrupt—poetic justice! The new government will sell this company on the international market and strip away its monopolistic powers.

Nenad Ivanković, editor in chief of *Vjesnik*, resigned. The newly appointed editor is Igor Mandić, a well-known journalist who had been unemployed during the past few years because of his independent viewpoints. Mandić has already changed editorial policy. Journalists are no longer to use hate speech, and they are to apply professional reporting standards once characteristic of this eminent newspaper.

Miroslav Kutle, the flamboyant media tycoon, was arrested because of illegal financial transactions. He had destroyed *Slobodna Dalmacija*, Tisak, and several radio stations as he grabbed up profits and other benefits for himself. Kutle became a poster boy for the illegal activities involved in the HDZ's privatization of Croatian companies, especially media companies and banks. Kutle's associates, Vinko Grubišić, owner of OTV,[6] and Jura Hrvačić, manager and owner of several national frequency radio stations, were interrogated for their connections with Kutle.

Parliament founded a special commission to find out who really owned *Večernji list*, the best-selling daily newspaper. The Croatian Pension Fund once owned the majority of shares of *Večernji list*, but almost overnight, during the Christmas holidays in 1998, the paper had been sold to the unknown Caritas Limited Trust from the Virgin Islands. It was the biggest media sale in Croatia, but still nobody knows who is behind this mysterious company. Parliament hopes to find out.

Independent TV, Moslavina, has pressed charges against the commission for frequency licensing, because they lost their frequency to a phantom television station where a 2-year-old boy is one of the owners.

Journalists working for Hrvatski radio (Croatian Radio)—which is part of HRTV—are asking for independence and turning the station's operations into a real public radio format. Journalists with Radio Pula, a local radio station in the HRTV system, have called for the resignation of Elvis Mileta, editor in chief, hopefully on the grounds that he was a willing propagandist, not that he is now a member of an opposition party.

Are these actions sufficient to bring Croatian media up to standards expected for truly free and open communication? As positive as they seem we must wait and see. A new government has to create a new media environment, and that means flying in the face of Croatian history. Almost fifty years of media control have left deep societal fissures and caused severe distortions in news coverage, distortions we must address in subsequent chapters if we are to understand fully the shaky foundations on which the "new" Croatia stands. It will take much more to fortify the news and information system needed to support the developing democracy in Croatia because values of a civil society must be implanted and nurtured to sustain the public support necessary for genuine democratic rule.

This democratic rule, as stated earlier, requires three strong columns of support: the political system, the press, and the people. In the end, the people are the key. They are the ones who must support the papers that probe and challenge and dissent. They are the ones who must choose the broadcasts and build the fires under elected officials, and they are the ones who must continue to elect governments that, at long last, promise to return the power of rule to the people themselves. As we say in chapter 4, snatching power from an ailing dictator is no sure thing. It was nip and tuck for forty-one frenzied days, as the dictator lay dying and his supporters kept lying.

NOTES

1. Held at the International Center for Education of Journalists (ICEJ) in Opatija.

2. Workshops were co-sponsored by the British Know-How Fund, the Thomson Foundation, the Council of Europe, and the BBC Training Trust.

3. Stipe Mesić got 9.7 percent and was not among the serious candidates.

4. *Vjesnik* was an eminent daily newspaper, with the same respect usually given to the *New York Times*.

5. Of course, Mesić was right to decry the inaccuracy of phone-in polls. They generally offer biased samples that tap only portions of the voting population. News organizations use such polls for entertainment and not predictive value.

6. OTV (Open Television) is the first private TV station in Croatia. Located in Zagreb, OTV covers one-fourth of the population. Owners are close to the HDZ, which is the main reason it never became an independent voice like Radio 101.

PART II

DEMOCRACY, MEDIA, AND GOVERNMENT: HISTORICAL ROOTS

3

Theory of Free Press/Open Societies

The American Founding Fathers knew "that it is hazardous to discourage thought, hope and imagination; that fear breeds repression; that repression breeds hate; that hate menaces stable government; that the path of safety lies in the opportunity to discuss freely supposed grievances and proposed remedies; and that the fitting remedy for evil counsels is good ones."

Justice Louis Brandeis, *Whitney v. California* 274
U.S. 357, 375 (1927) (Brandeis concurring)

The relationship between a free press and a democratic society, so ingrained in American history, is not well known in Croatia, nor, for that matter, in any country arising from Communist control. Assurances of a free press are now gelling in Croatia, along with the concepts and practices of democracy, although the mutually supportive nature of a free press and a free people may not be understood entirely by the people or the lawmakers. In this chapter, we lay out the precepts of that relationship as a foundation for the discussions throughout the book. This review draws heavily from the American experience, which obtains much of its impetus and direction for a free press and for democracy from European precedents. The American perspective, however, is unique and has, for many countries, become a model.

INTRODUCTION: FREE PRESS AND DEMOCRACY

Thanks to Justice Brandeis and other historic defenders of the First Amendment freedoms, Americans enjoy almost too much of a good thing—the problem of media overload. President John Kennedy once observed that the more you have of something the less you value it. Media coverage of government and politics illustrates that adage. Another campaign story, another commentary, another public opinion poll load up the media and turn off Americans who simply tire of political reporting.

Our never-ending political campaigns and never-resting journalism make for a wearying mix in any society, especially one intolerant of stories without endings or of plot lines with little evident appeal to voters. Many voters find it difficult to discriminate between analysis and advertising, between fair reporting and partisan snipes, thus jumbling genuine political news with hype and tossing it all on the pile of what they sense as information clutter.[1] Oversaturated but underinformed, they walk away from electoral politics. How sad that half of eligible voters sit out national elections.[2]

Chances are, Justice Brandeis would scoff at our whining about too much information and remind us of what happens when there is too little. The founders got it right when they gave the press a franchise to cover the news with immunity from government meddling, because it *is* "hazardous to discourage thought, hope and imagination." In light of the alternative, the clutter of information itself is a testament to the success of an open society. Better too much information than too little; better too many voices than too few. Better democratic confusion than tyrannical order. Or, as Mae West observed with a leer, "Too much of a good thing—is a good thing!"

The information glut suits an open society. Brandeis understood that the path of political safety "lies in the opportunity to discuss freely supposed grievances and proposed remedies." People seeking the truth are more likely to find it among the blizzard of reports and analyses than they are from accounts issued by the state, even if they must work at assembling that truth.

America's premier essayist, E. B. White, made that point in an editorial that appeared in *The New Yorker*, September 11, 1948, when he responded to the criticism that you can't learn *the* truth from a newspaper. He said, that's right, you cannot learn *the* truth. "You can, however, buy at any newsstand a[n] . . . assortment of biased and unbiased facts and fancies and reports and opinions and from them you [can] . . . assemble something that is a reasonable facsimile of the truth . . . and that's the way we like it" (see Rebecca M. Dale, ed., *E. B. White, Writings from The New Yorker, 1927–1976* [New York: Harper Perennial, 1991], 58–59).

Such truth finding requires that publishers be free to report the news and that the people be free to access it. Both supply and demand must be in force, and they must be driven by the market, not the state. Other than preventing broadcasters from crossing signals and obeying minimum rules, like truth in advertising, democratically elected governments are wise to let the marketplace determine what information gets out and what information gets used in public debate.

Advocates of a free press like to dwell on the journalist's right to put out the news. To be sure, the publisher's right to expression has been paramount in

English jurisprudence from William Blackstone's writings in the 1700s[3] to present-day debates about the Internet. That's a critical perspective. But it can eclipse the equally important right of the people to access the news. Press freedoms guard the rights of the listener as much as they ensure the rights of the speaker; that's a perspective made clear more than sixty years ago by First Amendment scholar Alexander Meiklejohn, who saw communication as a two-way street. He said, "Shall we give a hearing to those who hate and despise freedom, to those who, if they had the power, would destroy our institutions? Certainly, yes! Our action must be guided, not by their principles, but by ours. *We listen, not because they desire to speak, but because we need to hear*" (italics added).[4]

A free press, by this reckoning, is as much a freedom of the people to receive information as it is a freedom of the press to dispense it. Any clampdown by the government on media, accordingly assaults not only the owners of broadcast stations and newspapers but the people as well. It converts a violation against publishers to a strike at the people.

FOUNDATIONS FOR FREE EXPRESSION

In 1941, Harvard University law professor Zechariah Chafee Jr. asserted that the First Amendment protects two interests in free expression:[5] It safeguards the interests of individuals to make known their positions on public matters, and it protects the collective interests of self-government. Thomas Emerson, expanding on Chafee's list, wrote that free expression is necessary "1) as a method of assuring individual self-fulfillment, 2) as a means of attaining the truth, 3) as a method of securing participation by the members of the society in social, including political, decision-making, and 4) as a means of maintaining the balance between stability and change in the society."[6]

The hampered flow of news and information in countries like Croatia robs democracies of what democracies cannot do without: the open examination of ideas, the public debate, the contest between competing philosophies and contrasting solutions to society's problems. All very true, but if you reread Chafee and Emerson, you discover a double rap on censorship. They're saying that restricting freedom of expression does psychological damage to individuals and, therefore, damage to society at large. Ultimately, the pent-up hunger for information bursts forth from the dams of censorship, flooding the country with revolutionary force.

In the following section, we look at the other side of the coin—the benefits bestowed by guarantees of free expression, first for individuals, then for society.

Individual Benefits

The First Amendment of the U.S. Constitution and free expression guarantees in many other countries, emerge from a philosophy that elevates the natural rights of the individual over the arbitrary authority of the state. Most often associated with eighteenth-century philosopher John Locke, this view proposes that, by forming into societies to create a common culture, individuals agree to yield autonomy and to accept common rule. Central to this thinking is the notion that the individual does not become a subject of the state but remains a master of it. Consequently, the state's authority is conferred by its constituent members, guided by laws that they accept mutually.[7] The people who join the collective may yield autonomy but retain their rights as individuals. Professor Thomas Emerson points out that "the purpose of society and of its more formal aspect, the state, is to promote the welfare of the individual. Society and the state are not ends in themselves; they exist to serve the individual."[8]

Locke's idea of surrendering autonomy while retaining individual rights—a radical view at the time—stands in sharp contrast to the harsh philosophy of Thomas Hobbes. Hobbes, in his *Leviathan*, advocated an absolute authority of the state and a surrender of individual rights, especially the right to self-government.[9] In Hobbes's formula, the state is omnipotent; the individual is insignificant. All power is invested in the sovereign, whose decisions, policies, and enforcement of rules cannot be challenged.

The political philosophies of Hobbes and Locke paint useful contrasts of the individual's role in governance. Hobbes casts the individual as a powerless subject whose sole obligation is blind obedience. Locke broke all the rules with his amazing assertion that the power to govern is "on loan" from the people, who retain original ownership but lease it out to government as a concession to order and justice. In Hobbes's scheme, individuals have no need for information, for the exchange of ideas, for debate and discussion because they have no responsibilities for governance. Communication about public matters has no point, so free expression is irrelevant. Locke's radically different theory of governance won't work without free expression and the open flow of information from an unfettered media. If people are to participate in collective decision making, they must have access to objective information and then have the freedom to examine and test solutions through public debate.

This takes us back to professor Emerson's comment about freedom's impact on self-fulfillment. Many First Amendment theorists have built their entire defense of free expression from such a focus on the individual. They argue—no one can prove it, of course—that safeguarding the right to present one's point of view fosters the development of self-esteem, that quality which enriches personal growth.

The liberty to communicate, an inherently human trait, is essential to the realization of one's character and potential; it contributes to the discovery of meaning and the finding of one's place in the world.[10] More than an abstract philosophy, this translates into constitutional bedrock for open societies. Justice Brandeis, again in *Whitney v. California*: "Those who won our independence believed that the final end of the State was to make men free to develop their faculties."[11]

Neither Locke nor Brandeis, however, approved of sheer individualism, the kind that leads to "freemen" movements. Locke would have been appalled at the militia members who fear that the government threatens to limit their "freedom" to do whatever pleases them. They forget that the other side of freedom is yielding autonomy to a citizen-owned government.

Personal fulfillment cannot occur apart from the culture in which social creatures calibrate and sustain their personal values, beliefs, and opinions. Self-realization and self-evaluation, although individual processes, take place in the context of a social group; self-fulfillment, then, must be viewed through a larger lens that captures the individual within the social panorama. John Donne was on to this when he wrote, "No man is an island, entire of itself, but a piece of the continent, a part of the main."

An individual's associations are especially important in collective governance where members contribute to the group and are not merely defined by it. Individuals judge themselves, in part, by their capacity to influence group decisions; their self-perceptions grow with their capacity to participate substantively in those debates and to sway their outcomes—and to be swayed when won over convincingly.

Participation in public debates and public judgments relies on access to public information. Particularly with respect to matters of politics and government, members need facts and objective analyses with which to know the score, to assess conditions, and to make up their minds. Access to knowledge is central to the power of participation in common governance. On what other basis would people form wise judgments and engage in useful public dialogue if not on factual accounts and reasoned commentary derived from objective reporting and uncensored presentation of news? Individual fulfillment, played out in larger groups, is ample defense for a free press. Bridle the media? The words of Brandeis are worth repeating. When the state discourages thought, hope, and imagination, "fear breeds repression . . . repression breeds hate . . . hate menaces stable government . . . that the path of safety lies in the opportunity to discuss freely supposed grievances and proposed remedies; and that the fitting remedy for evil counsels is good ones" (see *Whitney v. California*).

Society's Benefits

The metaphor called "the marketplace of ideas" arose from the writings of John Milton in the mid-1600s, when the English poet and essayist argued for a total abolition of restraints on publishing and other forms of expression.[12] The author of *Paradise Lost*, like most poets, had a nobler philosophy than most philosophers. He believed that all ideas and all sides of an issue must be on the table in order for the people to judge the truth for themselves. Moreover, the only acceptable process by which these ideas should arrive for public scrutiny is for them to rise freely from the people themselves. The state, Milton argued, has no business censoring information, screening publishers, or controlling information that enters the public domain. He wrote harshly against licensing, which he saw as an especially pernicious form of censorship, arguing that it was "the greatest displeasure and indignity to a free and knowing spirit that can be put upon him."[13]

Milton's objection to controls on information came from his belief that the truth could be known only after it had done battle with conflicting ideas. For him, the truth is the outcome of process, and to deny truth a contest against competing ideas assaults its validity. He wrote elegantly on the power of truth to emerge from the confrontation: "And though all the winds of doctrine were let loose to play upon the earth, so Truth be in the field, we do injuriously by licensing and prohibiting to misdoubt her strength. Let her and Falsehood grapple; who ever knew Truth put to the worse, in a free and open encounter?"[14]

Three centuries later, Judge Learned Hand also saw truth as a process when he wrote that it is an essential American interest to disseminate "the news from as many different sources, and with as many different facets and colors as possible. That interest is closely akin to, if indeed it is not the same as, the interest protected by the First Amendment; it presupposes that *right conclusions are more likely to be gathered out of a multitude of tongues*, than through any kind of authoritative selection"[15] (italics added). Judge Hand made it clear that for the process to work, information sources could not be hampered and information users could not be kept from access to all points of view. For him, legislated rights to free expression set in motion a process that began with the availability of information and continued with the people deciding for themselves what to make of the information and how to use it.

Many other writers have picked up the truth-as-process concept. E. B. White, as we noted earlier, believed that truth was revealed by the intersection of many reports in a process of information triangulation—the arrival at truth from the convergence of facts and viewpoints. For White, each person constructed his own truth because each person compiled his own information. Truth does not come ready-made; it requires assembly.

While White saw truth as specific to an individual, Thomas Emerson saw truth as specific to a point in time. The perceptions of truth change, Emerson said, as people confront new information and engage in new analysis. Truth, like a prize fighter, must endure constant challenge to hold the title. The process is unending, and judgments on truth are never absolute.

[A]n individual who seeks knowledge and truth must hear all sides of the question, especially as presented by those who feel strongly and argue militantly for a different view. He must consider all alternatives, test his judgment by exposing it to opposition, make full use of different minds to sift the true from the false.

The process is a continuous one. As further knowledge becomes available, as conditions change, as new insights are revealed, the judgment is open to reappraisal, improvement or abandonment.[16]

Judge Hand's views that truth must be gathered, White's notion that it must be constructed, Milton's belief that truth is a battle, and Emerson's sense that it is an endless transaction all recognize the discovery of truth as a process. Each relies on the capacity of people to access wideranging issues and many points of view, to examine the evidence for themselves, to debate their thoughts with others, and to draw their own conclusions.

The availability of information and the rough-and-tumble of debate and analysis are known collectively as the "marketplace of ideas." The marketplace is sometimes seen as a collection of information only, but it is more than that, because all of the elements must be in place for it to function. Emerson put it this way: the "suppression of information, discussion, or the clash of opinion prevents one from reaching the most rational judgment, blocks the generation of new ideas, and tends to perpetuate error."[17] The functioning marketplace needs information, yes, but it also must allow discussion and confrontation for it to be effective.

The breakdown of the marketplace, accordingly, can occur in two places: First, the state can disable the media by limiting the information supply. In the previous chapter, we saw how the Croatian government employs a number of tactics short of censorship to control the news. With a lock on distribution, heavy taxation, licensing fees, and a docket packed with lawsuits and prosecutions, the government pretty much keeps opposing ideas in check. At the same time, by controlling the dominant print and broadcast media lock, stock, and barrel, the state raises its own view above all others. The result is a stripped-down marketplace where competing ideas are edged out of the public view, much to the impoverishment of society.

Closed societies force a second breakdown in the marketplace by limiting individual debate and discussion. In the most obvious cases, the people are prevented from engaging in public (or sometimes even in private) conversation about proscribed topics. The state may employ informants to keep track of errant souls and to disclose their misdeeds. George Orwell called them "thought police."

Suppression of public discussion can be subtle as well as overt. People exposed each day to the state's point of view and no other have little chance to practice their skills at judging and weighing the facts, at sizing up differing opinions, and at evaluating the merits of competing policies. When the morning paper and the evening newscast are in perfect alignment, when there is no information about policies that have failed, officials who have cheated, programs that have foundered because of bad judgment or deceit, there is little chance to develop the skills cultivated in free societies where people are flooded with conflicting reports, forcing them to judge the truth for themselves. What can people do with news reports that are bare of analysis and larded with party-line views, with stories that paint the government in glowing colors and render the opposition in strokes of black? In places where news is controlled, the analytic skills of the people wither and their capacity to engage in debate decays. That's what Brandeis meant when he warned against the hazards to thought, hope, and imagination.[18]

Single spigot news gives the people nothing to evaluate and debate; it deprives them of the perspective that they need to triangulate the truth. Without the "facts and fancies and reports and opinions," the people are denied the elements they need to discover a "reasonable facsimile of the truth."[19] Eventually, they lose the knack of winnowing out truth from trash, because this is an acquired skill. People in closed societies are deprived of the raw material that forms political wisdom. Compliant and accepting citizens must be taught to become doubters, challengers, and debaters of their information supply. Facing the democracies newly budding from closed societies is a marketplace as unfamiliar as free enterprise itself: the challenge from competitive media to use the information supply intelligently.

Does the West—particularly the United States—use its information supply intelligently, or is there a fly in our ointment? Critics have challenged the information marketplace, alleging that not all points of view surface for public examination, no matter what the theories promise. Without access to all perspectives, they claim, people cannot argue the merits of an issue rationally, because public opinion is channeled into preordained conclusions through the selective presentation of information. And who controls that information and, so, the public agenda? The government and corporations, according to Herbert Marcuse, who takes a decidedly leftist view of the American media: "The 'concentration of economic and political power' allows 'effective dissent' to be blocked where it could freely emerge, and the 'monopolistic media' prejudice 'right and wrong, true and false . . . wherever they affect the vital interests of the society.' "[20] This Marxist suspicion grows from a belief that the state is unable to keep its hands off the media because the media are key to state power. As long as government controls the information on the street, it controls the public mind, and when it yields control, it yields power. True marketplace principles are a threat, so in practice the state blocks them to preserve its authority.

For Marcuse, the real offense of the marketplace is its inherent deception. People in open societies, he says, are confident that they have access to a full range of views, and that is their failing. They believe they are deprived of no perspective because they are blinded by the profusion of media, and they swallow, hook, line, and sinker, the constitutional promises (such as the First Amendment). But they fall victim to what Marcuse calls "spurious objectivity,"[21] which is a selective presentation of views disguised as the full picture.

Jerome A. Barron, Zechariah Chafee, and others also challenge the validity of the marketplace concept, which, they say, is riddled with economic biases. Their arguments, focused on the economics of media ownership, play off the old saw, "He who controls the purse strings controls the world." Their economic quarrel with the marketplace is that in a capitalistic system, the only views to hit the streets are those of the moneyed elite. The well-heeled class owns the papers and the broadcast stations; people with modest means cannot start up a medium because the costs of entry are simply too high. This leaves ownership and control of information pipelines in the hands of wealthy individuals and corporations who, many believe, use the media to advance their own biases and economic self-interests and to suppress competing views.

As a result, critics charge, the public is deprived of issues and treatments from across the political spectrum, even though the illusion of openness prevails. News that threatens the corporations or the ruling class is killed, moderated, or downplayed; advocates of threatening views are shut out of the mainstream market.

The underground press, active on college campuses during the Vietnam War, is a good case in point. Opponents of that war, shunned by the mainstream media, were driven to produce their own newspapers in a vain attempt to change public opinion. Meanwhile, the mainstream press, at least during the early phases of the war, published articles that supported the dominant political and corporate views. The failure of the media to present a full range of opinions kept the public unaware of significant opposition to the war. Thus economic interests controlling the media set the public agenda, which influenced the political debate and altered national policy.

Remedies for economic control of the media are not easy to swallow for societies that are proud of their press freedoms and cautious of government intrusions. In most free societies, the print media are free to publish without restraint (short of libeling private citizens) and without a censor's hot breath on their backs to demand accuracy or evenhanded treatments. Broadcasters, once subject to standards of fairness and balance, are now limited only in their presentation of obscenity and, to some extent, violence. This liberal public policy reflects a faith in the marketplace and demonstrates a belief that the widest freedoms yield the greatest range of views.

Critics believe otherwise, and some, like law professor Jerome A. Barron, have proposed legislative remedies that force the news media to accept views contrary to their economic and political interests. He advocates requiring all papers to accept editorial advertisements without regard to content and allowing public figures to reply to stories in which they feel they have been maligned.[22] In practice, these remedies often occur in the absence of the legislation, but of course, there are no guarantees and guarantees are what critics want. As it stands today, in a hands-off-the-media environment, there is little chance that such legislation could be enacted. We don't tell newspapers what they cannot publish; we're not likely to tell them what they must publish.

But the critics should take heart. Within the past several years, the world has witnessed an extraordinary development in global communication that few could have envisioned a decade ago. The Internet may offer a solution to media monopoly and do it in the best tradition of an open marketplace. It could be the answer to limited public access and to financial and state controls. Financial barriers of conventional media are largely absent on the Internet, and at least for now, government regulators have stayed at arm's length from it. Anyone with an inclination and a few dollars can set up a website and present his point of view, no matter how far from the mainstream. It's true that the website may not draw the beefy audiences that gather around television networks or established newspapers today, but the Web offers a stage on a public medium, and that's more than any other medium can promise.

The size of the Web audience depends on the publisher. Although most site proprietors crave large audiences, websites do not need large audiences to survive, and this allows the sites to single out small groups for individual treatment. Aggressive promotion, smart positioning, and, most of all, strongly argued, well-presented ideas have a chance at getting an audience, and it can be accomplished without treading on the rights of free expression. Essentially void of economic constraints, ownership limitations, and political pressures, the Web is the first real test of an open marketplace of ideas, as we shall see in chapter 14.

Critics of the marketplace concept should find comfort in knowing that this new medium, operating under different rules, provides opportunities for public access previously denied by conventional media because of economic and political pressures. The potential for this open medium is found in its ungovernable nature. It was designed to withstand a nuclear war; advocates of free expression are counting on it to hold up against an onslaught of regulators and powerful financial forces.

Stabilize Change in a Society

A major societal benefit of free expression is stability. The marketplace, while disorderly and cumbersome by some standards, contributes to balance over the long haul and promotes society's orderly change. Stable, evolutionary development occurs when the people have access to information, when they can participate in the analysis of policy, and when they can contribute to key decisions affecting the community.

Cloistered environments, by contrast, provoke revolutionary change. Denied the information and the opportunity to participate in the making of public policy, the people are forced to swallow state decisions as *fait accompli* or to take to the streets in anger. Professor Emerson said that in any society "change is inevitable; the only question is the rate and the method. . . . Freedom of expression offers greater possibilities for rational, orderly adjustment than a system of suppression."[23]

Free expression, then, serves as a safety valve. It allows the public to participate in community decisions, and this sense of involvement brings people along in the policy-making process at every step. The open flow of information allows access to the full public agenda so that festering problems cannot be tucked away until it's too late. This forces government to deal openly with national problems and to bring the people into the picture at the earliest possible time.

The information marketplace stabilizes change within society because the people themselves are responsible for the direction of that change. In open societies, the public is in on the planning of government programs and policies, and this allows the people to edit the blueprints before the stones of public policy are set in mortar. By monitoring public comments, government leaders can see if their trial balloons sink or soar, then modify their proposals for greater public acceptance. Bringing the people along in public policy-making allows for gradual course corrections that keep the people and their leaders on the same track.

The state's thumb on the information marketplace also keeps looming societal problems from public view. Control of the media's agenda allows the state to pick and choose the issues it discloses, so problems the government finds embarrassing or awkward remain invisible to the public until they can no longer be concealed.

In open societies, the people have a right to know about the problems facing the country, and that knowledge imposes on them a shared responsibility to resolve those problems. Denying public access and blocking public discussion deprive people of their rights and their responsibilities, and they rob the state of the people's insights and involvement along the way.

Obstructing the flow of information to hamper the public debate, Thomas Emerson says, "promotes inflexibility and stultification, preventing society from adjusting to changing circumstances or developing new ideas."[24] People locked in the past and shielded from new ideas become brittle, headstrong, and unyielding. Forced to deal with new problems, they trot out old solutions.

Societies kept from a free exchange of new ideas likewise fail to grow and change with evolving conditions. Over time, as they fall further out of sync with other societies, they are driven further into isolation and alienation, and they grow increasingly incapable of adjusting to transitions occurring elsewhere. Inflexibility is especially difficult for closed societies during a time of globalization, when economic and political boundaries everywhere are dropping and reforming with rocket speed. While the rest of the world forges new alliances in commerce, education, the arts, sports, and other human-level transactions, the "single spigot" countries, deprived of input from every side, suffer from isolation, which contributes to stagnation and national paranoia.

In no society can every group have its way with public policy, but in open societies, the groups whose views have not been adopted at least will have had their turn to speak. Emerson says that "when the decision goes against them, they will be more likely to accept it knowing that they have had a shot at convincing others."[25] Often, they will have inched the outcome even slightly toward their position, thereby finding comfort in the knowledge that their efforts have contributed to the ultimate outcome. Acceptance of settled judgments is harder to swallow when groups have been denied access to the public and to decisionmakers. Public policy-making without public input leads to discontent and instability within the society—just check letters to the editor when a group feels excluded.

Finally, the process of free expression, including a free press, allows the public to observe the interactions, the arguments, and the judgments at each step along the way. Emerson said that even if the outcome of the decision process is disagreeable, "its presentation and open discussion serves a vital social purpose. It compels a rethinking and retesting of the accepted opinion. It results in a deeper understanding of the reason for holding the opinion and a fuller appreciation of its meaning."[26] In open societies, the observation of policy-making is instructive and involving, and by giving the public a ringside seat to the process, it stabilizes the society and, so, tempers extreme reaction, even to outcomes that may not meet with public approval.

Self-Governance

Of the arguments offered in defense of free expression, nothing rises to the level of importance of granting people the tools of self-governance. Self-governance cannot take place without a free press, without editors and publishers outside the government's reach who make decisions on what stories to cover and how to cover them, and without the right of citizens to access the media, discuss freely their views, and make their own judgments. That's a tall order, but it comes down to the tenacity with which the press and the people practice the art of free expression.

And a demanding art it is! The right to self-governance is not the same as the right to vote. Voting is an act; self-governance is a process. Claims that the people rule because the people vote are simply wrong. To know if the people truly govern, one must look beyond the lines at the polling booths and into the process that leads to electoral judgments.

Like truth-finding, self-governance is the process of information presentation, examination, and analysis, which leads to informed decisions. Interference by the state at any point tampers with the people's ability to arrive at the truth. It cramps their ability to discover for themselves the wisest leaders, the fairest laws, the best public policies.

Here once more is the Lockean tension between the "leased" sovereignty of the state and the original sovereignty of the people. Meiklejohn put it well when he wrote, "Though they govern us, we, in a deeper sense, govern them. Over our governing, they have no power. Over their governing we have sovereign power."[27] By this thinking, if the state influences the raw material of democracy—the information on which people make judgments—it exercises a power that fundamentally corrupts self-governance. The message to government is "hands off media!" It's a message many nations emerging from Communist rule are yet to receive.

An example of government jury-rigging was evident in the Croatian elections of 1997, when the government control of print and broadcast media led to a lopsided allocation of time and space to leading party candidates. Not only did news about the party dominate, but the stories gushed with praise for the party while reeking of criticism for the opposition. The selection and treatment of news stacked the public agenda and led the voters unfairly to electoral decisions. Tampering with the information pool thus set in motion a series of events that ended with a corruption of the process that leads people to political judgments.

Americans would do well to admit their own sins, as Senator John McCain tried to do with the campaign reform issue in his losing primary battle with George W. Bush in 2000. The U.S. system of political information corrupts the principles of self-governance, not by state control, but by financial control. Earlier, we alluded to the formula, more money equals more media. It is no secret that candidates with large bankrolls have greater access to the media and, thus, greater access to the public, greater ability to control the public agenda, greater opportunity to tell their story than candidates vexed by fewer resources. Obviously, wealthy candidates can buy more media time and space.[28] But that advantage is doubled, because they also draw more free attention from the news media. Reporters track the leading candidates more closely, and except for a novelty story here and there, they give little attention to third- and fourth-string office seekers, most of whom run hand-to-mouth campaigns. Thus the multiplier effect, whereby leading candidates able to buy more time and space get more free coverage, bring in more money, become better known—and on it goes.

Doesn't this financial advantage tinker with the information pool that is critical to self-governance? Doesn't financial control of the media set in motion a series of events that leads voters to electoral decisions, much as state control of the media leads voters to decisions?

The answers come from two directions, and the first answer cannot be denied: Yes, campaign funds set candidates apart, and the simple fact is that, in getting the message on the street, the advantage goes to candidates with the biggest bank accounts. The information pool is affected; thus self-governance is affected.

The inequity of public access conferred by money has been the rallying cry of reformers who demand limitations on the collection and expenditure of campaign funds. Sadly, the U.S. Supreme Court has rejected previous attempts at campaign financing controls, ironically offering the First Amendment as a rationale. The argument is ironic because the court contends that controlling campaign finances denies political speech to contributors and that is something the First Amendment cannot allow. The court does not deal with the argument that failure to control campaign finances also inhibits political speech, and that is something the First Amendment does not address. It comes down to whose speech is controlled, those with more money or those with less of it, and in the American political system, it has not been much of a contest.[29]

Nevertheless, money's influence in the United States falls far short of the Tito-to-Tuđman legacy in the Croatian system. In Croatia, candidates outside the party had no chance of success at the polls. Media ownership was so airtight that a challenger had no hope of becoming a serious rival to a party-backed candidate. He or she simply could not gain reasonable public access no matter what resources were available. In the United States, candidates with more money have an advantage. True, but poor candidates are not blocked from access to the media or to the public. They have the right and, thus, the possibility of obtaining the support necessary to attract media coverage. On occasion, the candidate with less money comes out ahead. The playing field may not be even, but it is open, and better candidates with grassroots support have a chance at scoring.

In Croatia, the state directly and overtly managed media activities. Editors and publishers of the country's leading media—especially television—answered to the party. No TV broadcaster was independent, and newspapers suffered subtle controls of the party.[30] The U.S. government, by contrast, has no direct ownership of the media, it holds no sway over the content of publishers and broadcasters, and it has nothing to do directly with the political coverage that flows from the news rooms.

Finally, the major media in Croatia were allied with party candidates and made no pretense at fairness. In the United States, most major media work at fair play on the news pages. Liberal and conservative papers typically offer both sides of a political argument, even though their political leanings may be quite pronounced on the editorial pages. The major U.S. television networks traditionally have been evenhanded in the coverage of national campaigns, down to the fastidious allocation of air time for competing candidates. This does not hold for minor candidates, of course, the coverage of whom at the national level would become a practical impossibility, but for the principal races and the major parties, the networks have been reasonably evenhanded, and the public therefore obtains a fair account of the leading candidates.

In the end, the proof is in the pudding. Croatian election results over the past decade have been predictable. The ruling party (HDZ) candidates, to no one's surprise, have consistently swept the elections; an HDZ loss rises to the level of "man bites dog." In money-rules-the-roost U.S. politics, by contrast, changeovers are quite common. Control of the White House swings regularly between the Republicans and the Democrats. The majority party in the halls of Congress trades off from time to time. Individual seats routinely alternate between the two major parties, and on occasion, they include an independent. As plodding as the changeovers may sometimes seem to impatient voters, movement between the parties is reasonably fluid despite the fund-raising advantages of incumbents.

To control the media is to control the electoral process and, ultimately, to control self-governance, and since no system is free of all influences, the impact of media control on the success of democracy is a matter of degree. How tight is the clamp on information? How many alternatives exist through which political messages can flow? How freely can the spirit and the function of the media market operate in order to allow voters to form an accurate picture of the leaders and of the issues facing the country? Tight locks on the press, few alternatives by which to get out information, and restraints on the marketplace of ideas choke off the information and the free exchange of ideas that sustain a government run by the people.

CONCLUSION

Free expression is sometimes seen as a *product* of an open society, but that is backwards: free expression is the *foundation* of an open society. It allows the media to set their own agendas and cover stories as they see fit. It ensures the rights of people to access that information, to analyze it, and to discuss it freely among themselves. An open society and self-governance start with information. If the people are denied that access, they lose control, forfeit their ownership of the government, and become its subjects. A society cannot be open if its media are closed—that's the decisive word, the Continental Divide between societies free and unfree.

Thankfully, James Madison and his like-minded colleagues were around during the birth of the United States to ensure constitutional protection of a free press. Wisely, they accepted Locke's notion of a sovereign people, not a sovereign government, and Milton's idea of truth's power to subdue falsehood on a free and open battlefield. Madison capped their ideas in the famous words with which we began this book. "A popular government, without popular information or the means of acquiring it, is but a Prologue to a Farce or a Tragedy; or, perhaps both."[31]

The application to Croatian communications is suitably theatrical: From the tragedy of Tito to the farce of Tuđman, Croatian politics has reached a hopeful phase in which the curtain is down on Acts I and II, and that's good. What we don't know, however, is what is going to happen now that the curtain is up for Act III. From the backstage actions of the newly elected parliament, we sense a new day of press freedom. On the other hand, new leaders may opt merely to rearrange the furniture and return to the old familiar ways of a state press dominating a variety of semi-independent newspapers and electronic media. In the next chapter, we trace the ringing down of the curtain on the Tuđman era— the encouraging election of 2000—as it was played out in the media.

NOTES

1. To make the point, a poll conducted in the United States in the spring of 1999 by the First Amendment Center at Vanderbilt University found that 53 percent of respondents said they believed that the press has too much freedom. This was a 15 percent increase since 1997. Associated Press report, "Poll: Public Feels Press Has too Much Freedom," *San Francisco Chronicle*, July 4, 1999, A-14.

2. The percentage of voting age population casting a vote for president was 51 percent in 2000 (Federal Election Commission, <www.fec.gov/pubrec/summ.htm>.

3. For a brief discussion about William Blackstone's interpretation of press freedoms as "previous restraints upon publications," see T. B. Carter, Marc A. Franklin, and Jay B. Wright, *The First Amendment and the Fourth Estate: The Law of Mass Media*, 5th ed. (Westbury, N.Y.: The Foundation Press, 1991), 25–26.

4. Alexander Meiklejohn, *Free Speech and Its Relation to Self-Government* (New York: Harper & Brothers, 1948), 65–66.

5. Zechariah Chafee Jr., *Free Speech in the United States* (Cambridge, Mass.: Harvard University Press, 1941).

6. Thomas I. Emerson, *Toward a General Theory of the First Amendment* (New York: Random House, 1966), 882.

7. The core element of this philosophy contrasts radically with an opposing view supported by Thomas Hobbes, an eighteenth century contemporary of John Locke. Hobbes, picking up on a view expressed a century earlier by French philosopher Jean Bodin, asserted an absolute authority of the state. It is the role of the state, he believed, to impose an order to what is otherwise an unruly horde operating by the brutal laws of nature, the survival of the fittest. To impose an order to this chaotic condition, individuals must yield their rights of self-government over to the state. By this view, the state is not comprised of the people; it is above the people and not answerable to them. This is the core difference from Locke's philosophy. In Hobbes's prescription, sovereigns are charged to accomplish an end (the establishment of order and control) and the means by which they do that are beyond question or influence of the people. Hobbes's view is discussed by Edward G. Hudon, *Freedom of Speech and Press in America* (Washington, D.C.: Public Affairs Press, 1961), 30–31.

8. Emerson, *Toward a General Theory of the First Amendment*, 5.

9. Hudon, *Freedom of Speech and Press in America*.

10. Emerson, *Toward a General Theory of the First Amendment*.

11. *Whitney v. California*, 274 U.S. 357, 375–77 (1927). Note the following comments: "In some cases, the social goals are viewed as sub-values that may derive from the achievement of the primary goal of individual self-fulfillment." Carter, Franklin, and Wright, *First Amendment and the Fourth Estate*, 34.

12. In light of the authorities we have quoted, it's intriguing to note that Milton's life overlapped the younger Donne and Hobbes and the older Locke. And if living longer is the sweetest revenge, then Hobbes, at 91, was the winner.

13. John Milton, *Areopagitica*, Vol. 21 (New York: E. P. Dutton, 1927).

14. Ibid.

15. Judge Learned Hand's views are reviewed in Carter Franklin, and Wright, *First Amendment and the Fourth Estate*. These authors quote the judge in *United States v. Associated Press*, 52 F. Supp. 362 (S.D.N.Y. 1943), affirmed 326 U.S. 1 (1944).

16. Emerson, *Toward a General Theory of the First Amendment*, 8.

17. Ibid., 7.

18. A curious exception has occurred in Communist dictatorships. In order to circumvent censorship, novelists and poets were forced to invent metaphors and circumlocutions that were not only more damning than prosaic discourse but were also superb literature. Ironically, when the walls came down, many observers believe, the literature and films declined in quality.

19. E. B. White, "A Voice Heard in the Land," *The New Yorker*, September 11, 1948, reprinted in Rebecca M. Dale, ed., *E. B. White, Writings from The New Yorker, 1927–1976* (New York: HarperPerennial, 1991), 58–59.

20. Carter, Franklin, and Wright, *First Amendment and the Fourth Estate*, 37.

21. His remedy is to shatter the illusion by suspending "the right of free speech and free assembly." This, he believes, will force people to react harshly against the political Right, said to be responsible for the corrupt system. See Carter, Franklin, and Wright, *First Amendment and the Fourth Estate*, for additional analysis of Marcuse's views.

On the matter of objectivity in the press and the presentation of one political viewpoint,

E. B. White once chastised the Democrats for complaining about the Republican right-wing control of the media. He also offered a suggestion: "Democrats do a lot of belly-aching about the press's being preponderantly Republican, which it is. But they don't do the one thing that could correct the situation: they don't go into the publishing business. Democrats say they haven't got that kind of money, but I'm afraid they haven't got that kind of temperament, or, perhaps, nerve." (This is from E. B. White's, "Bedfellows," an essay run in the February 6, 1956, edition of *The New Yorker* and reprinted in *Essays of E. B. White* [New York: Harper and Row, 1977], 80–89.)

22. Jerome A. Barron, *Freedom of the Press for Whom?* (Bloomington: Indiana University Press, 1973).

23. Emerson, *Toward a General Theory of the First Amendment* 14.

24. Ibid.

25. Ibid., 15.

26. Ibid.

27. Alexander Meiklejohn, "The First Amendment Is an Absolute," *Supreme Court Review* 245(1961).

28. FCC regulations stipulate that no licensed broadcaster can reject the political ad (1961) vertisement from a bonafide political candidate. Candidates better able to afford radio and television time, therefore, have a greater opportunity to get out their message on the most popular media.

29. More recently, legislation that observes Supreme Court objections has come to a halt in Congress. In a move frustrating to many supporters of campaign finance limits, House leadership, thumbing its nose at bipartisan, grassroots organizations, refused even to allow the measure to come up for a vote. Incumbents, after all, are the primary beneficiaries of funding inequities and, thus, enjoy financial and electoral advantages over their challengers. Legislators are not known to put themselves at a disadvantage, violation of self-governance principles be damned.

30. See a discussion of government control of the media in Croatia in chapter 1.

31. James Madison, Letter to W. T. Barry, August 4, 1832, in Gaillard Hunt, ed., *The Writings of James Madison*, vol. 9 (New York: G. P. Putnam's Sons, 1910).

4

The Croatian Government's View of the Media

HISTORICAL BACKGROUND

Government control of the media in the former Yugoslavia is legendary, and to understand how such control came about, we must trace the roots of the present totalitarian regime to its source in Bolshevism. Why Bolshevism? A quick primer: Going back to Plato, communism (small "c") envisioned a society based on the communal holding of property. Today, a hippie commune might come close to that idea. By contrast, Communism (Capital "C") envisioned a classless society in which all goods would be socially owned after workers overthrew their capitalist masters. That's when the Bolshevik Party, led by Lenin, became Communism. The key was a disciplined, centralized elite of party members, no longer classless or commune-like, but a hierarchy leading up to a leader with absolute power, surrounded by a few core officials. Central to party control of the masses was the leader's control of the press. That is the legacy of Bolshevism.

Tito's Yugoslavia was built in the tradition of the Soviet Union, but with a few minor modifications: Tito's "soft Communism" opened the borders and granted a little more freedom within the country. Nonetheless, it was inherently the Soviet model, with the roots of Stalin evident everywhere. Even in 1948, when Tito said his historic "No!" to Stalin, he never really changed his way of ruling. Yugoslavia, like the other Communist countries in Europe, was based on the rule of a small group of party members, which wielded unlimited control and held for itself absolute authority over everything.

The communist social model relies on an ideology derived from the theories of Karl Marx and Friedrich Engels. Lenin turned theory into actuality. The "Red" revolution resulted in a new state that was organized on principles of Communism. But it takes more than ideology to run a state, especially one as large as the former USSR. Lenin therefore was faced with the problem of how to govern the country and keep control firmly in his own hands. His approach was simple and almost natural: He organized loyal soldiers of the revolution, who remained from the ruins of the former Czar's government, and gave them authority and near boundless power, but under the control of the Communist Party. Bolshevism thus started a long period of Communist rule, and even after the remarkable changes during the last quarter of the twentieth century, the Bolshevik model is still present in most formerly Communist countries. In some places, like Cuba and China, it is relatively unchanged from years past and conspicuous for all to see. Elsewhere, as in the countries in transition, it is less conspicuous but no less controlling; the Bolshevist model exists deep at the core of the new, "democratic" governments.

Consider these items. The democratic elections after the fall of Communism throughout the former Soviet block countries were run with the mottos: "No to Communism" and "Yes to the independent, national state." But more than a decade later, nationalistic movements are almost gone and the "reformed" Communists are back in power. Is that a paradox? No, because the day-to-day grind of governing is not bound to ideology. The old guard changed labels but continued to govern.

After his rise to power, Stalin wasted no time establishing his iron control of the country. Unfortunately for the people, his control of daily life was cruel and harsh. The party encroached on every facet of the society, no feature was too small or too unimportant to escape the hot breath of the party. Loyal party members, watching and listening, were present everywhere, in the factories, the businesses, the theaters, on every block, in every house. Party control of the media goes without saying.

Party members immediately reported to higher authorities any violation of the general line. This information went through the pyramidal party structure to the highest authorities, decision makers who literally judged life and death for individuals and organizations. Orwell's *1984*, viewed often as a parody in the Western world, held more closely to the realities of life in the Communist countries than people elsewhere may realize. Orwell was seen by many people in Communist countries as a prophet, and his *1984*, as a bible. Many intellectuals had been arrested because they smuggled the book into their country and handed it around from person to person.

The inner party was the sum and substance of pervasive government control. Its powers were unchallenged; its reach was unrestricted.

Countries throughout the Communist empire followed this rigid system of control. Even Tito, whose historic break with the Comintern gave him the unusual opportunity to develop a new form of socialism, never gave up on absolute rule. His soft Communism allowed open borders, minor Western influences, international connections, limited private business, and the development of tourism. It even enjoyed brief periods of relaxed government control, but those periods did not last for long, and for most of the time, the inner party officials in Yugoslavia kept their hands tightly on the levers of control.

Who were the members of the inner party? They were the hard-liners who were the servants of Tito and ardent supporters of his personal policies. All of their power flowed from Tito; all of their allegiance returned to him. Tito, however, was smart enough to realize that while he had a firm grip on his own country, he needed an external affiliation to sustain his power. The Soviet model was based on the hegemony of the Russian nation. Tito decided that his power would be linked with the hegemony of the Serbian nation in Yugoslavia. The reasons for this decision are instructive.

The Serbs were the largest ethnic group in Yugoslavia. During the Yugoslavia of 1918–1941, the kingdom was ruled by the Serbian royal family which promoted the Serbian national dream to create an all-powerful Serbia that would dominate other south Slavic nations.

This political dream was realized by Tito, who gave Serbs power in the party and control over the Secret Service Police (UDBA) and the Yugoslav National (People's) Army (JNA). This power was strong enough to provide the authority of rule they sought. The weakness of the system was that it raised questions of unsolved relations among the various nationalities represented in Yugoslavia, and it elevated, perhaps exacerbated, problems inherent among the various religions and nationalities. Tito himself was born a Croat with Slovenian roots, but he never expressed national feelings. He was interested only in his own control and authority, so his adoption of powerful Serbian hegemonism was a decision based solely on the pragmatics of power.

Tito's integration of the inherent differences within Yugoslavia proved to be most efficient. He drew up divisions based on several characteristics:

- The three major religions (Catholic, Orthodox, and Moslem);
- The six republics (Slovenia, Croatia, Serbia, Bosnia and Herzegovina, Macedonia, and Montenegro) plus two autonomous provinces of Vojvodina and Kosovo;
- The five major nationalities (Slovenes, Croats, Serbs, Macedonians, and Montenegrins) and numerous national minorities living throughout the country. (Tito allowed the Moslems to declare themselves a separate Moslem nationality.)

Consider the divisions within each group and then the combinations and permutations of the various groups to understand the complications of Tito's scheme. Clearly, Tito did not foster the concept of a melting pot after the fashion of the American model.

His idea was to build the new Yugoslav nationality, a concept supported by Communist ideologists. Many young people, mostly the product of mixed marriages, declared themselves as "Yugoslavs." Some "Yugoslavs" tried to hide their Croatian or other national roots, counting on better promotions and better party careers.[1] But the brutal events that took place in the 1990s showed that the idea was without a future. National feelings and ethnic identity were much stronger than artificial Yugoslav identity, and the public reaction clearly demonstrated that the melting pot concept was not possible in the Balkans.

The concept of the artificial country solved none of the major problems that continued to brew over nationalism, religion, politics, and economics. Beneath the surface of the powerful Tito government awaited a legion of dissatisfied political, national, and religious movements preparing for the right moment to release their pent up frustrations and to realize their political objectives.

The problems started immediately after Yugoslavia was established in Versailles after World War I. Creating an artificial country is like assembling a powder keg; one spark is enough for an explosion. Even after the cruel events during World War II and the most recent conflicts in the nineties, the problems are not yet solved, and even worse, the draft of a workable solution is not even on the table.

To understand why conditions are so intractable, it is crucial to understand what happened during Tito's fifty years of Communist rule. Government's absolute control of society, including the media, has much to do with current conditions. Western analysts were often fooled by "democratic" laws, the development of a new socialism, the principles of self-management, the apparent participation of the working class in government operations, the freedom of expression, and the other signs that gave the impression of a country moving ever closer to Western democratic values.

Tito was a master in creating a double reality. On the surface it appeared that he was building a "new socialism" comprised of self-management, collective government, a non-alignment movement, brotherhood, unity, and other warm ideological creations. But, whenever his personal authority was in danger or a deputy became too ambitious or expressed an interest in grabbing power, Tito's reaction was quick, sharp, and brutal, and it showed none of the benign, humanitarian values that floated on the surface of his new socialism. Tito's second reality displayed his competence at secret political games, false promises, tactical negotiations, and public manipulations. Each opponent during his half-century rule was knocked down like a profile on a shooting range. Tito left in his wake a long list of purged young revolutionaries whose dream was to take over the party, but a few ambitious ones survived.

Milovan Ðilas is well known in the West for his metamorphosis from cruel party commissar to the dissident who finally recognized and acknowledged the cruel face of communism.

Ðilas, however, never had a chance to replace Tito or to change the system. Tito was too strong; he controlled the police and the JNA. Ðilas' criticism of Bolshevism was well accepted among party intellectuals and liberals, but it was not enough to take over leadership.

The same was true of each of Tito's opponents, none of whom was strong enough to dislodge the supreme leader, whose iron grasp prevented even the most stalwart opponent from rising to power. These failures included tenacious leaders of the mass movements that formed in the Croatian Spring of the 1970s and serious attempts from diverse geographic regions in Slovenia, Serbia, Montenegro, and Kosovo.

Tito's durability became the stuff of many jokes, most of which are a variation on this one:

Tito became old and sick, and his advisors told him how he should write his last will and testament.
  "Why should I write the testament?" Tito asked his advisor.
  "Just in case, comrade Tito, just in case," answered the advisor.
  "OK," said Tito who then started dictating his will: "If I ever die . . ."

Tito's deceptive appearance belied the reality beneath the surface. The people were informed of every rule and regulation in the official party register, and they were instructed in obedience to each of the party's demands and expectations. Nobody abused the party line in public, for that would have been foolish, but in private, most citizens continued with their cultural, social, and religious practices. For the average person, double morals and parallel life tracks became a common way of living. Each citizen became a master of disguise, wearing an official mask in public, revealing his real face in private. For instance, the party directed people to despise the church and to cease celebrations at Christmas and Easter. Sunday masses were taboo.[2] Yet with curtains drawn and windows shut, the people celebrated the religious and, to a limited extent, the secular features of the holidays, and they found ways of holding masses in the shadows of private homes and faceless buildings. Discreetly and privately, nearly everyone celebrated Christmas and Easter, the majority baptized their children, and a small minority even risked the wrath of the secret police by attending Sunday mass.

In order to preoccupy the people at the times of greatest temptation—for instance, on Christmas eve—local party organizations set up official meetings. They would use these events to argue the negative influences of religion on workers and, especially, on intellectuals, in the hope of inculcating in the people a disdain for the church. But, for most people, the meetings were like a cork in a bottle of Champagne. After the meetings, people rushed home to celebrate Christmas with their families, perhaps to sneak off to a midnight mass, trusting that the secret police would be too drunk to see who was going where.

The rules were strict and the surveillance mechanism was efficient at detecting the public violations, even though the private violations sneaked beneath the party's radar. When behaviors were indiscrete, the police took names, the consequences of which might be a lost job or the destruction of a promising career. Everyone was subject to this watchful eye, but under the strictest control were party members and certain professionals, including teachers, managers, and journalists.

The dual reality, the public and the private, was a metaphor for Tito's Yugoslavia. Nobody talked publicly about it; nobody admitted a double life. It was a matter of survival, even for the children, who were conditioned to enact the dual roles from the earliest ages. Children were aware that they could not declare religious beliefs in school. They knew how their families celebrated Christmas and who celebrated it with them, but none spoke about it with their teachers, who came to the classroom sleepy after midnight mass. What a farce!

In the face of conditions imposed by Tito's rule, the people employed a convoluted rationale to justify the maintenance of their private lives. It went something like this: Communism voided private ownership, so everything was owned, therefore, by the state, and the state, in turn, is owned by everyone and by no one. In that case, the logic went, it was not immoral to cheat the state, to steal state property, to disobey the laws, because nobody was really behind the government authority (since everything, including the government, was owned by no one). The inner party ruled because it took over power from the people and from democratic institutions, so party power is unnatural and illegitimate. All this comes down to one question: Why is it immoral to disobey a party that has illegitimately taken power from the people?

Generations were raised under these suffocating social conditions. Despite their daily experiences, the people knew that the system was wrong, inhuman, and based on the tyranny of a small group of party members. Each generation had to face these cruel facts, all the while knowing from contacts with the Western world, from reading, studying, and some traveling, that conditions were unnecessarily harsh and fundamentally unfair to the Yugoslav people.

Awareness of Western freedoms and frustrations with domestic constraints pushed people to ask questions and to seek relief from the Communist model. Sensing this discontent, Tito was wise enough to allow the release of a safety valve from time to time. Whenever the economy became particularly severe, whenever waves of the national feelings became too strong, whenever members of the inner party became visibly corrupt and incapable of governing, he loosened the rules, if only a little, and introduced just enough democratic freedom to ease public pressure.

Tito had a sixth sense about these things. When Yugoslavia entered a deep economic crisis in the late 1950s and early 1960s, he allowed small economic changes, such as permitting self-management and opening the borders to allow citizens access to jobs in Third World countries. Tito soon recognized that opening the borders also invited in tourists and the influx of tourism dollars, which proved to be a mild tonic for the ailing economy. But with Western dollars came Western ideas about politics and the economy. A sense of entrepreneurship washed into the country along with other ideas about capitalism and democratic values.

Tito's liberalizations brought in new political ideas. The 1960s saw a rise in influential political movements throughout Slovenia, Serbia, and especially in Croatia. Rigid Bolshevism was no longer possible in handling rising problems in the country, and young Communist leaders were not satisfied with their role in governing. Tito realized that the time had come to give way to liberal streams. But this liberalization was not well accepted among strong party leaders. Aleksandar Ranković, the powerful party leader from Serbia, second to Tito in party hierarchy and chief of the secret police, did not support Tito. In fact, Ranković took control over the country using strong police forces. He even controlled Tito himself—up to a point—by bugging the leader's private quarters.

In 1965, Tito was forced to replace Ranković after a dramatic meeting of the politburo on Brijuni Island. Tito's control over the JNA was crucial because JNA loyal units were the breakpoint in the fight among politburo members. Ranković was replaced and spent the rest of his life as a private citizen, far away from politics.

Replacing hard-liners Ranković and the Brijuni politburo plenum was a clear signal for younger party leaders in the republics to raise their particular interests. The iron grip of the UDBA was relaxed, the party line got more liberal, and Tito allowed reforms that resulted in economic growth and a wave of optimism.

Liberal movements, especially in Croatia, were connected with the expression of suppressed national feeling. The famed Croatian Spring raised the great mass movement that was brutally stopped by Tito. Serbian liberalism also was broken. Tito confirmed his personal dictatorship by establishing the collective leadership in 1978. Members of the collective leadership of the state, party, or any political organization in the country, at all levels, were obliged to switch their jobs with each other every year. Yugoslavia was overwhelmed by one-year presidents of the state, party, republics, city councils, companies, war veterans, youth organizations, and even the Boy Scouts. Ordinary people quickly dubbed the one-year leadership cycle "deciduous"!

Tito's death in 1980 was a shock for the nation, and his funeral was the last expression of "surface unity" in Yugoslavia. The collective presidency of the state and the party adopted the slogan "After Tito—Tito!" in an attempt to convince the people that nothing would change and that Tito's policy would endure forever.

The first few years after Tito's death were void of visible candidates to assume Tito's authoritarian role. It was like the bicycle races in the Velodrome, where contestants ride several laps bike to bike, the race never engaging until one rider starts to accelerate. The trick is timing: Don't start too early, but finish on time. Tito's successors played by this rule, showing the public only a mild interest in the post while they prepared to finish the run successfully.

The media picked up the cause of the public in the political fights. Party leaders in each republic used their local media to spread political ideas and to assault party leaders in other republics. The media became political weapons and played a significant role in spreading nationalism.

Of the challengers lining up to be Tito's successor, Slobodan Milošević became the key player, because he was the one who started the race and set the pack in motion. His timing was off by a beat, however, because he had not counted on the Slovenians to be so strong and steadfast in their resistance to his objectives. The unfinished congress of the Yugoslav party in January 1990 ended in collapse when the Slovenians left the congress, the Croats were close to leaving, and the Serbs let it be known that they intended to rule the country. The lines were drawn, war appeared on the horizon, and the bitter tone Slobodan Milošević set was exemplified by his defiant declaration in Kosovo in 1990: "Serbs may not know how to work, but they know how to fight!"

INFLUENCE ON MEDIA

Why is this background so important in understanding the media in former Yugoslavia and, specifically, later in the Croatian state? Because one cannot grasp the current problems of the media without first recognizing how the Communist system set in motion the political, economic, and social conditions that prevail today. Then all political decisions were made under the strong influence of Bolshevism. The role of the media under that system was not to provide honest, accurate, and impartial information but to inform the public about the party's view of events. The media's sense for news and the journalists' values and objectives, were not the same as they are for Western reporters. The market had no influence on the media, real life had no relevance, and real events were covered only if the party commissar instructed an editor to cover them. It was the duty of journalists to explain the party line, to pass along party directives, to point out how policies, actions, and events would influence public life. Period.

Media in the former Yugoslavia were cast in the Soviet mold, and to understand Croatian media, it helps to understand how the Soviets viewed the role of the press. Downing et al. described it this way:

It is important to recall that Soviet media were originally conceived according to yet another normative theory, namely, that media existed for the purpose of developing political awareness and commitment to work for a just and fair society, a socialist philosophy. One of the tragedies of the twentieth century is the process by which those ideas became perverted into their opposite under the Stalin regime and at the hands of most of his successors at the helm of the Soviet state.[3]

What are the priorities of the Soviet model of mass media? Paul Lendvai describes them as follows: "What is news? In the Soviet context basically anything which can be used to illustrate current party policy or economic progress is considered worthy of publication and almost anything else is considered unimportant and unworthy."[4]

Lendvai illustrates this news approach with a statement of N. G. Palgunov, a former TASS (official news agency of the Soviet Union from 1925 to 1991) director and head of Moscow University's Faculty of Journalism. Palgunov defined the Soviet news value as follows:

News should not be merely concerned with reporting such and such a fact or event. News or information must pursue a definite goal: it must serve and support the decisions related to fundamental duties facing our Soviet society, our Soviet people marching on the road of gradual transition from socialism to Communism. In selecting the object of information, the author of an informative report, must above all, abandon the notion that just any fact or just any events have to be reported in the pages of the newspaper. The aim of information must be to present selected facts and events.[5]

This was not just Palgunov's personal opinion, it was the official media policy of the Soviet Union. The same system was transferred to Tito's Yugoslavia. The media were simply an official propaganda tool of the ruling regime and were granted no other role. Whenever journalists, on occasion, ran after real news, the system struck out and forced the media back into its propagandist role.

Officially, the law allowed democracy—freedom of the press and freedom of speech—but as in so many things during that period, it was the difference between theory and reality, between what was posted for public consumption and what was enacted in daily life. Clearly, the media were hamstrung, and they were prevented from publishing the truth as editors and journalists saw fit. With a proclaimed openness of free press and free expression, how were the media controlled?

In the fifties and early sixties, Tito copied the Soviet model, but over time his relationship with "mother Russia" had changed, as he took up an increasingly independent role. The transition influenced all aspects of life in Yugoslavia, including the media.

The Yugoslavian socialist and self-management system required a specific mass media model. The Soviet model provided the basics, and Western media added additional elements, but the realization was a local Yugoslavian creation. So the media were a Tito paradox. They carried Tito's ideology, but the presentation was Western-like. The layout of newspapers bore the appearance of Italian, German, and British papers. Television broadcast music shows, radio stations played rock 'n roll, but news aired on both media was under party control.

Orwell's Big Brother, who watches citizens from every monitor or screen, was fiction, but the principle of centrally controlled information was an everyday reality in the former Eastern bloc countries. Governing ideology for all of Tito's Yugoslavia, including the doctrine for information and media systems, was adopted from the "Soviet brothers." Prohibited were private papers and radio and television stations; all outlets came under direct control of the state. The media were organized into big publishing houses, which were controlled by managers and editors appointed by the Communist Party. The system was in force at every level—federal, republic, and regional.

The publishing houses consisted of three basic units: the publishing, printing, and sales divisions, all supported by a central unit of technical services. These collectives were usually giants with thousands of workers; the largest, run on the federal Yugoslav level, were the Borba and Tanjug media companies.

In addition, each republic had its own house: Delo in Slovenia, Vjesnik in Croatia,[6] Oslobođenje in Bosnia and Herzegovina, Politika in Serbia, Pobjeda in Montenegro, and Nova Makedonija in Macedonia. The more developed regions within the republics also had publishing houses operating on the same principle. For instance, Slobodna Dalmacija in Dalmatia, Dnevnik in Vojvodina, and Rilindja in Kosovo. Those were the real media mammoths, powerful and unchallenged in their day, but when Communism fell, so did these big, state-run companies.

Operational functions of these publishing houses, from the journalists' work to distribution at street corner kiosks, were vertically integrated, and all production, printing, and sales were centrally controlled. The only exceptions were some small peripheral and specialized papers of no great significance (such as general science, agriculture, or fishing publications), which could be printed in smaller publishing companies. Some of the specialized papers were run by the Socialistic Union of the Working People (SSRN), a political organization under control of the Communist Party. All papers of even modest significance, however, were managed by one of the major printing companies, which kept books on every story, photo, and editorial to ensure strict compliance with party ideology.

A similar command-and-control structure existed for the electronic media. While broadcasters were not formally organized under an official government department, they were united as an association of Yugoslav Radio and Television (JRT). The local radio and television companies within each republic produced their own shows, but some program sharing among television companies in different republics provided material common throughout the country. Language differences provided a natural barrier for convenient exchange of shows, but these matters were often addressed with subtitles. Language remained a problem, nonetheless, and it offered a significant reason for most companies to continue with local productions. No matter if programs were shared or aired strictly at the local level, all productions in all republics remained under the watchful eye of the Communist Party. That was an experience common to all broadcasters, no matter where they operated.

That fact was important to the liberalization of the Yugoslav press, because when the central government weakened, it was possible for local party leaders in the republics to influence audiences with their own ideas. It was important to have their own newspaper or broadcasting companies, which were freed from external influences and control.[7]

As we noted earlier, the principal, Yugoslav-level media companies were Borba and Tanjug. Borba published two daily newspapers, *Borba* and *Večernje novosti*. *Borba*, a daily broad-sheet, was well known as the official voice of the government, and in the early fifties it was the best-selling newspaper in Yugoslavia. But this is a bogus claim because *Borba*'s circulation was augmented artificially through compulsory subscriptions for all local party branches, governmental offices, JNA barracks, and company managers. The party used *Borba* like a company newsletter to send official messages to field workers. It was a typical party paper, with pages of official documents and speeches by party leaders printed in nine-point font without photos or page frames. One could hardly read it. Among journalists, the name for *Borba* was "The Sheet" (read as "The Shit"). *Borba* was composed and printed in Belgrade for the Cyrillic alphabet versions and sent by overnight train to a printing plant in Zagreb for publication with Latin letters.

The second daily newspaper published by Borba was *Večernje novosti*, a very well-edited evening paper. It was a modern tabloid with short news, human interest stories, big photos, well-written headlines, and lots of sports, city, and regional reports. The results were obvious. For a long period of time, *Večernje novosti* had the largest circulation in Yugoslavia. Only *Večernji list* from Zagreb occasionally beat them.

Vjesnik was by far the largest and most popular newspaper company in the republics. For instance, Vjesnik always followed the latest publishing and printing methods. It was the first in Zagreb to offer full color and offset printing, the first to outfit a computerized printing plant, the first to generate a computerized magazine (*Start*) and a computerized daily paper (*Večernji list*), and the first with electronic page transfers to a remote printing plant (*Večernji list*). It also produced the best-edited and the best-selling papers in the country.[8]

The Croatian press produced well-edited student and youth media whose influence was visible during the periods of liberalization. Two newspapers, *Studentski list* and *Polet*, were among the papers that influenced not only student populations but wider audiences as well. Some journalists from this period have become well known and even now influence the media in Croatia. Ninoslav Pavić, former editor of *Polet*, is now the largest private media owner in Croatia. Denis Kuljiš was editor and founder of *Globus* and *Nacional*, two new and influential political weeklies.

Today, student journalists have little such influence because of the current media conditions. In the former Yugoslavia, student media had more freedom than official newspapers, and those young journalists used their opportunities to put out papers that would never be tolerated from professionals. After several years at student papers, many found jobs in regular media, where they attempted to continue their liberal style. Sometimes they were slapped down.

Zagreb's radio and television company (today's Croatian HRTV) was also a leading voice in the former Yugoslavia. It was the first in the Balkans to put a radio station on the air when it began broadcasting from Zagreb on May 15, 1926. It broadcast the Balkans' first live report on November 7, 1926, when it aired the opening ceremony of the Bishop J. J. Strossmayer monument in front of the Yugoslav Academy of Science and Art. The first television station in Yugoslavia went on the air from Zagreb on August 3, 1956, and several months later, TV Zagreb started regular, experimental broadcasting. Belgrade may have been the Yugoslavan capital and political and administrative center but Zagreb, with its Western orientation, became the center of Yugoslavia's media and culture.

Central to the party's control of the country was the party's control of the media. If the party dared to loosen its reins on the journalistic corps, there was little question that the papers and broadcast stations would have introduced opposition views to the public, a prospect which the party feared. This was especially true in Slovenia and Croatia, the two Yugoslavian republics always spring-loaded to defy party control. It was this westward-looking stance that caused the party in Slovenia and Croatia to seek additional ways to assert its authority and control over the media.

Of course, the party's first means of control was the publishing industry, which served as a well head for all primary media. Another, more personal approach involved recruiting journalists to become members of the Communist Party. In one period, almost 95 percent of journalists were members of the party, while only about 10 percent of the population at large were listed as party members.

Why was party membership so important? Because as members of the party, the journalists themselves became part of the controlling structure, and for some there was a sense of ownership in the system. Besides, journalists were more easily manipulated and more vulnerable to the party's application of rewards and punishments. If editors or reporters disobeyed the general line, misused their position, and wrote against the official "directive," the party could quickly react with strong measures. Miscreants could be punished internally at local party branch meetings and transferred to another post. Editors could be reassigned as proofreaders, or they could be sent to the "morgue" as a file clerk. A reporter's beat could become irrelevant, with a punitive assignment to a trivial city desk, the crosswords, or some long-forgotten outpost. Disobedient or rabble-rousing journalists disappeared, and often nobody knew exactly why. The pending threat that always loomed over the heads of Yugoslavia's journalists proved to be an efficient and effective system in stimulating self-censorship.

In the next chapter, we will look more closely at self-censorship. Self-preservation or journalist's scourge—the practice has been the limiting force in the Yugoslav, then in Croatian, media since Tito.

NOTES

1. The number of citizens who declared themselves as "Yugoslavs" was rising. According to the census in 1953, 16,964 people declared themselves as Yugoslavs in the territory of Croatia. The number of Yugoslavs rose in 1971 to 84,118. The highest number of Yugoslavs was declared in 1981, with a total of 379,057. Tito's new nation almost was born. But after his death and during Yugoslavia's crisis, the number of Yugoslavs decreased to 106,041 in the last census in 1991. There are no further figures on the national structure of Croatian citizens, but it is all but certain that the number of

Yugoslavs is very small in the new Croatian state. This melting pot idea was not strange for communism, because its ideology relied on working class and proletariat values and not on national identity. Yugoslav feelings were also present in culture, art, and media. Yugoslav culture and art was presented to the world as a unique achievement, even if, like native art, it was created in limited, local areas.

2. In public, religion was condemned, and practicing religious rituals was only for the "enemies of the people." Priests were not allowed to participate in public life, for the church was all but illegal.

3. John Downing, Ali Mohammadi, and Annabele Srebery-Mohammadi, eds., *Questioning the Media* (London: Sage Publications, 1990), 139.

4. Paul Lendvai, "What Is Newsworthy—and What Is Not—in the Communist World," in *Comparative Mass Media Systems*, ed. L. John Martin and Anju Grover Chaudhary (White Plains, N.Y.: Longman, 1983), 68.

5. Ibid., 69.

6. The former leadership used to boast that, among all the media mammoths, Vjesnik was the biggest newspaper house in the former Yugoslavia, even the largest throughout the Balkans.

7. The federation and the republics always had conflicts of interest, including disagreements over the budget and the media. Republican leaders were interested in maximum autonomy, and the media were used to promote their positive image. Furthermore, the republics fought among themselves. Developed republics, like Slovenia and Croatia, were not happy giving money to Serbia and Macedonia. An often cited proverb said, "Croatians are working, Belgrade is building up." Today's version is "Dalmatia is working, Zagreb is building up." It is a constant conflict between metropolitan regions and the provinces.

8. "What *Večernji list* did in the last few years is one of the most serious lectures to our [Yugoslav] journalism . . . How to explain its popularity? My opinion is that *Večernji list* was very close to the readers." Jug Grizelj, journalist, Belgrade, *Večernje novosti*.

Vjesnik's leading edition was the *Vjesnik* daily broad-sheet, a very well-edited and extremely influential paper in landmark political events such as the Croatian Spring. *Večernji list*, the evening paper, created under the influence of the *Daily Mirror*, became the best-selling Yugoslav daily, with an average circulation of 370,000 copies and printings in twenty local editions. Vjesnik publishing company was known by its reviews and magazines: *Vjesnik u srijedu, Start, Studio, Arena, Svijet, Plavi vjesnik, Danas*, and others.

Besides Vjesnik, there were three very developed and influential regional publishing, printing, and sales companies: Slobodna Dalmacija in Split, Novi list in Rijeka, and Glas Slavonije in Osijek. Using the Vjesnik model, all three regional companies concentrated all functions in one central facility. Two local daily newspapers, *Slobodna Dalmacija* and *Novi list*, have had no significant competition in the last fifty years. Within their own regions, they are the undisputed newspaper powerhouses.

5

The Press and Self-Censorship

The journalism practiced in Tito's Yugoslavia was more developed and more professional, by Western standards, than the journalism practiced in the Soviet Union and other Communist countries. As with most other aspects of life in Yugoslavia, the reporting of public news was less burdened by state control because of Tito's embrace of a softer, kinder version of Communism, recognized in part by a greater tolerance of Western ideas. Openness to the outside nurtured a more liberal media and elevated the role of news and public information that was never seen in the Soviet bloc countries. By no means were the media in Yugoslavia free-spoken by Western standards, but neither were they government handmaidens, as they were in Eastern Europe. Through the lens of this history, present-day journalists view the profession and the practice of their trade. We will examine some of this history before looking at the views of today's Croatian journalists.

HISTORICAL BACKGROUND

The first newspaper written in the Croatian language was published on the Adriatic coast in the city of Zadar, on July 12, 1806. The language may have been Croatian, but the news was derived from information released by the French Occupation Army Forces and not compiled by Croatian reporters. From the earliest days, newspapers in Croatia were not entirely free to report Croatian news.

Božo Novak, a noted Croatian journalist, offers the poignant observation that press freedom in Croatia, to understate it, has been a persistent struggle. In the second half of the nineteenth century, the press faced serious restrictions and legal obstacles at the hands of the Royal Yugoslav government. The worst of these was in 1929, when the Yugoslav police confiscated leading papers more than 100 times.

Politics in Yugoslavia became more complex and confrontational after the 1934 assassination of King Alexander in Marseilles, and the resulting political chaos was reflected in the pages of the country's newspapers. The press played increasingly active and partisan roles in the political crossfire that took place among advocates of the extreme ideologies that fought it out during this period. For nearly a decade, newspapers became embroiled in the fierce battles among the Communists, Nazis, and Fascists from the outside and the Croatian Peasant's Party and the Ustasha movement from within.[1]

One of the more evident examples of the heated conflicts in this tumultuous period can been seen up to and during World War II. In the late 1930s and early 1940s, Croatia became a caldron for the searing mix of the profascist Independent Croatian State (NDH), linked to Hitler's Nazis, and the strong antifascist movement led by the Communist Party, headed by Tito. Journalists became embroiled on both sides of the conflict, not as objective reporters of news but as opinionated supporters of ideologies, movements, and parties. This troubled period in Croatian history fostered an advocacy journalism of partisanship and promotion and offered no opportunity for the rational reporting of facts and the honest appraisal of news. Wars usually put reporters' feet to the fire, but during this war in this place, the conditions vastly overwhelmed the media.

Novak explains the changing role of the press under Tito:

In Tito's Yugoslavia the Croatian press went through several stages. The period after the liberalization until 1962 was strongly dominated by "Bolshevization" of Yugoslavia and Croatia, and the intensification of the great Serbian domination, suppression and plundering of Croatia.

The next period ended with the suppression of the Croatian Spring Movement on the 1st December 1971 in Karađorđevo. This was a time of economic and political reforms in which Croatia started to gain independence from the political center in Belgrade. The pluralism of the press and public opinion was on the increase. At that time the newspaper company Vjesnik and RTV Zagreb, together with numerous publications of the *Matica Hrvatska* and youth or student magazine, represented the burst of democratic freedoms and the hope of the total breakdown of Bolshevism and great-Serbian hegemony. The period until the first democratic elections was characterized by massive persecution of the press, journalists and intellectuals. Between 80,000 and 100,000 followers and supporters of the Croatian Spring Movement, particularly intellectuals and journalists, underwent repression.[2]

The tumultuous history of Croatian journalism created an image of the profession among reporters and the public that lingers even today. Yet more than an image was at stake. Years of media control had established professional practices and expectations and formed a general image of the media's role in public life and in political responsibilities. In earlier days, journalists were seen as the servants of government rather than the defenders of free expression. They transformed government policy papers into news copy, and given these mundane assignments, they knew little of the investigative skills practiced by their Western counterparts.

From years of repression, the public, too, formed perceptions of the media, accepting them as an organ of the state. To them, a newspaper was, by definition, a tool by which the government talked to the people. It would have been inconceivable to most readers that a paper would challenge the government or attack public policy. Indeed, a story about corruption in high places would have been seen as dangerous fiction. The public had no experience with an aggressive, probing media, and those impressions, which formed years ago, linger today.

It is difficult for westerners to understand why Croatian reporters, even today, practice a relatively passive journalism rather than adopt more aggressive practices. By the same token, it is hard for westerners to accept the reality that the Croatian public has been neither disappointed in the journalism recently practiced nor eager to see the hard-hitting stories typically found in more open societies. Maybe the following anecdote helps explain their inability to grasp the situation.

A Croatian fisherman cast his line into the Sutla River, which is the border between Slovenia and Croatia. On his side of the river, the fish were not biting. On the other side, in Slovenia, a young boy was reeling in fish by the bucketful. The fisherman, eager for such success, wanted to cross the river as quickly as possible, but with no bridge or boat in sight, he shouted to the boy, "How did you cross the river?" The boy looked at him and answered, "I was born here!"

It's that simple. The fact that you were born under Communism—on one side of the river—determined your entire life. It provided experiences and a lifestyle, and it set up expectations. Only 200 kilometers west was freedom and an entirely different set of experiences, a different lifestyle creating altered expectations. At heart, of course, the people are the same; they have only been molded differently by their environments. Those born under Communism are no less educated or less sensitive to the human condition; they do not appreciate any less the brilliance of science, nor do they value less the elegance of good art and literature. Surely, they would value the benefits of good reporting—and the payoffs of investigative journalism—if only their experiences could let them sample it.

Immediately after World War II, the Yugoslav Communist Party assumed control of all segments of life, including the practice of journalism. Special bodies within the party, called Agitprop (*Agitacija i propaganda* in English is agitation and propaganda), ensured media purity. They guaranteed that the media "kept the party line," informed the public about the party's achievements, and reminded readers endlessly that the party was headed by "the beloved" and infallible President Tito. Journalists did not assemble their own news agendas or pursue an independent reporting schedule. Their role was propaganda, pure and simple. Events as far from politics as the wheat harvest were made to serve the party, and it became the press's job to lavish praise on the genius of Marx, Engels, Lenin, and Tito for creating favorable conditions in which the wheat could grow.

The party asserted itself into every aspect of life, and it fell to the press to remind the people that the party was indispensable. The official party line was disseminated by *Borba*, the leading newspaper, which each day told the people the opinions they were obliged to hold. The editors were joined at the hip with Agitprop members and with other party officials who kept careful watch on every line that appeared in print. Editorial policy was, thereby, directed by the party, lock, stock, and barrel.

Maintaining control over the press was simple. Journalists were obliged to be members of the party, and like all party members, their primary charge was to obey and promote party policies.

The internal mechanisms that enforced discipline were quite efficient. When a party member disobeyed the policy, the "comrade secretary" set in motion a disciplinary mechanism that was both subtle and effective, having been refined by years of practice. Everything was internal; all actions were quiet. There were never public scandals, never embarrassing incidents, never judicial involvement. Unlike loud, public punishments, which would have enabled people to monitor government control and measure the level of dissent, the silent, furtive retaliations fed the imagination and fostered a sense of the unknown, heightening the fear.

Errant party journalists were punished for "not being awake in realization of the party line" and removed from their media posts. If the offender held a minor position, say, as a reporter or a secondary editor, and his "mistake" was relatively small, he might be transferred to a regional publication or assigned as a proofreader. More senior players and more serious mistakes could land the offender in the newspaper morgue (a dead-end job, no pun intended) or in an irrelevant administrative post. He would be forbidden to publish stories or to engage in activities customary of the profession that might allow him to "sin" yet again. They called these people the "walking dead journalists," and the duration of their sentences—a month, a year, a few years—were at the discretion of the party commissar.

A journalist could not simply walk out of the newsroom and look for another job, since all jobs came under the control of the party. When the party punished someone, the sentence eclipsed all other options because each option would have required party approval. The punishment of errant journalists, therefore, was in the diminished tasks imposed by the sentence, in the futility of legal recourse, and in the blocking of alternative employment. The only slim chance a delinquent journalist had to escape this fate was to become a dissident, which almost always meant exile to a farm or to an assembly line in some remote outpost. Dissident status was not an attractive choice.

The intended impact of these cruel punishments was to pressure journalists into self-censorship. The plan was remarkably effective, if laughably transparent.

The basic rule said that a single venture into taboo territory will be your last; the cost for violations is absolute. So, if your beat is the steel mill, your role is to tout the success of the operation, the wisdom of the party, and the eminence of President Tito. It was your job to explain the inspiration of Marx and Engels and the vision of Tito and to applaud the brave workers at the mill. With such a job description, journalism training was a snap, and anyone could hack it in no time at all.

Discoveries of malfeasance, corruption, negligence, health dangers, black market involvement, and other problems that would be fair game for Western reporters, were off-limits for Tito's press corps. Journalists simply could not investigate such things, for even showing a professional interest in these matters might trigger an official reaction and bring about the awful consequences noted above. Self-preservation—in the journalist's lexicon, self-censorship—told the reporter that he had nothing to gain and everything to lose by such pursuits.

It isn't difficult to understand how self-censorship killed stories—and thoughts of stories—even mildly uncomfortable to the state and the party. Furthermore, it's easy to see how the system molded a generation of journalists to become little more than writers of advertising copy, with few opportunities to study, observe, or practice reporting skills common in Western versions of the profession. Seen from the outside, then, reporters in press-controlled countries may seem to be compliant serfs of the system who have little interest in aggressive journalism. Seen up close, however, it was a different story.

The restrictions were a nightmare for the journalists and an assault on their personal and professional dignity. They knew full well that they were pawns in a larger strategy to control the public mind, and they knew, also, that their daily efforts served the masters who killed the spirit and the practice of their noble profession. They were, thus, the victims and the victimizers, and that thought was a constant torment and an enduring disgrace.

Many journalists found comfort in alcohol, and many attempted to get around the system but failed. The party was strong, the commissars were eager to chase down each insubordination, and there were no exceptions. There was no agency, watch group, or public monitor to lend a hand or to sit in fair judgment on appeals. The system was efficient and effective and served the shameful ends of Tito and his party.

But, once in a while, during periods of liberalization, when Tito wanted to curry favors with the West, when he decided to show the nice face of Yugoslav governance, the reins would slack some, and reporters would seize the opportunities to practice real reporting. These were infrequent periods, and they usually coincided with Tito's quest for new loans and grants and grace from lenders whose payments were due. The doors would open, and the country would display its soft Communism for the world to see.

Adventurous journalists used these periods of liberalization to play a game called "attempts and punishment" with party hard-liners. To understand the game, you must know that even in these lighter times, all controversial and challenging topics remained taboo. There never was an official pronouncement, of course, but reporters were reminded of the items to avoid, lest in their euphoria they trip the wire and suffer the party's wrath. For instance, they were cautioned to stay at arms length from praise for the church, discussion of dissidents, coverage of free market values, and analysis of philosophies that did not in some way originate from Marx, Lenin, or, naturally, from Tito himself. They could not challenge the party, the army, other pillars of socialism, self-management, and other canons of the state.

But journalists sensed a weakness in this concrete wall, and the more spirited of them occasionally tested that theory. For example, one eminent scientist (Prof. Dr. Ivan Supek) dared publicly to discuss ideas which were not based on Marxism. It happened when he was invited to a party-sponsored "scientific" workshop, where, predictably, everyone competed to extol Marx's brilliance and to explain how Yugoslavia's academic community, led by Tito, was contributing to modern Marxist theory. Without warning, this scientist ventured to explain ideas not in keeping with this hackneyed old theme. Although he shocked party ears, it was too late to stop him; the cat was out of the bag. Journalists covering the workshop seized on the event and rushed their stories to the newsroom. Word from the party was slow to reach the editors and, coincidentally, all other safeguards failed. By the time the party reacted, papers everywhere had reported the fresh new ideas of the maverick scientist.

Of course, the offending reporters and editors paid a heavy price, and the scientist suffered the punishments of a dissident. Such a story, for most dissidents, would have ended here, but this one goes on. Dr. Supek was not only renowned throughout Yugoslavia, but he was central to many key government activities. Whatever the embarrassment, he was still invited to official meetings, still allowed to speak. Then, in spite of official annoyance, some impudent journalist dared mention Supek's name in a story. An angry editor deleted it, but in a subsequent story, the persistent journalist put it in again. Again the editor penciled it out, and again the reporter sneaked it in.

Finally, the editor, worn down or overwhelmed, said "Maybe we can give it a try" and published the scientist's name. Nobody reacted; the party was silent. Sensing a weariness, another journalist published a Supek statement on a different subject, and, once again, there was no reaction from the Yugoslav committee. At that point, a popular science revue interviewed the scientist, who finally had an opportunity to vent his radical opinions publicly.

Despite such isolated victories, journalism during the periods of liberalization opened up slowly and with uncertainty. The party never expressed new policies, never suggested that it would free up some space for journalistic ventures. It just sat back and watched, sometimes not too closely. Meanwhile, journalists proceeded with blindfolds, moving ahead carefully until they hit a wall or tumbled off the cliff. When they occasionally found an open path, they were followed by other journalists, tiptoeing quietly, all holding their breath to see how far they could go before being slapped back.

Sometimes the absurd is humorous, and methods of repression during this period were occasionally very funny. For instance, the Croatian Independent State and the Ustasha movement during World War II were declared to be the biggest enemies of Tito's Yugoslavia. Uttering the name Ustasha was prohibited, and if it were mentioned at all, it had to be in a negative context. Party commissars even suspected the letter *U* at the beginning of a paragraph.

Now, the letter *U* at the beginning of a word is quite common in the Croatian language, and it is also a word in common use as an adverb of place (it means "into" in English). Simply put, a writer has to use the letter *U* quite often.

The commissars even counted how many paragraphs started with letter *U* and interpreted a piece well populated with the subversive letter as evidence of Croatian nationalism. Journalists who wished to avoid problems with such stupidities simply skipped using the letter *U* in the beginning of paragraphs. So strong was this paranoia that even in 1987, during the international Univerziada Sports Games in Zagreb, the logotype was not in the normal shape of the letter *U*. Instead, the *U* in Univerziada Games was replaced with a *Y* to read "Yniverziada"! The absurdity of banning "bad" letters in one's own alphabet provided a first-rate contribution of the Communists to world comedy.

Party commissars also routinely analyzed the language in the Croatian media, and writers who used too many Croatian verbs or nouns were severely criticized. There was great concern about the proper use of language. In true Communist form, all republics were to use a blended language—Serbo-Croatian or Croatian-Serbian—and not pure Croatian or pure Serbian. Use of the pure form was seen as a statement of rebellion and a departure from strict party doctrine.

Without party permission, the truth could not be published. In fact, the truth was especially prohibited. Take the case in 1972, when the city council in Zagreb dramatically replaced the mayor. Reporters present at the council meeting were preparing the story when the party secretary directed that it could not appear on the front page, nor could it be given a conspicuous caption. How could any newspaper published in Zagreb avoid such a political scandal on the front page? How could a paper not flag it with a conspicuous headline?

At the time, one of the authors was a young editor of the city chronicle and eager to publish the news of the scandal. The editor in chief of the *Večernji list* was new on the job, coming from his four-year mandate as a correspondent in Moscow. Despite the directive from the committee, he published the news as a main headline on the front page. The next morning, the newsroom was shaken by a thunderstorm from the committee. The instructions were simple: The editor would be replaced, and he would be punished at the party branch meeting. The script read like this: The guilty editor would criticize himself, and after a long discussion and ample consideration among the comrades, the committee would vote for his punishment. Luckily, the editor in chief was willing to fight, and he obviously got a "green light" from the higher powers. Nothing happened to the young editor.

Another example is connected to mass hysteria during Tito's death. At the time of his passing, press reports of Tito's life and the funeral ceremony ate up every column inch of space. Timing of the funeral ceremony, though, was not convenient for the newspaper production schedule. Deadlines fell as the ceremony got underway and for the first edition, editors prepared several heartbreaking stories about the great leader, how he was the beloved president, the father of Yugoslavia. One of the best reporters quoted verses written by the most popular partisan poet, Ivan Goran Kovačić, about the heroic days of the war against Nazism and the Ustashas. It was an absolutely positive text about Tito, even glorifying him as a great historic figure. But one quoted verse mentioned the president's "cut leg." Indeed, Tito's leg was cut during his illness. Editors planned to replace the story, however, with fresh reports as soon they reached a deadline. From an editing point of view, the account itself was trivial. But, given the national psychosis, several colleagues protested to the general manager of the Vjesnik publishing company about this blasphemy printed in *Večernji list*. Instantly, the managing editor stopped the printing process, directed the editors to change the "irresponsible verse," and ordered the destruction of almost 60,000 copies already printed. In this case, the editor was punished, but not the reporter who had been from the party.

During the period of political conflict in Tito's Yugoslavia, the media generally enjoyed a breath of liberalization. This was often the case because party control was not strong enough, or some factions within the party allowed media freedom as a means of advancing their political goals. During Tito's regime there were several highlights of media freedom, as mentioned in this historical overview by Božo Novak.

What was the role of the media in this short, but flourishing period of liberalization? Was it possible to forget overwhelming self-censorship and act as real media professionals?

The answer lies in Pešić's explanation. Journalists were aware of their professional role, but they have been desperately waiting for a moment of freedom to express it. The media products were professional: They had modern lay-out and design, good quality printing, well written stories and good broadcast productions that won numerous international festivals. . . .

Mitja Gorjup, a legendary Slovenian journalist and former president of the Yugoslav Journalists Association and editor-in-chief of *Delo*, wrote about the role of the media: ". . . many of us, journalists, regard journalism as a kind of apologetic service."[3]

The message was clear. Gorjup also said, "Journalists are free to use their freedom only to enable the working man to be responsible for his future, without any mentors and tutors. Manipulation over people has to be replaced by socialistic humanism as a natural freedom."[4]

Despite Gorjup's manifesto, independent organs appeared sporadically. The political weekly *Naprijed*, for instance, broke off relations with the central committee of the Croatian Communist Party on May 29, 1953. It billed itself as the "weekly for social-political and cultural issues," and by vote of the publication's journalists, Dušan Diminić was chosen editor in chief. This was the period of liberalization when Milovan Ðilas was trying to shift Yugoslav Communism to democracy. Immediately after Ðilas was politically liquidated, *Naprijed* was annulled on January 22, 1954.

The golden age of media freedom in Yugoslavia was the remarkable Croatian Spring, noted above. During this spring of 1966, Tito replaced the much feared chief of the secret police, Aleksandar Ranković and, in so doing, threw open the doors to new winds of freedom. Sadly, this period of grace came to an abrupt end in 1971, when Tito called a brutal halt to all democratic movements.

Before the clampdown, however, the media seized the chance to practice Western-style journalism, the result being a news industry strengthened with its new-found freedoms. Vjesnik, Slobodna Dalmacija, Novi list, and other publishing companies produced a wide range of publications. They enjoyed healthy circulations and supported many young journalists who entered the profession with expectations of promising careers. With self-censorship only a sad memory, journalists set about their trade with renewed enthusiasm, establishing their own own agendas, investigating stories in government and industry wherever their instincts took them. "There were no more taboos," said Božo Novak.[5] Indeed, the Yugoslav press seemed as free as the press in any Western nation.

But the empire struck back. Communism was too strong, and Tito's personal power was not sufficient to hold off the hard-liners. The Croatian Spring was premature, and it never had the chance to change significantly the Yugoslav model of socialism. More than that, the revenge of the party was severe. Over 2,000 "counterrevolutionaries" were imprisoned and almost 80,000 Croatian citizens suffered political and police repression.

The period that followed can only be called the dark ages of Croatian journalism, which reverted to the old model, where every move was controlled, every story analyzed for adherence to party dogma. The media were now officially—and conspicuously—under the jurisdiction of the parapolitical Socialist Union of the Working People (*Socijalistički savez radnog naroda*, SSRN). This organization was authorized to run all newspapers and radio and TV stations with complete control.

Making it even more dangerous, as a devil behind an angel's mask, SSRN fronted a democratic façade. It did this in several ways. For one, it ostensibly elected editorial and publication boards, whose task it was to appoint the newspaper editors. For another, each year the SSRN made a big deal of a wide and open debate on the editorial policy of the media. Editors traveled across the country like Monty Python's Flying Circus, visiting regional centers where they debated the fine points of "news coverage."

Their in-depth debates centered on how to arrange front-page photos for all local leaders and how to allocate to each leader an acceptable amount of airtime on the evening newscasts. These policy debates, along with everything else the

SSRN did in the name of journalism, were a shameful mockery of democracy and of the news profession. Still, everyone played it seriously, even the editors and professional reporters, who really had no other choice. Luckily, the road shows were held in good local restaurants, which lavished on guests the traditional hospitality of the Croatian people, so at least the editors could drown their sorrows in tasty local wines.

Along with the clampdown and controls, self-censorship among journalists returned with its subtle, dispiriting treacheries. The media became dull, gray, and vacuous as journalists reverted to the bad habits of bad reporting, which included no criticisms, no questioning, and no investigations of Tito, the army, or the party. They could attack private pub owners, crooked farmers, the church—especially the Catholic Church—slow waiters in the hotels, slow public transportation, but the government and all its patrons remained the "third rail" of journalism.

The paradox of the post–Tito period was that it limited media freedom even more severely, although thanks to the appearance of Milošević on the political scene, it curiously granted the non-Serbian press new freedoms. The Croatian press became a weapon against Milošević and the great Serbian plan to control all of Yugoslavia.

During this difficult period in Yugoslav history, the central committee met in nonstop sessions in an effort to resolve growing problems among the member countries—but it was futile as the dissolution of a united Yugoslavia was simply not in the cards, given the national, ethnic, and religious differences.

For the reporters, it was a gold mine. Finally, they were free to call their own shots again and to report serious political news. Newspapers even began competing with coverage of key political events. The competition was taken so seriously that deadlines often became a genuine concern. *Večernji list* even computerized its newsroom and, thereby, managed to beat competition to the streets by two hours. The two-hour deadline advantage became a strong incentive for other newspapers to invest in computers.

The Vjesnik publishing company cancelled the political weekly, *Vjesnik u srijedu*, and this created a void at the newsstand. The absence of a source for good political coverage inspired several journalists to start a modern news magazine. When approached for permission to publish such a magazine, Vladimir Bakarić, the Croatian Communist Party leader and uncrowned ruler of Croatia, said darkly to the management of Vjesnik, "You may start but I doubt that there are enough qualified journalists for producing a serious newsmagazine in Croatia." It was all the permission they needed, and in 1982 Vjesnik inaugurated *Danas* which became an eminent Croatian political weekly.

CONCLUSION

The history of Croatian journalism is a history of media repression. Media freedom and political freedom are mutually dependent, and when one fails, so does the other. It's easy to tout the virtues of a defiant editor shaking his fist at the system, but such an image flourishes only in a democratic society. In totalitarian regimes, the rebel editor is removed or killed, a memorable lesson to the rest.

The Bolshevik ideal of self-censorship and "patriotic" journalism existed right to the end of the Tuđman era. Despite the severe punishments, there have been a few stubborn, independent journalists who went beyond the boundaries, helping to expand, if only a little, the boundaries for all journalists. In more recent times, the influence of these journalists has been used to draw the attention of outside watch groups, who, in turn, have brought pressure upon the government. The power of the maverick journalists, the ability of reporters to abandon self-censorship, and the receptivity of the new Croatian government to an open press remain great unknowns as Croatia enters the twenty-first century.

NOTES

1. "Before World War II in Yugoslavia twenty-three daily newspapers were published, and ten of them were published in Croatia (seven in Zagreb, including *Morgenblatt* in the German language). In 1938, there were 132 regular members and 49 candidates for the membership of the Croatian Journalists' Association." Božo Novak: Novinstvo: Almanah hrvatskog tiskarstava, nakladništva, novinstva, knjižarstva, bibliotekarstava [*Almanac of Croatian Printing Business, Publishing, Journalism, and Library Science*] (Zagreb: Horizon Press and Kratis, 1997), 167.

2. Ibid., 244.

3. Mitja Gorjup, Samoupravno novinarstvo, Delatna enotnost, Ljubljana (Self-Governmental Journalism, issued by Delatna enotnost [Slovenian for Operational Unit] in Ljubljana), 1978, 51.

4. Ibid., 58.

5. Novak, *Printed Media*, 201.

PART III

MEDIA CHANGES: A SHUT, THEN OPEN CASE

6

Rise of the Press, Fall of the Secret Services

Spying, bugging, taping, and other methods of controlling the people and the press were seen as business as usual for Croatians. Under Communism and Tito, surveillance was an unchallenged tool with which the governmental maintained control of its citizens. But almost ten years later, free from Communist rule and Tito, the new Croatian government resorted to the same methods: eavesdropping, denunciation, terror—old ways die hard. Government eavesdropping on citizens became a well-known public secret as soon as Tuđman appointed Josip Manolić as his right-hand man. Manolić, who was known as an influential member of Tito's secret police, was in charge of reestablishing the Croatian secret police. It was a task he approached with enthusiasm, as he employed the old Communist methods and hired the old Communist operators who were still around from the days of the UDBA (the Yugoslav KGB). During the war with Serbia, the role of the secret service grew rapidly as HDZ developed several parallel agencies placed under different authorities and ministries, including interior, foreign affairs, defense, and the president's office. They all had the same task: to collect information on political enemies, mostly politicians from the opposition, and journalists.

Soon Croatia was webbed by a huge and complex network of secret service agencies, all of which were under the direct control of Franjo Tuđman, who it seems may have had more than a professional interest in this vast information system. The president demonstrated his personal curiosity in spying when he appointed his older son, Miroslav, a university professor of information science, to coordinate the secret service's network. This gave Tuđman control of the output, and it also put him close to the mechanics of clandestine information gathering throughout the country.

From time to time, information about the secret service's activities surfaced for public view, because infighting and power struggles would lead one branch to air the dirty laundry of another branch. Scandals among spies became an interesting topic for independent journalists, who enjoyed disclosing their operations. It was well known that some of the secret services were using the media to launch scandals and discredit politicians and public officials. One weekly tabloid, the *Imperial*, which regularly reported on security scandals, obtained its information from sources who were obviously secret service insiders.

Few people doubted, however, that the vast secret service network had become a regular activity supervised closely by elected officials including the president himself. A scandal broke out when Hrvoje Šarinić, head of the president's office and one of the strongest politicians in Croatia, explained in an interview with the weekly magazine *Globus* how strong the secret services network had become. To make his point, he presented Đurđica Klancir, *Globus* editor in chief, the secret service files on her and several of her reporters. Ms. Klancir was shocked as she read through her own secret service file, and when she reported the story, it was an even greater shock for the public. The explicit files made it unambiguously clear how Croatian citizens were controlled by the secret service. A long interview, published in *Globus* in mid-November 1998, became a hit with average readers, who passed the text from hand to hand. The story provided two key questions and answers, published in a glaring sidebar:

QUESTION: Is it correct that SZUP[1] has notes about all the editors and journalists working for *Globus?*

ANSWER: Yes. And for editors and journalists of *Globus* for whom there are no intelligence data, SZUP has included many personal facts, including information not connected with journalism . . .

QUESTION: This is, in fact, a confirmation of how SZUP is systematically wiretapping us?

ANSWER: Draw your own conclusion.

Šarinić also provided many previously unknown details about the lives of politicians, many of whom were his political enemies from his own party. The Šarinić scandal was the end of the first round of internal political fighting within the HDZ.

Under the iron grip of President Tuđman, members of the HDZ fought for better positions, and several factions used every possible legal and illegal means to achieve their political and financial goals. In this round, the losers were not only Šarinić but also the minister of defense, Andrija Hebrang, and the former prime minister Franjo Gregorić. This internal fight marked the beginning of the end of HDZ unity. Never again would the HDZ regain its unquestioned strength.

In fact, the HDZ's stunning electoral losses in the 1999 parliamentary elections can be traced back to this period.

Tuđman and the HDZ lost several leading politicians. One politician, Prof. Dr. Andrija Hebrang, was not only a founder of the HDZ and son of a legendary World War II leader but also a newly appointed minister of defense and head of Tuđman's personal medical team. Hebrang helped to keep the aging Tuđman in reasonably good health through the nineties. Despite his relationship with the president, he had many battles within the party. His losses were marked in his letter of resignation to the president in October 1998, in which he penned this haunting line: "May God help you know the difference between good and evil!" Like a prophet, Hebrang warned the Croatian public how difficult the future would become when even the authoritarian leaders were not capable of making decisions.

This period was also the beginning of the crucial role of the Croatian media to air the dirty laundry of politicians. Without courageous editors and journalists, the HDZ would have been free to hide its internal scandals. But starting with Hebrang's interview, no secret was beyond reach of Croatian journalists. That event marked the time when reporters from *Globus, Nacional, Novi list, Feral Tribune*, and Radio 101 dogged the secret service for every scrap of internal conflict.

The weekly magazine *Nacional* made the next move. Editor in chief Ivo Pukanić and reporters Jasna Babić, Mladen Pleše, Sina Karli-Šmigmator, and Srećko Jurdana pressed charges against the Ministry of the Interior for conducting wiretapping and surveillance operations on the paper's staff. Evidence was based on Šarinić's interview to *Globus* and eyewitness accounts of secret service stakeouts of Pukanić. Pukanić stated in court, "I will prove how Ivan Penić, Minister of the Interior, is lying to the Croatian public. As citizens, we are asking for our rights to privacy."

Nacional did not stop at its legal challenges. The paper ran a major story about the illegal activities of the police forces, using as prima facie evidence the internal secret service files maintained on *Nacional* reporters. These surveillance files described what each reporter had written and with whom they had met. They summarized the journalists' key interests and charted their psychological profiles. Pukanić, for instance, was characterized as extremely interested in money but not primarily concerned with politics, except if he saw a way to achieve some personal benefit from it. The report said that he was "arrogant, self-confident, and aggressive."

In fact, Pukanić was not interested in politics, although he had a passion for investigative reporting and for publishing good stories. Ironically, his best story was about the secret police surveillance of journalists and was published on January 20, 1999. At about the same time, he also published a list of names of people who, according to the minister of the interior, were "security problems" for Croatia. The list was surprising because it included not only journalists but also eminent lawyers, actors, politicians, generals, businessman, and diplomats.

Each was labeled in police files as dangerous and, accordingly, had been kept under police supervision.

Coverage in *Nacional* kicked off a trend, and soon all the media took up the scandal investigations. Even HRTV, never known to be a firebrand of aggressive reporting, got into the act, although in a strange way. The television network tried to explain how important it was for the police to protect national security and, by doing so, elevated the issue to national prominence. Meanwhile, the facts about egregious, official abuses published in independent media were strong and persuasive. Police came out looking more like thugs than heroes.

Secret police activities, reported in the press, kept the country on edge. The "Dubrovačka banka"[2] scandal initiated serious fights deep within the HDZ when some members of the party became aware of what others in the party were up to. The evidence presented in public revealed how the secret police were directing not only political but also financial and economic activities. Miroslav Tuđman, head of a secret police agency and a coordinator of secret services, was forced by his father, the president, to resign. Ivić Pašalić, the powerful advisor to the president, was the final winner in this long fight. HDZ, however, came away with a seriously damaged public image, especially after *Nacional* sunk its teeth into the story.

Nacional's muckraking serial on the secret police started on May 12, 1999. A short overview of the paper's front pages reveals how it took on the job:

May 12, 1999

The medical condition of the president was getting worse and it was becoming increasingly difficult for him to control his party. *Nacional*'s breaking story caused a stir in the media and throughout the country. One should remember that up to this point, the Croatian president bore the image of an all-powerful ruler, party chief, even father figure, who was always in control, always able to pull the strings of power. A public inquiry into his ability to use that power was significant news.

May 19, 1999

Division within the HDZ deepened when Tuđman was asked by the court in The Hague to arrest suspected war criminal Miroslav Kutle.[3] A press release, published by the state-controlled media, did not mention that the session of the president's Council for Defense and National Security in which this matter was discussed turned out to be heated and quarrelsome. *Nacional* spelled out the details of that meeting and, in so doing, provided evidence that the president did not have a firm grip on the players in his own council.

May 26, 1999

Tuđman surprised the international community in the middle of the Kosovo crisis by proposing to divide Kosovo. This suggestion created consternation among world leaders and provided evidence that Tuđman and Milošević shared similar goals. This perception of a kinship between the two leaders was further supported by a *Nacional* story that revealed that the real author of Tuđman's proposal was the great Serbian ideologist Dobrica Ćosić. How firm was Tuđman's grasp when he relied on Serbian strategists for Croatian initiatives?

June 2, 1999

Politics is politics, but soccer is religion in Croatia. When *Nacional* reported that the "Secret service followed an order by Tuđman to fix a final match of the football championship," the story created a shock wave across the country. The entire front page was dedicated to this national scandal. Included were documents to substantiate the claims, photos of the referees who were in on the scandal, and details of the wire taps made on club managers, journalists, and fan-club leaders.

Tuđman knew that nothing was more important to average citizens than soccer; he, too, was an avid fan and a regular visitor to home matches. In fact, he personally changed the name of Zagreb's best football club from "Dinamo" to "Croatia." The fan club, called the Bad Blue Boys, never accepted the new name because Dinamo had become so closely identified with Croatian independence from Communism. A popular song, "The Sacred Name of Dinamo," expressed the depth of public sentiments toward the name as a national symbol. But, Tuđman never accepted the public's wishes and never yielded his support for the name "Croatia." His passion for the team was almost irrational, and his drive to make the team the best in Europe reached fanatical proportions. In his mind, when the team was someday crowned as the finest on the continent, he wanted the headlines to read "Croatia is best in Europe." He could never accept the kudos going to a team called "Dinamo."

It was therefore extremely important that "Croatia" win the championship. But even for a powerful man like Tuđman, manipulating the outcome of a contest could be difficult. A local club from Croatia's Adriatic coast called "Rijeka" was in a playoff with another Croatian team called "Osijek." In the final round, if "Rijeka" beat "Osijek," it would win the championship, leaving "Croatia" in second place. If "Rijeka" lost, "Croatia" would be the champs.

The Bad Blue Boys still fighting against the name change of their "Dinamo" team, publicly supported "Rijeka." The game was as charged as soccer in Europe can be, and with a tie score in the final few seconds, "Rijeka" scored a goal. That ended the game. "Rijeka" was the national champ, and Tuđman's beloved "Croatia" ended the season in second place. But wait. The referee annulled the goal with an offsides call! "Rijeka" therefore tied with "Osijek," leaving "Croatia" as the champion. Tuđman congratulated the players, saying, "There is a God!"

Thousands of "Rijeka" fans went home dejected but without stirring trouble, which has been known to happen in the aftermath of a soccer match. On late-night, Croatian television, reporters covered highlights of the big game with their usual banter and videoclips. The show included a guest appearance of the president of the referee organization, who reflected on the fair and wise decisions made throughout the game.

But without advance notice, one reporter said that he had obtained a video clip from Slovenian POP TV, which filmed the controversial play from another angle. They aired the film, which showed conclusively that Rijeka was not offsides. The team's score was a textbook play, and in fact, the referee waved his flag even *before* the action began. Reporters in the studio were shocked by the clarity of the footage and by the unfairness of the call. It was evident to all that the championship had been stolen from Rijeka.

In that moment, and in front of the cameras, the referee association president resigned. This double shock was too much for what started out as a regular sports wrap show. The cameras suddenly changed studios, and programming continued on a totally different subject, never to return to the soccer story.

This big story got even bigger when *Nacional* published revealing stills taken from the POP TV footage and, along with them, documents that revealed how the secret service fixed the match. The compelling evidence pinned the rigging of the match on a cabal of three: Reno Sinovčić, a football referee, Ivan Brzović, an official of the secret service, and Zdravko Mamić, a businessman in Zadar, an Adriatic city.

The Croatian public was surprised that in addition to bugging, wire tapping, and maintaining files on all segments of Croatian life, the secret police were also in the business of fixing soccer matches. In the United States, it would be like the FBI rigging the Super Bowl.

That was not the end of the story, because soon after *Nacional*'s article hit the stands, the secret police struck back with attacks on *Nacional* and, personally, on Ivo Pukanić, editor in chief, and reporter Robert Bajruši. Not to take such abuses lying down, the attacks themselves became the lead story in the next edition of *Nacional*.

June 9, 1999

Nacional's front page, banner headline read, "Police searched newsroom and reporter's apartment."

The subheadline explained: "On Monday, June 7, 99, at 3:50 p.m. the police raided *Nacional* offices in what has become the strongest attack of the present regime on media freedom in Croatia." *Nacional* provided two pages of photographs and a lengthy story describing how uniformed and plain-clothes antiterrorism units of the Zagreb police force presented search warrants, then ransacked the offices looking for secret service documents published by the paper. These documents, according to the district attorney, were classified as state secrets and, thus, justified the warrants and the search. News of the searches, which quickly spread throughout the city, brought out many colleagues, political figures, and human rights activists to express support of *Nacional* and to protest the police actions.

While the government kept up the pressure on *Nacional, Nacional* kept up the pressure on the government. The same issue looked at the cost of Tuđman's sports passion in a story headlined "A New Scandal of Croatian Football, While People in Croatia Starve." The story examined how Tuđman approved the hiring of the failed Argentinean coach, Ardiles, for 2.5 million deutsche marks, money that could have gone a long way to ease the hunger of many poor citizens. The paper also ran stories explaining how the championship was fixed, and it began a new investigation on a secret service operation called "Election." This, the paper explained, involved wiretapping and other surveillance measures against opposition parties, trade unions, and student leaders.

The spying of secret police on independent journalists grew into a scandal as more and more was revealed by the investigations of independent media. For most people—even a population grown accustomed to government intrusion into private lives—this crossed the line.

Media investigations themselves brought about further police actions, as the secret service arrested members of its own corps believed to have collaborated with the press. They arrested and interrogated Miroslav Šeparović, former head of the Croatian Information Service (HIS) and one of the most prestigious leaders of the intelligence service. They searched Šeparović's apartment and opened his safe deposit box, where, they said, they found documents on secret police operations. Police investigators also brought in four members of the secret service accused of betraying national secrets to the media.

Croatian TV organized live shows dealing with the sports scandal and the broader matter of eavesdropping by the secret police. For an audience long deprived of anything but the blandest television news, this was an alarming display. Even pirated videotapes of the shows became an instant hit on the streets.[4] One of the more remarkable sessions was an interview with Markica Rebić, an influential secret police leader, who claimed there was nothing strange in these police methods. He proposed the list of names found in Šeparović's safe deposit box as evidence that hundreds of journalists were members of the former Communist secret police, the UDBA. This, he said, justified the control of people writing for the public media.

Journalists were offended, and Jagoda Vukušić, president of the Croatian Journalists' Association, filed charges against Rebić. After a brief trial in September 1999, the court decided there was insufficient evidence to sentence Rebić but that his accusations about the journalists were not based on truth.

June 16, 1999

Nacional's continuing investigations turned up new secret documents and further misuses of secret police powers: It said, "SZUP is wiretapping President Tuđman's closet confidants, and even has a wiretap on the President's private phone and fax lines." *Nacional* published three pages of original documents containing transcripts of conversations between Obrad Kosovac, the powerful television editor, and Rikard Gumzej, Tuđman's advisor. The documents showed that Gumzej sent a report of this conversation to Tuđman's private fax machine, and police tapped even *that* message. It left little doubt, that the secret police were out of control.

Srećko Jurdana, a columnist for *Nacional*, called for Tuđman's impeachment, arguing that he was responsible for such operations. Jurdana also criticized opposition politicians and their parties for remaining neutral in the face of such abuses. He expected their outcries and indignation and was disappointed when the opposition simply ignored the matter.

The opposition was always one step behind the media, driven by a fear of criticizing the president. The president himself made some noises about investigating the secret service, but the records later showed that this was a bluff and that nothing ever came of it. If anyone could have launched a serious probe into police misdeeds, it was Tuđman, and his failure to act provided further proof of his growing impotence as leader of the party and the country.

June 23, 1999

On this day, *Nacional* brought the secret service scare a bit closer to the lives of the average Croatians when it ran a front-page story with the headline "New evidence on mass wiretapping of Croatian citizens. SZUP agents wiretap even the coach of Croatian football team, Miroslav Blažević."

Nacional again published the original documents and transcripts, demonstrating that no one was beyond the secret services's ear, including journalists, business leaders, sports officials, Tuđman's enemies and friends, and people with no apparent public significance. In the same issue, reporters discussed the failure of official governmental investigation into the secret police scandal and examined the power struggles taking place deep within the intelligence service.

Meanwhile, Tuđman's official visit to the inauguration of South Africa's president turned out to be a diplomatic disaster for the Croatian president. The South African daily, *Sowetan*, wrote that "the presence of heads of states like Croatia's Franjo Tuđman, the crown princess of Morocco, the Saudi and Spanish royal houses and other high-ranking government representatives went largely unnoticed." *Nacional* republished this story. Tuđman also visited the local parliament, where he was greeted by low-ranking officials who were casually dressed. The biggest slam, though, came during his meeting with the community of Croatian emigrants, who criticized Tuđman's politics. Of course, all of this was covered by the Croatian press.

June 30, 1999

But the secret police were not discouraged by the growing public reaction, and they continued their attacks against journalists. *Nacional*'s aggressive coverage also continued. Today's headline read, "The government's strike at media freedom continues: 50 police are in action against *Nacional*'s editor-in-chief." The two-page story, illustrated by photos and documentary evidence, made a compelling case for a police force out of control. The article showed secret service agents ransacking the newsroom, searching Pukanić's apartment and even searching the home of Pukanić's parents. All of this was in pursuit of the original documents that could reveal the source of secret service leaks, who had become known as "Deep Throat."[5] Refusing to disclose the name of his informer, Pukanić said, "I would rather die than betray my sources." He then kept up the pressure on the police, aggressively publishing new secret documents on the wiretapping operations.

Meanwhile, new scandals were brewing. A front-page headline read, "By direct order of Franjo Tuđman, Miro Bajramović[6] regularly visited Pašalić in jail to learn the whereabouts of documents that could harm the Croatian government at the Tribunal in the Hague." This new story expanded the scandal from a largely domestic matter to one of international scope, involving Croatia's secret policies during the war with Serbia. While rumors of these issues had already appeared in the public media, until now prosecutors had no real documentary evidence. Even in the Hague trials, evidence was sketchy at best. Now, *Nacional* has reopened the case at the most sensitive moment, when it was said that courts in the Hague were investigating Tuđman's role in war crimes.

July 7, 1999

A week later, *Nacional* fed more fuel to the fire with a front page story bearing the headline "Exclusive document about the secret strategy of David B. Rivkin, the legal representative of Tuđman's policy in the Hague." Tuđman was jeopardized by the Hague because Gojko Šušak stopped the punishment of war criminals after "Storm," a Croatian military operation which liberated the country in August 1995.

It was revealed for the first time that American lawyer David B. Rivkin Jr., from the Hunton and Williams law firm, was representing Tuđman and advising him to cooperate with the Hague Tribunal. Rivkin's strategy was to press charges against Yugoslavia in order to preoccupy the tribunal and to postpone charges against Croatian general Gotovina. The paper also described how some prominent Croatian officials, such as Minister of Foreign Affairs Mate Granić,

Minister of the Interior Ivan Penić, Minister of Justice Milan Ramljak, and others, were eager to press charges against war criminals after the Storm operation. Minister of Defense Gojko Šušak, however, failed to accepted such suggestions. After Croatia backed down from the prosecutions of suspected war criminals, Tuđman's policy was questioned by the international community and, finally, by the Hague Tribunal that considered Tuđman's role in the matter.

Nacional put a lot of ink into the Hague story, but it had not forgotten the secret police intrusion; how could it? Its own offices and employees were still being investigated and harassed. In this edition, the paper ran this long headline: "Cleaning house in the intelligence community. The rising of Miroslav Tuđman to the HIS leadership jeopardizes the positions of Rebić, Brzović and Luburić,[7] who investigated him last year."

The comeback of Tuđman's eldest son as leader of the secret police illustrated how deeply the president was threatened by the scandal. *Nacional*'s persistent drumbeat of news about low dealings in high places raised the eyebrows of many people in a population not accustomed to aggressive reporting. Some even blamed the messenger for the bad news, and in defense of *Nacional*, Pukanić wrote in his column that the paper had not jeopardized the state through its disclosures. The government criminals were the threat, and they should be held responsible.

At the same time that the country faced problems with the secret police, the Hague, and other government scandals, crime soared in Croatia's streets. Private banker Ibrahim Dedić was killed in front of his home, and the presence of organized crime was felt throughout the country as criminals mixed it up in street fights and wild-west shoot-outs. Columnist Srećko Jurdana wrote a stinging rebuke of the police in the same issue of *Nacional*. He said: "Ibrahim Dedić did not get support from VONS, SONS, MUP or any of the seven Croatian secret services whose job it is to protect the citizens. Instead, they're investigating what Obi Kosovac swore into the ear of Riki Gumzej and vice versa; instead, they're black-mailing football referees, war criminals, and vice-versa; instead, they're analyzing the phone calls of Ćiro Blažević and invading journalists' apartments. Meanwhile on the streets of Croatian cities, terrorists are raising hell."

Nacional's editors and reporters practiced two bloody and intensive months of investigative journalism, but that was only the beginning. Despite the efforts of formidable government agencies, they continued with their aggressive work. Yet these were just warmup days for the times ahead, when the protracted illness of President Tuđman would present serious challenges to the independent press that refused to buy the official line.

What happened to the secret police after the scandals? The football referee, Reno Sinovčić, was arrested for criminal activities, but he was released, and immediately he bought the first private daily newspaper in Zadar. The government brought no major charges against the secret police until December 1999. The encouraging news is that the district attorney in Dubrovnik pressed charges against Luburić, an important member of the secret police. An official investigation confirmed all the data published by *Nacional*, then added even more details to the story, revealing that the scope of illegal police activities was even larger than *Nacional* had originally thought. Non-HDZ politicians have promised to bring needed changes to secret police operations and, further, to impose stronger parliamentary oversight on police activities. Chalk one up for a free media. Without the tenacious reporting of *Nacional*, it is unlikely that police activities would have been disclosed or that any of the reforms that followed would have made it to the official agenda.

NOTES

1. SZUP is one of the secret service agencies.

2. "Dubrovačka banka" was a successful local bank when, overnight, its general manager Neven Barać was arrested and accused of misusing funds. Overnight the bank went bankrupt, and citizens lost their savings. Barać tried to explain how he was a victim of political games initiated by Miroslav Kutle, the HDZ tycoon, and Ivić Pašalić, the powerful presidential advisor, who was the secret, fifth owner of the bank.

3. Miroslav Kutle is one of the most important Croatian tycoons, who became extremely rich and influential, well connected with Ivić Pašalić, the president's advisor. Kutle controlled media and banks.

4. There was a rumor that Tuđman himself had been asking for videotape of this show.

5. Deep Throat refers to the still undisclosed *Washington Post* information source who, in the early 1970s, provided reporters Bob Woodward and Carl Bernstein with inside information about crimes in the Nixon White House.

6. Miro Bajramović, a member of special police forces during the war, admitted to the *Feral Tribune* how his unit tortured and killed Serbian prisoners in jail in a small village, Pakračka Poljana. Bajramović and several other police were accused, but found innocent.

7. All are influential members and officials of the HIS (Croatian Information Service).

Case Study: Forty-one Days that Changed the Country

Looking back on the 2000 elections, it is hard not to be optimistic about the emergence of a free press in Croatia. Remarkably bold coverage of President Franjo Tuđman's illness during the leader's final days demonstrates a significant step in the Croatian media's advance to an open journalism. The conspiracy of silence about the president's fatal illness was punctured by vigilant journalists, and as a result, the ruling party was unable to keep a lid on public awareness of the president's failing condition.

At first, when Tuđman sought overseas medical assistance in 1996, the clampdown was reasonably successful, but when news of his illness leaked out, concealment became almost impossible, not that the government didn't try. But once independent journalists learned the truth, they became relentless in their search for every detail, just as the old guard with the old media was persistent, often ludicrously so, in hiding the truth.

"Each man has a right to be tired, even to get cold, to act like a normal person! Do not serve those who would like another Croatia, or those who would like to reestablish another Balkan state." This was the cryptic, defensive answer of an angry President Tuđman, responding to a question by Nino Đula, a young reporter from *Jutarnji list*. During a press conference at the Zagreb airport, Đula asked Tuđman immediately after landing if he altered his obligations at the Vatican because of personal exhaustion. Such a direct question shocked the crowd because no one before dared to ask the president about his illness. The subject had been taboo ever since Tuđman was hospitalized several years earlier at Walter Reed Army Hospital in Washington, D.C.

Tuđman's fury was evident in his voice and on his face; clearly he was incensed at the flippant question from the brassy young reporter. But the visible signs of the president's illness were unmistakable and evident to the cameras, and the reporter's question was, no doubt, on everyone's mind. It had become evident to all that the "Father of the Nation" the invincible leader who had led the country from Tito's Yugoslavia to the new Croatia, was human after all. And he was dying.

That press conference at Zagreb Airport marked the beginning of a long and dramatic period that ended in Franjo Tuđman's death. While his personal tragedy caused a painful struggle for political power, it also led to an awakening of the Croatian public, which, for the first time in a generation, faced the reality of life without this towering figure.

Tuđman's protracted illness also became a time for dramatic change in Croatian journalism. During this period, the media practiced real investigative reporting that it would not have dared to attempt in the previous ten years. Not every journalist seized the moment, of course, but large numbers of independent reporters, editors, and publishers engaged in hard-hitting journalism worthy of any Western media. Tuđman's personal tragedy and the ensuing political fight for power became the topics of headlines and the subjects for exemplary independent reporting. The weeks of Tuđman's agony changed the Croatian media. This period, from November 1 to December 10, 1999, is critical for any understanding of the democratic overthrow of the ruling party—and is, as well, the exciting stuff of history.

Croatia's best-known public secret had been Tuđman's ill health. In November 1996, the president was secretly transported to Walter Reed Army Hospital in Washington, D.C., where he was diagnosed with stomach cancer and given only a few months to live. CNN immediately broadcast the news (on November 15), which shocked the Croatian public. Before this, Tuđman's condition was unknown even to his most intimate contacts, including the Croatian ambassador to the United States.

Coincidentally, on the same day, over 120,000 citizens attended a rally in Zagreb protesting government policies toward Radio 101. The protest and the public announcement of his condition infuriated the ailing Tuđman, and the Croatian medical team was instructed to deny the reports of cancer and to say instead that the president had a stomach ulcer and would soon recover well enough for him to play tennis.

That report marked the beginning of official denials that remained in force until the last few days of Tuđman's life. The next official report was released some three months later, on February 7, 1997, when Prof. Dr. Andrija Hebrang,[1] head of the president's medical team, announced that "after successful treatment, the present health condition of the President allows him to return to work in full capacity." It was rumored, but never officially confirmed, that experts from the Gustave Roussy Institute for Cancer in Paris cured Tuđman with a new chemotherapy treatment. Speculation was rampant, and stories in the independent press proliferated about his cancer and a possible cure, but the government never issued an official confirmation of any aspect of the president's health.

Some media, including *Nacional*, reported in the spring of 1998 that Tuđman also had brain cancer and that his chemotherapy had to be repeated. A visible result of the treatment was Tuđman's hair loss and his obvious use of a wig to hide it.

In the two and a half years that followed, all outward signs suggested that his health had improved. His illness was all but forgotten in the media and public discussion until February 12, 1999, when he returned visibly ill after an official visit to Turkey. The official explanation was that the president had the flu, although the government issued no medical press release to substantiate the claim. Several months later, Tuđman cancelled several official obligations during a visit to South Africa, with the explanation that he was exhausted from a heavy schedule. Again, despite a groundswell of press and public interest, the government failed to issue an official medical report to explain the nature of the president's exhaustion.

So the illness started as an official secret, and silence became the official policy. As unreasonable as this may seem to Western observers, in Croatia, as in many countries arising from the Communist system, a president's medical condition is not public information, and the media have no access to medical records or consulting physicians. Officially, at least until early 2000, Franjo Tuđman never had cancer. Unofficially, the media reported the president's illness from what scraps it could assemble, sometimes from the foreign press and other foreign sources.

For instance, two weeks before Tuđman's important visit to the Vatican in September 1999 and in the middle of the political crisis caused by a secret police scandal, *Nacional* reported that the president's medical condition was deteriorating. Front-page headlines on September 29, 1999, accused the government of a silent conspiracy on the president's health. The paper asked why the medical team had not spoken up and charged that the police scandal (discussed in chapter 6) proved that Tuđman could no longer fulfill his duties. *Nacional* offered two pages of details on the president's health and claimed that the once active Tuđman could no longer play tennis. The paper said that, in fact, he couldn't even play cards with his friends.

This regular edition of *Nacional* hit the streets while Tuđman was traveling in Rome. Normally, such an official visit would stimulate coverage of the president's audience with the pope, highlighting the diplomatic skills of the HDZ and Tuđman himself. This time that agenda did not evolve. *Nacional*'s black prognosis became a reality as the trip became a nightmare.

The crisis started in the morning of October 29, when Tuđman was unable to participate in the morning prayers in Saint Jerolim's Institute or to conduct an important ceremony at the Croatian embassy in Rome to decorate high-ranking Vatican officials. Rumors of his illness immediately flared and were confirmed two days later at the evening press conference at the Zagreb Airport. Tuđman sped away from the airport, but the visual evidence showed that his cancer was growing worse. HRTV broadcast the press conference live, so the cameras were first to tell the story. The next morning, the independent papers were thick with details of events in Rome and at the airport in Croatia. The story was now unstoppable. The last day of October marked the beginning of Tuđman's personal crisis and the first of the forty-one days that changed Croatian media.

A day-to-day analysis of media coverage of the crisis reveals a stark contrast between outlets that toed the government line and outlets that reported the truth. This was a remarkable period of public education with extraordinary impact on the population. During these forty-one days, the fraudulent reporting of state-fed media stood beside the investigative stories of the independent press, and the public could judge for itself the virtues of a press freed from official restraints. If the issues were not so serious, the effects might have been amusing at times.

The public education started on All Saints' Day, when the country witnessed for itself the televised image of the gravely ill president. The next day readers were asked to believe, by government-allied *Vjesnik* and *Slobodna Dalmacija*, that Tuđman's health problems were minor. The disparity between what people saw for themselves and what the papers told them simply strained credulity. In the following section, we examine the media coverage and see why, for Croatia, this period amounts to Media Freedom 101.

CASE STUDY

From Day 1 (November 1, 1999) to Day 41 (December 11), the independent press, long constrained, fought out its battle of truth with the hireling press, still in command of the public mind. We trace the seesaw action through this period.[2]

Day 1

While All Saints' Day in the United States has become trivialized as Halloween, in Croatia and many European countries, it is traditionally a solemn occasion. People visit graveyards to honor the dead. They set out elaborate flower arrangements and light candles at the graves of family members. On All Saints' Day, Tuđman visited the Medvedgrad Memorial Center on the hill overlooking Zagreb, just like tens of thousands of other citizens. Traditionally, the president paid his respects at the grave of the unknown soldier.

This year, as in years past, prime-time television news covered Tuđman's visit. The startling images projected throughout the country on this morning were of a seriously ill man. Tuđman's wife, Ankica, physically supported him, and the strain on her face confirmed the seriousness of his condition. The coverage was minimal, showing only his arrival, and it provided no news of additional protocol obligations, including the visit to his parents' burial site that was originally scheduled for that afternoon. This thin coverage, contrasting with detailed accounts in previous years, reinforced the talk of the president's grave health.

Speculations were confirmed in the midnight news, which reported that the medical team issued a press release saying that the president was taken to a hospital in Dubrava. It said that a medical team performed surgery, and the diagnosis was a "perforation of the diverticule of the large intestine." There were no complications, postoperative procedures were going well, and the patient was feeling better.

Day 2

Tuesday was the first full day of news coverage of the president's hospitalization and subsequent surgery, and differences in content and style between the state-influenced and the independent press could not be more pronounced. Each of the controlled media (Croatian radio and television, *Vjesnik, Slobodna Dalmacija, Glas Slavonije*, and several private radio stations) adhered to the official line without pursuing the story through independent sources.[3]

By contrast, the most influential independent media, including *Nacional, Novi list, Jutarnji list, Globus, Feral Tribune*, and Radio 101, pushed the boundaries of media freedom. *Nacional* was almost always a step ahead of the others, running no-holds-barred stories that reported every available detail about Tuđman's condition. It told when the surgery took place, how long it lasted, what procedures were involved, and what the likely outcomes would be. These reports cut to the hard facts of the president's condition. For instance, Ivo Pukanić, *Nacional*'s editor in chief, wrote: "The chemotherapy is having no effect. As a consequence, it appears there are complications in the stomach and large intestines. This is a clear indicator of an alarming prognosis for the total health condition of the Croatian President."[4]

Beyond reporting Tuđman's health condition, *Nacional* described implications of the president's illness on the Croatian political situation, particularly focusing on how, at the time, the state was being run outside established constitutional provisions.[5]

Jutarnji list also covered the unfolding events in detail, supplementing official information with independent investigation and analysis.

In stark contrast to the independents, *Večernji list* published only the official story, including verbatim transcripts of the government's press releases and statements issued by the censored medical team.

Day 3

Croatian photojournalists staked out the entrance of the Clinical Hospital in Dubrava and remained firmly in place until December 10, when Tuđman died. Every movement around the hospital was photographed; everyone with business related to the president's illness entering and exiting became a study of media photographers.

By this time, now two days after events began to unfold, even in the state-influenced press, news of Tuđman's health led the lineup of stories.

Average citizens were treated to a study of differences between manipulated and free coverage, between a closed press and an open press. In a sense, the state-controlled media, at this point, were serving the people and the political process very well.

Day 4

Representatives of six opposition parties expressed their concern to Vlatko Pavletić, speaker of the Parliament, that the media were wasting their time on meaningless coverage of issues surrounding the president's illness. In his editorial, "Civilized and non-civilized Croatia," Josip Antić wrote in *Vjesnik* that Croatia was now divided by new journalistic criteria. He challenged the media for ignoring the dignity of the patient and concluded that in the past few days, Croatian journalists had been split into two camps: the civilized and the non-civilized. Ironically, his editorial exemplified a few of the differences between media that are free and media that are handcuffed.

Day 5

The medical team issued an optimistic report today that led to generally positive press stories. Ankica Tuđman, the president's wife, issued the statement "Of course, he is better!" and her remark was widely reported. Some physicians, however, for instance, Dr. Nikola Ivaniš, a gastric expert, told *Novi list*, "His condition could be very serious, even alerting."

Meanwhile, *Jutarnji list* published results of the first poll conducted after the onset of Tuđman's illness. It found that 61.4 percent of Croats believed Tuđman should resign because of his illness! Increasingly, Tuđman's illness was proving to be a laboratory in free expression.

Day 6

Today, the medical team released its most optimistic assessment, reporting that the drainage equipment was removed from the president's body and that the patient remained in intensive care, but only as a matter of routine peritoneal treatment.[6]

Meantime, the HDZ-controlled media shifted into high gear. *Vjesnik* was the most aggressive, leading with this headline: "Tuđman will actively participate in the campaign and he will be HDZ's principal candidate on all electoral lists."

The glowing optimism of the controlled press did not derail the independents from examining the story from a different perspective. Sanja Modrić, editor of the home politics section in *Jutarnji list*, wrote that it was nice to hear good news from the hospital, but in political circles such reports must be seen as no more than "the air and water of political survival." She said this strategy was an attempt at survival, "not only for the HDZ as a party, but for all HDZ politicians individually."

Many Croatian print journalists writing for the independent press actively investigated the story from outside sources in a remarkable effort to inform, explain, and analyze the evolving political situation. Unfortunately, television, from which nearly 90 percent of Croatians obtain their news, remained under the party's control. Accordingly, the evening newscasts stubbornly reported the official version of events without acknowledging the growing number of reports and rumors that suggested conditions were rapidly deteriorating in the hospital and in the halls of government. News producers conducted no outside investigations, asked no questions about Tuđman's health, and assigned no camera crew to observe the stream of visitors passing through the hospital entrance.

As noted earlier, the official media's steadfast adherence to an increasingly unbelievable version of the story fostered a growing skepticism throughout the population. These intransigent media became their own worst enemies and provided the Croatian people with the best arguments for a free and open press.

Day 7

On this Sunday, President Tuđman arose. He was reported in the media to have signed laws on election matters. Front pages of the papers were filled with photos of the family visiting the hospital. *Jutarnji list* reported that Ankica Tuđman visited the hospital at 6 A.M. and that Tuđman's son, Miroslav, visited the hospital several hours earlier, at 12:30 A.M. Newspapers published more details on activities at the hospital. *Večernji list* ran a front-page photo of the postman who twenty times a day brought the president cables and letters filled with good wishes.

Day 8

The heavy reporting of the day fell to *Jutarnji list*, which became the first to publish a chronology of the dramatic events that took place in the presidential mansion, Pantovčak,[7] on the day Tuđman underwent surgery. The paper discussed how an informal consortium was now running the government and revealed the startling news that the official successor to the president, the speaker of the Parliament, was not in charge.

These political revelations were serious enough, but *Jutarnji list* dropped the other shoe when it reported that Prof. Dr. Andrija Hebrang, former head of the medical team, had declared that Tuđman's diagnosis was cancer and today's illness was a consequence of the chemotherapy. Although rumors and unofficial reports of such a serious illness had been around for some time, the government line was still that Tuđman had stomach ulcers. Such news from an authoritative source had particular weight.

Day 9

Again optimism flowed from official sources. A governmental press release avowed that Tuđman's health was improving by the day.

By contrast, *Nacional* wrote, "The President is fighting for life." To help make the case that the president was suffering from more than a mild ailment, *Nacional* published a large photo of an obviously afflicted Tuđman, taken days earlier during the press conference at Zagreb Airport. The caption read, "Could this man be a little tired and cold?"

Messages in the Croatian media remain mixed and conflicting.

Day 10

The media faced another denial, this time from Speaker of the Parliament Pavletić: The press office said that there was no reason for fear, even though the president remained in the hospital. A press spokesman, ostensibly quoting Pavletić, reported that the president told the speaker, "I am in excellent health, so everything is OK." Of course, the official version is that Pavletić, and his office, never contacted the media and never quoted the president saying anything like that.

Such confusion. What was really happening in the hospital, and what was the truth? Was *Nacional* making up stories, or were official sources misinforming the public about the president's health?

Day 11

Vjesnik reported that the Croatian Parliament would lodge an official complaint against *Nacional* to the Croatian Journalists' Association's Council of Honor. To no one's surprise, the state-influenced paper, *Vjesnik*, did not like what it saw reported in the independent daily.

At the end of the day, the government issued a jarring press release: "Capillary bleeding in the internal organs required a new set of medical treatments." At long last, the government acknowledged that Tuđman's condition was critical.

Day 12

Yesterday's press release rocked the media and this morning's banner headlines in nearly every paper proclaimed that the president was fighting for his life. Only *Vjesnik* sought to minimize the news, with its PR-heavy, front-page headline stating that "President Tuđman is under additional cures."

Day 13, November 13

Once again, pessimistic headlines filled the media. Except for *Vjesnik*. If nothing else, this paper's policy had been consistent: It shielded the truth when the truth revealed government weakness. Today's headline was "President's health condition is still heavy."

Meanwhile, *Večernji list* ran the headline "Dr. Tuđman is in intensive care." The story explained how, for the past twenty-four hours, the president was on life support and that two experts from the French institute, Gustave Roussy, were closely monitoring his condition. *Novi list* was even more grim: "Physicians can no longer help Dr. Tuđman." Even state-controlled *Glas Slavonije* ran a front-page headline that read "Dr. Husedžinović: 'Things are not good . . .' "

The crucial question on this day was, Who is ruling the country? The controlled media reported that the affairs of state were proceeding by provision of the law. The independent press protested an abuse of authority by power-hungry officials who, it said, were using the president's illness to grab power. Again, differences between the free and the controlled media were startling.

Day 14

Finally, even *Vjesnik* conceded. For the first time, the paper published a banner headline containing the word "critical" and a story with large photos of Tuđman's wife and daughter entering the hospital, grave concern evident on their faces.

Croatian television, by contrast, remained a hold-out to the official line, adhering to information contained in the standard-issue press releases distributed by the medical team. While this may have been a minor problem in the many places where a television station is merely one of many competing sources of news, in Croatia, remember, television is the primary news source for nearly 90 percent of the population.

In today's edition of *Nacional*, television critic Ivan Starčević wrote that prime-time coverage on November 8 was sorely lacking. He said: "In that newscast, several days ago, we heard nothing about the President's health. Such directed and careless coverage has become caricatured in the past 24-hours with news transcribed from today's newspapers about the archbishop praying for the President's health."

On Friday, however, one program on Croatian television changed its reporting strategy. While the prime-time news continued to provide only brief press releases by the medial team, a special late-night news show called *Motrišta* said that the situation was evidently more serious. It employed an old trick of television journalists, used sometimes during the Communist period, of rebroadcasting news from foreign television outlets such as the BBC and Slovenian television. This got out the truth, but with less risk than if the stories were produced in-house. Further, *Motrišta* sometimes quoted early editions of daily newspapers to get out the news. This, too, offered a second-hand account of the news and afforded a little protection from official challenges.

Day 15

An official press release issued late yesterday and first reported today, alarmed the country with the news that President Tuđman required an operation once more. Following a pattern now well established, the medical team issued a brief statement without the detail one would expect, given the significance of the news.

Differences between the media once again were becoming more and more visible, and tension between the two camps was growing. For instance, Radio 101 journalists made jokes about the president's condition, and although management subsequently punished them, the harm was done. Josip Antić, writing in a *Vjesnik* editorial, excoriated the station and asked how anyone in the public light could be so unethical as to poke fun at an ailing man, especially the ailing president. Antić charged that all media, left and right and irrespective of their views of the current issues, were obliged to accept the dignity of the people and the institutions involved.

Editors of *Feral Tribune*, the popular satirical weekly, had a different opinion of media ethics, however. Throughout the Tuđman episode, they continued their long-standing tradition of political derision in a section called the "Greatest Shits," where they spotlight the stupid public statements of government leaders. For instance, a typical "Shit," called "*Feral*'s Amen," referred to a press clip taken from *Slobodna Dalmacija*, where Drago Krpina, chief secretary of HDZ said, "Tuđman even now has the final word."

Day 16

On a slow medical news day, Croatians turned to sports. One of HDZ's vice presidents, Zlatko Canjuga, president of the Zagreb Council and president of the football club "Croatia," caused a sensation when *Jutarnji list* ran a headline stating that Canjuga would return the name Dinamo. The Dinamo story was well known to Croatians.[8] President Tuđman, who fought bitterly with Dinamo fans (called the Bad Blue Boys), stubbornly refused to allow use of the name Dinamo. The over 100,000 citizens of Zagreb who, in 1996, gathered in support of Radio 101, sang "The Sacred Name of Dinamo." Tuđman, however, never yielded. And now Canjuga said, if the people want that change, I will listen and return the name of Dinamo. He said that he once thought that the return of Dinamo meant the return of Yugoslavia, but now he knew that was not so. Canjuga's initiative was understood to be the first nail in Tuđman's political coffin, because it directly tied the president to the most publicly visible scandal.

Day 17

Prime Minister Zlatko Mateša was the lead on HRTV and in the afternoon papers, with news that he visited Tuđman in the hospital. This was news, because he was one of the only people outside the family to visit with the ailing president during his hospitalization. But Mateša brought no substantive news of Tuđman's condition; the story peg was simply that an outsider had laid eyes on Tuđman.

Day 18

All the morning dailies were filled with news that Prime Minister Mateša had visited the president and that his condition was good. ("I saw Tuđman and he is well.") The official's testimony, so heavily reported, once again raised public optimism that Tuđman, in fact, was recovering and would soon resume control of what appeared to be a disintegrating political situation.

Although the Mateša news dominated, the papers reported other topics related to the presidential crisis. One topic that concerned many papers was HRTV's coverage of the events. Criticism, even in controlled media like *Slobodna Dalmacija*, was unusually severe. For instance, Ante Tomić wrote: "This serious hospital drama of the country's President is covered casually in the few first minutes of prime time news with a few simple quotes from a medical team press release, and—ciao boys! HRTV does not even try to offer more . . . [and] the cameras have not attempted to come close to the officials visiting the hospital. It is a huge human and journalistic tragedy that not a single television journalist has shown any initiative or even tried to offer more depth. They sit on their hands waiting for messages to arrive at their fax machines with the seven disinfected lines that they will read on the 7:30 news. A dog could do as well."

Day 19

This was another day without a press release, and the government-influenced media sustained their customary optimism. Headlines told that the president was recovering, and now even HRTV had footage of an official standing at the hospital entrance proclaiming positive news. *Novi list*, by contrast, ran a front-page story that examined the meaning of the fact that the president's family had not been seen at the hospital for three days.

Day 20

Again, there was no reported change in Tuđman's condition.

While the politicians were talking about a solution, family members were pressed for a response to yesterday's questions, published in *Novi list*, about their apparent absence from the hospital. *Novi list* said, "Ankica and Nevenka were without any comment," and asked why press inquiries were met with silence. *Vjesnik*, ever the optimist, reported that there was no constitutional crisis and that by the end of the week, the president would be making decisions about the elections, approving the temporary state budget, and reviewing other laws passed in the Parliament.

Day 21

From the beginning of this crisis, photos of the family had become a good barometer of Tuđman's condition. During the first nine days, the photos of smiling family members leaving the hospital projected an image that the president was doing well and that doctors had the illness under control. That changed around the tenth day, when the mournful expressions in the photos telegraphed a message that Tuđman's health had worsened. Photos in today's editions left little doubt that the family was distressed by what it had seen.

Day 22

It was now clear to even the most tenacious believers in a speedy presidential recovery that the December elections could not be held, so the country turned its attention to a new term in January 2000. The need to postpone the election provided convincing evidence that Tuđman was, indeed, very ill, but even so, *Vjesnik* pressed blindly on, telling readers in a front page story, "There is a real possibility that the President himself will issue the writs for election today."

Prof. Dr. Žarko Puhovski, an eminent sociologist from Zagreb University, said to *Novi list*, "Who will be the first to say, 'The king is dead'? That person will lose his head."

Not only would few of the controlled media approach the subject of the president's demise, but most now even avoided negative news entirely. HRTV, the country's most popular news source, had not even mentioned the postponement of election day, nor did it report any other unpleasant or controversial issue.

Day 23

The relative calm of the past few days abruptly ended when *Nacional* hit the streets with a banner headline declaring in huge red letters, "The End of the Tuđman Era," followed by the bold subhead, "Tuđman is in a deep coma, Pavletić becomes the President of Croatia on Friday." *Nacional*'s story became even more compelling when, on the second page in a brightly colored sidebar, it stated that the Zagreb City Council was secretly preparing to build a grave for Tuđman and that architect Ante Vulin had been chosen for the job.

Again *Nacional*, a weekly, was faster with the news than were the dailies and much faster than Croatian television. *Nacional* was also most critical of the rosy official who promised Tuđman would recover and return to work. Columnist Srećko Jurdana wrote: "Confusion in the Court caused by Tuđman's departure is reminiscent of a scene from Frank Tashlin's slap-stick comedy, *Disorderly Orderly* starring Jerry Lewis. In the past few weeks, HDZ has been providing joke-tellers with a bottomless well of material."

Day 24

Journalists reported on the activities of Tuđman's sons. The press reported that the older son, Miroslav, spent the entire night by his father's side. The younger son, Stjepan, was interviewed about Canjuga's initiative to change the name of the football club. Stjepan Tuđman's response was surprising. He said, "It is possible that papa whispered something to Canjuga." Reporter Tomislav Židak's last question was, "Was your father informed that Canjuga will organize a referendum to change the name of the football club?" His response: "No, my father is fighting for his life."

Day 25

Reporters tracked family members and watched day and night who entered the hospital and through which doors. They noted how many limousines arrived, when helicopters landed and departed, which members of the medical team were in attendance. The press had become so persistent that security officials issued orders to prevent photographers from taking photos of the president's daughter, Nevenka.

The media today began looking at the story from a different perspective. With the outcome of the presidents's illness all but certain, press attention turned from reporting on Tuđman's illness to asking what will happen when he dies. They began to ask the questions that most had until now avoided: Where he will be buried? Who will build the grave? How will the media and the country react?

Day 26

The political situation was becoming more sensitive. For the first time in its history, the Croatian Parliament passed a law proclaiming the temporary incapacity of the president. This new legal status gave serious journalists a lot to analyze and explain to the public.

As usual, *Novi list* went a step beyond the other media. It committed an entire page to comparing the illnesses of Josip Broz Tito and Franjo Tuđman. It was only a matter of time before the media would run a head-to-head comparison of the protracted illnesses of the two presidents. It may be difficult for people born and raised in a democracy to recognize the significance of such an analysis. For them, the passing of a leader is of little personal consequence. Leaders, who yield their offices after a few years, exercise minimal power over the daily lives of citizens.

The relationship between a leader and the Croatian people is quite different. Since 1945, they have lived through only two presidents, and in that time, the leaders have held significant power over every aspect of public and much of private life. To Croatians, the president is a protector, punisher, sage, father, a walking God. Here, a compare-and-contrast, microscopic examination of the presidents' illnesses is much more than a clinical exercise. It is a reminder, in the most graphic terms, of the president's mortality and a notice that the country is led by a man, who, like the least of its citizens, in the end, must face the indignity of death.

Novi list analyzed similarities and differences in Tito's and Tuđman's agony. It found that one of the biggest differences was how the media covered the events. Tomislav Klauški reported: "Tito's illness was not a topic for journalists until he was about to die. While Tuđman's style of ruling was similar to Tito's, in his illness, news and public reaction were significantly different."

Day 27

The big stories were that Vlatko Pavletić took over as the acting president and election day would be scheduled for January 3. No news was reported about Tuđman's condition.

Day 28

The weekly papers were having problems covering the rapid-fire sequence of daily events, leaving the action to the satirists.

Feral Tribune took off on a comment by television critic Đermano Senja-nović, who noted how everybody has been waiting to witness, on the prime-time news, the formal signing of the Election Law. *Feral*'s parody:

Nothing happened. He could not even sign the law. My mother asked me why Tuđman could not sign the law: "Why didn't he just push his finger into the ink and press it on the paper?"

"Mother," I said, "it is impossible, he is plugged into instruments."

"What is he plugged into?" asked Ivan, my son.

"Into everything!" I replied.

"Is he logged onto the Internet also?"

"Idiot, shut up!"

Day 29

Vjesnik ran a heartbreaking front-page photo of younger son Stjepan, his wife, Snježana, in a fur coat, and their two children accompanied by Tuđman's military aide, General Kašpar, coming out of the hospital. There was not much else.

Day 30

It's Tuesday again and *Nacional* was on the streets. In this issue, the hard-hitting weekly reported that the mystery of Tuđman's grave seems to have been solved. A large, front-page photo of the Mirogoj graveyard was captioned, "Here is where Franjo Tuđman will be buried." The information would later prove to be correct, and *Nacional* could again take credit for being the first with the story.

Nacional's valuable sources in the intelligence service again provided the paper with crucial information. While the president was dying in the hospital, a power struggle was raging within the HDZ for control of the party and the country.

Other independent media also investigated the struggle for control. The news agency, SENSE, reported that the HDZ decided that, when the time came, it would not keep the president's death a secret. According to SENSE, the news would be published forty-five minutes after the president's death. As it turns out, that was not far from the truth (it took three hours).

Day 31

Stories in the independent media reflected the reality of Tuđman's impending death. At this point, they were already looking beyond the death, probing for information on such items as construction of the grave, graveside visits of the family, and similar events that would follow the president's passing.

In this wait-and-see period, where the "what" was certain and only the "when" was unknown, even little side shows drew media interest. One such event occurred when acting President Pavletić arrived at HDZ headquarters in Tuđman's armored BMW model 740 IL. The large black sedan provided a sensational photo, especially after Pavletić promised only a few days earlier to use his seven-year-old Mercedes.

Day 32

The image of acting President Pavletić was everywhere in the media, not only because of his new political role, but because of his flamboyant style. Pavletić made a point of regularly visiting the green market, shopping for vegetables and checking off the list made by his wife. He wrote a diary for the weekly news-paper *Globus*. In this column, he told about his life as the acting president, offering details about riding in Tuđman's BMW, inviting the minister of the interior for conversations, and asking security to sweep his offices for signs of wiretapping. He was thorough and eager to share the tiniest details of his fascinating role with an adoring public.

Day 33

Media coverage today offered a mixed bag. *Večernji list* and *Novi list* didn't even mention Tuđman's illness on the front page. *Vjesnik* ran a press release on the first column, and *Glas Slavonije* covered the front page with news and an old photo. *Globus* ran a big interview with Mate Granić, minister of foreign affairs and vice president of the HDZ, who said, "After Tuđman there will be no Tuđman!" It was a significant play of words. After Tito's death, the official Communist slogan read, "After Tito—Tito!" Speculations about HDZ's politics were similar: Should the party continue the Franjo Tuđman cult or launch a column of new leaders?

Day 34

Reporters on watch in front of the hospital entrance were finding increasing evidence of the president's impending death. *Novi list* reported that Obrad Kosovac, HRTV editor in chief, sent a crew to the hospital, and this was a clear sign that acting President Pavletić would soon arrive there. Foreign journalists were also present. For instance, at the hospital were a Slovenian television crew, John Reed of the *Wall Street Journal*, and others.

Day 35

Feral Tribune continued to report on the "Drama of Franjo Tuđman." In one sensational story, it reported several significant details. It said that Cardinal Franjo Kuharić administered the last rites to Franjo Tuđman on November 25. On December 3, the story said, doctors found that only the heart muscle was functioning.

Another *Feral* story compared Tito and Tuđman. In a long table, it posted side-by-side similarities and differences, such as the preferred vehicles of each leader, their favorite football clubs, their residences, brands of drink and wine. Tito preferred poker, while Tuđman liked other card games. Tito drank whiskey, and Tuđman sipped graševina wine by Enjingi. Tito's favorite journalist was Dara Janeković; Tuđman delighted in Maja Freundlich. Both preferred white uniforms, a residence on Brijuni Island, the villa Zagorje in Zagreb, a personal army guard unit, and Obrad Kosovac as television editor.

The story, of course, was a joke with a point. It was an efficient tool for making the case that from the public point of view, the ends for Tito and Tuđman were quite different. *Feral* was not joking when it compared photos of Zagreb's streets in 1980 and in 1999. In the earlier photo, hundreds of thousands of people crowded the streets, lamenting the death of their leader and showing respect at his passing. The later photo depicted Zagreb streets filled with rioters.

Day 36

The papers did not say much about the Tuđman crisis. *Slobodna Dalmacija* skipped the story on the front page; *Jutarnji list* published a small, one-column headline reporting no changes. Only *Glas Istre* posted a front-page headline that read, "Dr. Husedžinović: 'nothing new.' " The accompanying story explained that intensive care continued without major improvements.

Day 37

News about Tuđman had been overtaken by interest in the upcoming parliamentary elections, but Tuđman has not dropped from the media agenda entirely. Dr. Ivica Kostović, head of the president's office, was reported today trying to convince people that the medical team press releases were, in fact, accurate. That was a tough sell, to say the least. *Nacional*'s television critic, Ivan Starčević, wrote: "No brave television journalist has dared to ask one simple question which would be asked by any peasant's aunt: 'Is my child still alive?' Therefore, our best information may be the news show for the deaf. One of these days, the lady doing the signing will tell the truth about the number of leukocytes, and that will be how the information slips by television editors."

Nacional did not even mention Tuđman on the political pages. Its cover story was that the secret police wiretapped the phones of acting President Vlatko Pavletić. *Nacional* had been like a bulldog grabbing the bones of the secret service. Somehow, they had obtained access to secret files, which they seemed eager to publicize.

Day 38

Huge headlines filled the front pages with news of Tuđman's imminent death. *Večernji list* posted this: "On Tuesday night, Dr. Tuđman's heart almost stopped." *Feral Tribune* wrote that Cardinal Kuharić was reluctant to confirm that he secretly visited Tuđman to administer last rites. (Later, after the funeral, the cardinal publicly said it was true. He also told the public that Tuđman fulfilled all of his duties as a Christian, including a church marriage.)

Day 39

While the Tuđman story was drawing to a close, a second, related, story was evolving. In this morning's *Vjesnik*, editorialist Josip Antić wrote:

If anybody will write the history of journalism's dishonor he should not avoid the date of December 9, 1999, and he should particularly not miss the front page of the weekly magazine *Arena*. This Europapress edition published images of a deathly sick Croatian President and his wife in the hospital room. This story—from inception to publication—is the biggest media dirt ever published, including *ST*[Slobodni tjednik] and the non-crowned king of supermarket journalism, the late Marinko Božić. Readers got the impression that *Arena* got exclusive photos from Tuđman's room in the Dubrava hospital, like it was a photo of Tito in the Ljubljana Hospital.

What happened? Nobody, including *Arena*, was able to gain access to the seventh floor and take photos of Tuđman. *Arena*'s editor decided to make an artistic illustration. Antić was shocked by such an approach, judging it as unethical and asking the Croatian Journalists' Association to condemn such journalism.

Day 40

At around 11 P.M., President Tuđman died. The government, however, delayed release of this news for three hours, so no media, broadcast, or print made it to the streets with the news until the following morning. History will record that the first word of the president's death was released December 11, 1999, on the forty-first day of Tuđman's hospitalization.

Day 41

At 2 A.M., Croatian television used all three channels to broadcast the anticipated news of Tuđman's death. Vlatko Pavletić, speaker of the Parliament and acting president, held a meeting of high-ranking officials in the government and the Parliament, after which he read a short statement, broadcast later on HRTV. Croatian television was the only medium present at this historic meeting of the Parliament.

The world media picked up the story immediately after HRTV broadcast the news. Meanwhile, HINA, the Croatian news agency, was very late with the story, a delay that caused anger among officials and governmental news agency reporters and finally brought about the resignation of the general manager, Ljubo Antić.

The media did a credible job presenting the news. They issued special editions filled with details of Tuđman's life and political role. But even now, after the president's death, differences were visible. Media close to the government (HRTV, *Vjesnik, Slobodna Dalmacija, Večernji list, Glas Slavonije*, HINA, and others) painted Tuđman in the best possible light, without a hint of the controversy surrounding the ruler's life. Day and night, on all three channels, HRTV broadcast programs celebrating the dead leader. One channel even showed a continuous loop of film depicting the march past Tuđman's grave.

By contrast, independent media like *Novi list, Jutarnji list, Nacional, Feral Tribune*, Radio 101, *Globus*, and others did not shy away from presenting the good and the bad features of Tuđman's life and of his role in Croatian history.

NOTES

1. Andrija Hebrang, a physician, expert in radiology, professor at Zagreb University's School of Medicine, and eminent HDZ leader. His father, Andrija, was an interim Communist leader during World War II, but he was replaced by Tito and killed in the Communist Yugoslav prison. His son became very close to Tuđman. Hebrang was minister of health and minister of defense. Tuđman replaced him because he wanted to limit Herzegovinian influence on the Croatian army. Hebrang was even the head of Tuđman's medical team, but he was fired.

2. Note that analyzed issues of daily newspapers are reporting on the previous day's events. Radio and television reports cover the actual date.

3. Some media under the influence of the ruling party, which also had an eye on the bottom line, like *Večerniji list* and OTV, started out telling the official story but later engaged in investigative journalism, which, of course, offered a very different account of events.

4. Ivo Pukanić, "President Tuđman suffers by carcinoma in late phase with no more effects of chemotherapy," *Nacional*, no. 207, November 3, 1999, 5.

5. By constitutional provisions, the speaker of Parliament serves as acting president during the president's illness. While Tuđman was ill, the power was concentrated in the hands of his advisors, even his son, and constitutional provisions were ignored.

6. Only a few days later (November 9), *Nacional* would report what really occurred.

7. Remarks of authors: Official Presidential Residence, the former villa of the late President Tito.

8. Dinamo—a football (soccer) club from Zagreb—was, during the Communist period, a symbol of Croatian national independence. Being a fan of Dinamo was a clear sign that one did not support Communism. Dinamo fans, called Bad Blue Boys, started the fight for Croatian independence.

PART IV

THE ROLE OF THE PRESS IN CROATIA'S POLITICAL EVOLUTION

8

The Transition and the First Elections (Late 1980s, Early 1990s)

From the fall of Tito's Communism to the first democratic and free elections, it was a short but sparkling time for the Croatian media. Immediately, the press opened the door for coming democratic changes by presenting even-handed coverage of all political views and all political parties. The press also led the resistance to Serbian dictator Slobodan Milošević, and this clearly demonstrated that, given sufficient provocation and opportunity, the press could rise to greater heights. Unfortunately, lessons learned during the war years have not endured.

The mid-eighties were a period of many changes in Europe. Gorbachev's new communism initiated movements throughout the Eastern bloc: in Poland it was the Solidarity movement; in Hungary the old leader, János Kádár, was replaced; in Bulgaria the "palace revolution" changed the character of governance; in Czechoslovakia Vaclav Havel took office; in Romania the bloody revolution ended with the execution of Ceaucescu and his wife. In East Germany, the very symbol of communism, the Berlin Wall, came tumbling down, and so ended the era of Communist hegemony in Central and Eastern Europe.

Meanwhile, Yugoslav Communists did not share in this liberalization; instead, they dreamed of power, and their visions led them and the entire region into a series of bloody wars. By the time it all ended, more than 250,000 people would be killed and another 2.5 million would become refugees and displaced persons.

Prof. Dr. Vesna Pusić from Zagreb University, explained the roots of the Yugoslav crisis:

Tito left behind a personalized regime (he was even mentioned by name in the 1974 Constitution) with a power vacuum at its core. Things held together by inertia for a while, but eventually there arose a politician—Slobodan Milošević of Serbia—ruthless, ambitious, and cunning enough to take advantage of the situation. That his power grab coincided with a time of general upheaval across Eastern Europe only made his task easier.[1]

The Yugoslav Communist government could no longer keep all the republics and regions under its iron grip, and slowly each republic separated and developed strong autonomous governments. Then, in 1987, Slobodan Milošević came to power on the wings of the Greater Serbian Plan. From the beginning, the danger of his policies was evident as he implemented his "bureaucratic revolution," a part of which was suppressing the autonomy of Vojvodina and Kosovo.

Milan Kučan, president of the Communist Party of Slovenia, developed a workable model of soft Communism, based on the Eurocommunism created in Italy. Slovenians, thus, paved their own way to a free, independent, and democratic state. Meanwhile, Stanko Stojčević, Croatian Communist Party president, came up with the well-known "Croatian Silence," where he never opposed Milošević as he tried to keep Croatia under strong party control. Other republics sat it out while they waited for the results of Serbian, Slovenian, and Croatian decisions.

President Tuđman's political advisor, Prof. Dr. Zvonko Lerotić from Zagreb University, analyzed this wait-and-see period as follows:

At the time of the worst clashes of interest between Serbia and the other constituent republics and provinces, the Croatian communists invented the "Yugoslav synthesis" as a program that they hoped would reconcile the very distant Slovenian and Serbian views, remaining faithful to the 1974 Constitutional solutions and the technocratic solutions proposed by the then federal Prime Minister Ante Marković.

Marković sought to replace the already defunct communist ideology by the idea of reform as a new foundation on which to build the unity of the Yugoslav State. . . . Most people refused to trust Marković and his "Yugoslav synthesis" because they failed to help the Kosovo Albanians defend their autonomy and save them from the brutal persecution by the Serbian police. . . .[2]

Yugoslavia entered a period of intense political life, and especially interesting was the new political environment in Croatia. Here the power of the Communist Party was ebbing in the face of burgeoning democratic parties and organizations. "Two political alliances emerged in Croatia in 1989, to remain important and influential until the present day—the Croatian Democratic Union (HDZ) and the Croatian Social Liberal Party (HSLS),"[3] explained Zvonko Lerotić. He stressed how Croatian Communists were already politically disoriented at that time, as they found themselves caught in a whirlwind of irreconcilable forces at work in Yugoslavia.

Mass rallies were held, at which public demands were voiced which enjoyed the support of the whole world. The Croatian League of Communists renounced the single-party system in December 1989, and in January the following year the Croatian and Slovene Communists left the Yugoslav communist organization. A month later, the Croatian Parliament called for free and multi-party elections to be held in the late April.[4]

The mass media became a crucial part of the change, because they brought to light a wide range of events, and they even disclosed hidden political plans, trends, and ideas, something unknown in previous years. The media were organized within the republics and provinces; consequently, they presented the policies of their political centers. The Slovenian media supported Kučan's policy, Serbian media backed the Milošević policies, and the Croatian outlets were between the rigid Communist leader Stojčević and new democratic movements.

The transitional period was painful, and it was not an easy time to find out how to exercise media freedom while surviving the pressures of the Central Committee. Croatian journalists struggled during this period to explore the freedom of speech so central to democratic governance.

Their first steps took place during the rigid Communist rule of Stanko Stojčević, who efficiently controlled all the newsrooms in the country, thanks to the obligatory membership of journalists in the party. "If we know that 80 percent of the 12,000 members of the journalists' association (in Yugoslavia) are in the Communist Party, we have to ask ourselves of which Party we are the members?" asked Nenad Unukić, a journalist from *Večernji list*.

Are we members of the Party which has clear class ideas and democratic ideologies or of a Party that is nationalistic, hegemonistic and absolutistic—one that is bullying with beatings and arrests. The Party that does not allow pluralistic opinions, does not respect pluralism of interests, does not admit obvious rights to differences. And, there is no pluralism of truth, because eight views to the reality (or six) doesn't means the truth.[5]

Journalists, even scientists, were confused. How should they react, and how should they report on events when the Yugoslav Communist building is falling apart? Prof. Dr. Pavao Novosel conducted a survey among prominent journalists and editors from print and broadcast in four republican centers (Belgrade, Ljubljana, Sarajevo, and Zagreb). He gathered data from thirty reporters in each center. His findings were instructive:

To us, the grand opening of the public communication in this country should be attributed to:

1. The withering away of the one and ultimate authority center with the ensuing decentralization of the power structure at the republican level,

2. The economic, cultural and ideological differences among the existing republican centers, which prevent their consolidated control of the public communication,

3. The general economic and the resulting social crisis in the country,

4. The inability of the elite to find fast and effective solutions for the country's plights,

5. The correlative uncertainty of the elite in their role of the "ultimate receptacle of the wisdom."[6]

A conference for Yugoslav scientists and journalists was run by the school of Political Science and the Croatian Journalists' Association in 1989 and titled "Journalism in Function of Development." There were visible differences, especially among scientists who were still following the old Marxist information models.

Prof. Dr. Zdravko Tomac, of Zagreb University and later minister in the government and vice president of the Social Democratic Party, asked some probing questions:

Is the media war a consequence of bad moral character of journalists or of something else? Can we stop the media war by moral measures, calling on common sense, changing or rehabilitating the people? How much is ideology and the system responsible for the present situation?

The life of the journalist, like the life of the other public figures, becomes a hell, when two epochs cut across each other; when the value system of one epoch falls apart and the other value system is not yet defined.

Dr. Muhamed Nuhić from Radiotelevision in Sarajevo said that the key to the problem is in the centers of political power, not journalism. The new role of the journalist is not as a social-political worker but as a free intellectual. S/he is not forced to be a member of the party but can search after truth and present his and other's opinions, not just the official opinions, said Dr. Neda Todorović-Uzelac from Belgrade University.

Fear of a new media war was on the mind of Prof. Dr. Davor Rodin of Zagreb University, who said that we are facing the loss of media freedoms when journalists attack, insult, lie, and twist the truth about the past, present, and future. He said: "The only medicament against the loss of media freedom, which was achieved by the transition from censored and self-censored press, is the free public. It is not an abstract media freedom formed by two hostile, political forces facing each other."[7]

Dr. Manca Košir from Ljubljana University presented an initiative for the new journalists' association, which would change journalism from a semiprofession to a genuine profession with strong, professional standards. She also presented a list of old and new media paradigms.

OLD PARADIGMS	NEW PARADIGMS
revolution	evolution
autocracy	democracy
monism	pluralism
political activism	social activity
dependence	independence
information	communication

At the end of the 1980s, the war among media in the republics was at a climax. But was it really media conflict generated by journalists or promoted by the politicians? Stjepan Andrašić, editor in chief of *Večernji list*, the best-selling daily newspaper at that time in Yugoslavia, said, "Yugoslavian journalism is at the crossroad of social processes which include the pluralization of the Yugoslavian society and the evolution of a market economy."

Yugoslavian journalism was understood to be part of the political environment. "Journalists are social-political workers and their media are the tools for bringing about the working class' right to be informed. The public information system will be developed only when Yugoslavian journalism will be recognized as an intellectual, impartial profession whose goal it is to serve the public by its knowledge, honesty and social-moral engagement."[8]

Similar voices could be heard from the other part of Yugoslavia. Pavle Milivojev, a journalist from Novi Sad, the capital of the Vojvodina province, explained how journalists are prosecuted with no protection: "Only the independent journalist can be really a journalist and only the journalism liberated from all chains, dogmas and restrictions can fulfill its tasks."

But the wise voices were not in the majority. The mass media in Yugoslavia were divided into those that supported local politicians and the independents. Sadly, most journalists were obedient servants of local politics and never tried to become independent. They were in the service of politicians, presenting only political views of their republics and attacking other opinions.

The media war began in Belgrade under Slobodan Milošević (who created an efficient propaganda machine during the Kosovo crisis in 1999). Dr. Jozo Grbelja said: "It was the transition period when republics and provinces accused each other; the republics accused the Federation, and the Federation attacked everyone else. Attacks, insults and manipulation filled the media whose common approach became: 'The worst the better!' Readers were confused as they faced dilemmas and uncertainties, and they lost faith in the politicians, trusting only the home media."[9]

But the liberated media could not be silenced. Each week magazines such as *Mladina* from Ljubljana discovered a new scandal among the Communist leaders. They wrote about how the "red bourgeoisie" misused their power by building apartments, summer houses and villas. For example, they described Admiral Branko Mamula in Opatija, who ran shops with special discount prices. They told how he enjoyed free vehicles, held secret bank accounts in Switzerland, and benefited from many other personal fortunes.

The main task of the independent media became support of the war effort. Some of the media crossed the line and served local politicians and their nationalistic ideas as an answer to Milošević's Greater Serbian Plan. Serbian propaganda machinery regularly attacked anyone in the former Yugoslavia who expressed positions contrary to those advocated by Milošević. All of this readied the population for the real war, which began in 1991 in Slovenia.

Meanwhile, what about the media in Croatia? During the 1980s, the Communist government tried to stop dissident journalists. The Central Committee of the Communist League of Croatia published the notorious *White Book* created by the hard-liner Dr. Stipe Šuvar, who listed all the "mistakes" of the Croatian media. Inclusion in this list became a serious matter for each journalist or medium whose name was mentioned. Communist leaders or officials warned that the media were not under the firm control of the party. Some of them asked for more political and police control.

In 1982, Radio 101 was founded in Zagreb under the name of Omladinski radio (Youth Radio), and it quickly became the symbol of media freedom. The so-called youth press (*Studentski list*, later called *Polet*), open-minded weekly newspapers, became influential among large portions of the population. Many of Croatia's most noted journalists began their careers with the youth press or radio, so from the beginning they had a taste of media freedom. Later, working in larger, more commercial media, they continued with the practices of a free press.

The Communist Party had lost much of its power as hard-liners were replaced in December 1989 by new moderate politicians (such as Ivica Račan, Zdravko Tomac, and Branko Caratan) who knew that they were facing the end of Communism. Early in the year 2000, most of them were running the Social Democratic Party, leading Croatia more fully toward an open, democratic system.

Journalists backed out of party membership. Some did so publicly, but most were quiet about it, refusing to pay membership fees, asking to be deleted from the membership rolls.

Wishing to end organized political influences in the newsroom, journalists of *Večernji list* dissolved the Communist Party organization within their paper. *Večernji list* declared itself "an independent newspaper" and printed this banner regularly on its front page. Later, almost every newspaper printed this or a similar line, even when it was obvious that the editorial policies were not independent at all.

Croatian newspapers at that time were remarkable compared to those of other countries in the Soviet block, and of the Croatian papers, *Večernji list* was the leader. It became one of the most modern daily newspapers in Yugoslavia. It was the first daily to use offset printing methods, the first daily to print simultaneously in Zagreb and Osijek, the first to use a computerized newsroom, and the first Croatian daily printed in Germany by page transmission. Remarkably for the time, the paper published over twenty local editions throughout Yugoslavia. In 1990, journalists of *Večernji list* were the first to elect their editor in chief by secret ballot.[10]

The beginning of the weekly magazine *Danas* demonstrates the initiative of journalists during this period. For many years, the Yugoslavian magazine *Vjesnik u srijedu* was the best publication of its kind, but for various reasons, it ceased publication. Journalists from that magazine were interested in starting a new publication, so a group of them arranged a meeting with Dr. Vladimir Bakarić, the old and ailing Croatian Communist leader. When the journalists asked for his blessing, the elderly leader was surprised and said: "What? You would like to publish a news magazine? Personally, I do not see journalists in Croatia capable of carrying out such a project." Bakarić's answer was not a "yes," but it also was not a "no." So interpreting the Communist leader's words in the most favorable light, the journalists set up the *Danas* project and soon produced one of the most important and influential news magazines in the country. It was run under the leadership of top Croatian journalists, such as Joža Vlahović, Dražen Vukov-Colić, Mirko Galić, Jelena Lovrić, Gojko Marinković, and Mladen Maloča.

The Croatian press flourished during this period. Readers were eager to buy and read newspapers, and the political situation provided plenty of good stories. The big company Vjesnik was out of business by this time, and Večernji list became an independent company. Clearly, the media environment was changing.

Local newspapers were also developing quickly. *Slobodna Dalmacija* was already mentioned as one of the best-edited daily papers. *Novi list* from Rijeka appointed Veljko Vičević as editor in chief. Vičević turned this local daily to one of the best, most open-minded papers of the nineties. Drago Hedl, editor in chief of *Glas Slavonije*, reorganized the newspaper and computerized it, thereby improving the editorial content and efficiency of production.

Unlike the print media, Croatian Radio and Television did not adopt liberal policies, and the principal reason was strong government control. HRTV, for instance, couldn't make a move without government oversight. When general manager Veljko Knežević left his post at HRTV, he became the first Yugoslavian ambassador in Croatia. It was not easy to practice media freedom under his management or the rigid management of his successors.

Local radio stations, especially Radio 101, played an important role in the story of Croatia's media. The station, which later became an icon of free media in Croatia, hosted all opposition politicians, including Franjo Tuđman, giving them the opportunity to discuss their political ideas and programs. Ironically, open discussion was a freedom that Tuđman, as president, later denied other political candidates.

The legal status of private newspapers remained uncertain, and some early start-up attempts show how some entrepreneurs approached the job. One private construction company asked the Ministry of Information in Croatia for permission to publish a weekly paper called *Oglasnik* (free classified adds). The minister said "yes," but with the condition that the Socialist Union of Zagreb, the union responsible for the media, went along with the idea. The Socialist Union gave its okay, but it did so quietly, without ever informing the Central Committee. In the West, this means nothing, but in Croatia at this time, not clearing such a proposal with the Central Committee of the Communist League of Croatia was unthinkable.[11] Nonetheless, the deal went forward and the first private newspaper in Croatia, *Oglasnik*, was founded in 1988.

A similar situation occurred with the first nongovernmental television channel. The youth organization (*Savez socijalističke omladine*), founder of Omladinski radio, today's Radio 101, asked Croatian TV for the rights to use an available channel (called the 3rd Channel). A similar procedure ensued. This time television manager Goran Radman publicly declared the acceptability of pluralism in television ownership and gave his okay to the proposal. Today the channel is known as OTV, Open Television.

In Yugoslavia, private ownership was limited. Individuals could not own factories, banks, hotels, or newspapers. The system was called "social ownership," and the workers themselves managed the factories and companies. Over time, privatization slowly became acceptable, but it was available only to a select few. Ante Marković, Yugoslavia's prime minister, allowed privatization under a special law known as "the Marković law on privatization." The media could also be privatized, a fact recognized by Ivo Novačić, manager of the weekly magazine *Arena* (published by the Vjesnik Company).

After careful planning, *Arena* became the first privatized newspaper in Croatia, and the paper's journalists became its shareholders. Again, by Western standards, this is a yawn, but at this time in a place so long under Communism, privatization and employee ownership were extraordinary developments. *Arena* became a well-edited weekly with an impressive circulation. Its employee-shareholders became wealthy by Croatian measures.

Novi list, a daily from Rijeka, followed the *Arena* model. That ownership, in fact, served as the foundation of the paper's independent editorial policy. Unfortunately, it was too late or too premature for the others to get in on the privatization deal. *Večernji list* tried, but the ruling party killed the deal, largely because this paper was too big and too important to the party to lose control. *Slobodna Dalmacija* also tried, but it, too, was cut down by newly elected government officials.

Thanks to the *Oglasnik*, though, it was possible to set up new private newspapers. In February 1990, Marinko Božić founded *Slobodni tjednik*, the first tabloid in Croatia. Božić's paper became popular among large audiences, as it published a wide-ranging assortment of stories in the best free-wheeling tabloid style. Because the paper published political secrets, sensational gossip, and details of scandals, its political influence also became quite remarkable. Somehow, its sensational, off-the-edge style granted it a measure of immunity from political interference not afforded the more staid, traditional papers.[12]

The Croatian Journalists' Association was also active during this period. Newly elected president Ante Gavranović and her staff corrected earlier injustices toward members who were expelled from the organization during the communist regime in 1954, 1972, and 1973. On February 27, 1990, Croatian journalists expelled during that period were welcomed back into the association.

The Croatian media environment had changed significantly by the time of the first free and democratic elections, held in January 1990. At this time, it was obvious that Yugoslavia was breaking up. Slovenian Communists, led by Milan Kučan, made a big scene of their departure from the "Sava" congress center in Belgrade under the glare of television lights and the unbelieving stares of Communist delegates from throughout Yugoslavia. The Croatian delegation, which also did not support Milošević, failed to leave that session of Congress—which later became known as the "Unfinished Congress"—and that proved to be a great mistake. An early demonstration at that point may have headed off some of the wars and political problems that followed during the next five years. Returning back to Zagreb, the Croatian League of Communists declared free and democratic elections for April 1990.

Croatia now faced new conditions. The Communist government allowed free elections, and this was almost unbelievable! So unbelievable that most people suspected the election was a front for deals being made behind the curtains.

The country prepared for the elections by founding parties, looking for candidates, preparing for the campaigns. None of the players had experience with electoral politics, so every step was a venture onto new ground, and this was especially true for the media. Journalists did not know how to cover free elections, how to present candidates and their policies, how to choose and write stories that gave all sides an even hand in coverage. Meanwhile, the politicians knew the power of the media, and they knew what they wanted from the journalists and editors who covered their campaigns.

On March 28, 1990, the Croatian Journalists' Association accepted a list of guidelines governing the principles of professional media activity during the elections. The simple standards recognized the need to present different ideas and opinions, to protect human rights, to strengthen civil society, and to support basic democratic doctrine—that people control the government and politics.

Journalists agreed to write the truth but also to retain their right to offer their own opinions. Rules for election coverage were drafted by editorial boards of each major medium. Editors presented their guidelines to political party representatives and asked them to obey them. Each party got equal space and time to present their programs. Most of the parties were new and unknown to the public, but even these got a share of exposure.

The media campaign was something fresh and new in Croatian political life. For the first time ever, voters had access to live debates, position papers, and speeches from familiar and unknown parties. The media were filled with political information, and the voters ate it up.

At the same time, most citizens did not quite understand what the election was about. The electoral law had voters selecting representatives to Parliament. They were not voting for the parties or the president—not directly. No one cared for these Yugoslav election laws, because they obscured the primary aim of the people, and that was to dig Communism from the system. They wanted an independent Croatia and the abolition of Communism, and they did not particularly care which member of the Parliament won from any particular town. Yet these were the kinds of choices they were given.

Candidates associated with the Communist Party had no chance of winning, so the contest centered around two leading alternative parties: the Croatian Democratic Union, led by Dr. Franjo Tuđman, and the Coalition of the People's

Agreement, led by a former leader of the Croatian Liberation Movement. Tuđman's approach for his party was direct and simple: Say "no" to Communism and "yes" to an independent Croatia. His campaign was efficient, and it was no surprise when he won the election.

The media contributed satisfactorily to the democratic process. Croatia became an independent state without bloodshed or riots, and it was now ready for Europe; the Croatian media were ready for complete freedom of expression. At this optimistic time, few people could have seen the clouds of war and repression on the horizon. Few could have anticipated that media freedom and true democracy in Croatia, and in the rest of Yugoslavia and former Yugoslavia, was still far away.

The heady bubble of freedom was soon punctured by Tuđman's Democratic Union. Could history repeat itself after the high hopes of election 2000? How sure can we be that an even more tragic disenchantment is not in the cards—today, tomorrow, or five years from now?

The transitional period was exciting for most of the Yugoslav journalists. Liberated from the Communist Party's iron grip, they wrote and published freely and reveled in the lifting of government restraints. But this lively period was not to last. Although the old Communists were off the political stage, the new leaders were even more dangerous because they were better skilled in public manipulation. The new government promised a "thousand-year dream of national freedom and independence"—wasn't that Hitler's promise as well?—but, in fact, they offered more of the same. The rhetoric was a hit, though, and the people did not see the old despots hiding beneath their new clothes.

In the beginning, it was not easy to recognize the dangers. Milošević was a hero to Serbians, because they saw him as the enabler of their vision: a greater Serbia, including Kosovo and major portions of Bosnia and Croatia. The slogan "Serbia is wherever there are Serbian graves," became the foundation for a serious political program that would soon result in great tragedies. Again, the Liebestraum theme of Nazi Germany.

The breakup of Yugoslavia meant that, for the first time in memory, information came from many voices in Ljubljana, Belgrade, Zagreb, Sarajevo, Split, and Novi Sad. News now arrived in different languages, covered different ideas and positions, attacked politicians who held different points of view. All of this was entirely new to people who had been fused as one under the previous government. Tito's Yugoslavia, although a patchwork quilt of people, was stable.

The transition period, however, was demanding on people who rarely faced choices. Now, they were forced to take a side, to vote, to support one of dozens of newly founded parties. They were confronted with a fresh menu of newspapers and radio and television stations. Which should they trust? All of these choices were new and difficult for people not used to making such important decisions. Life under Tito was hard, but decision-making then was easy.

The simple solution for people was the best: be loyal to your fellow countrymen, your language, your heritage, your historical and cultural origins. Be loyal, especially when confronted with aggressive and dangerous ideologies like those offered by Milošević. The end of a fused Yugoslavia was obvious. The election results were inevitable.

The role of the media under such circumstances was to cover local politicians and not the range of issues facing all of Yugoslavia. So readers in each of the republics got reports only from their local media about local politicians. The agendas were limited and parochial.

Restricted news agendas endured through the nineties, as media in each republic tended to fix on its own issues and political topics. This was certainly true during the war years, when the media played an active role in marshalling public support. Serbia, however, appears to have taken this to an extreme, as is evident in coverage of the Kosovo crises during the 1999 war. Months of conflict in the region, with stories of Serbian atrocities filling evening newscasts in countries around the world, were unknown to most Serbian citizens. Many people in Serbia were shocked when NATO began bombing their cities and towns; they had no idea what Serbia had been up to.

The Kosovo story offers a clear example to present-day audiences of how citizens of the former Yugoslavia could remain uninformed. When government controls the press and limits media access to officials, it sets the agenda for the people and prescribes the truth for them. Such control was in full force—on all sides—during the war in Croatia and Bosnia-Herzegovina.

NOTES

1. Vesna Pusić, "Croatia at the Crossroads," *Journal of Democracy*, 9, no. 1 (January 1998): 11–24.

2. Zvonko Lerotić, "The Democratic Foundations of Croatia's Independence," *Croatian International Relations Review* 1, no. 1 (Institute for Development and International Relations, Zagreb) (1995): 26.

3. Ibid., 27.

4. Ibid.

5. Nenad Unukić, "Journalism in the Service of Profession of Politics," in *Proceedings of Journalism in the Function of Development Conference* (Vinkovci: Novost, 1990), 39.

6. Pavao Novosel, "Wonders Still Happen: A Case of Communication Opening in One-Party System," *Communication and Society*, Informatologia Yugoslavica, special No. 7 (Zagreb, 1998): 48.

7. Davor Rodin, "Beyond the Free and Censored Press," in *Proceedings of Journalism in the Function of Development Conference* (Vinkovci: Novost, 1990), 60.

8. Stjepan Andrašić, "Developmental Problems of Yugoslav Journalism," in *Proceedings of Journalism in the Function of Development Conference* (Vinkovci: Novost, 1990), 102.

9. Jozo Grbelja, "Censorship in Croatian Journalism 1945–1900," Ph.D. thesis, University of Zagreb, 1996, 165.

10. *Večernji list* and *Večernji novosti* from Belgrade were in constant competition as the best-selling dailies, each always improving editorial policies and implementing new technologies to inch ahead of the other. *Slobodna Dalmacija*, a daily paper from Split, became one of the best-edited newspapers in Yugoslavia in that time, practicing open-minded editorial policy, thanks to Joško Kulušicć, editor in chief. Magazines such as *Start, Danas*, and *Nedjeljna Dalmacija* were also noteworthy for their good editing and professional productions.

11. Malović, a co-author of this book, was the president of the Central Committee of the Communist League of Croatia.

12. *Globus*, a weekly, was started by the Vjesnik publishing company, but it soon became independent and part of Ninoslav Pavić's media empire.

9

The Media Role in the Croatian-Serbian War

The start of the Croatian war in 1991 forced journalists to face a conflict between their professionalism and their patriotism. How could they honestly report on the homeland war without covering the crimes of Croatian troops? No army had clean hands in this war; balanced journalism at the time would have been seen as a betrayal to the country. So objectivity became a casualty of the war, no surprise given the huge obstacles faced by this tiny, struggling country. The abandonment of objectivity, however justified, reestablished the press culture of self-censorship that flourished under Tuđman.

The war in Croatia, then in Bosnia and Herzegovina and Kosovo, opened old questions among the international media about journalism ethics, objective reporting, sensationalism, and political advocacy in the press.

The wars in the former Yugoslavia were no sudden explosions. The crisis which brought them about began with the elections in the republics. When Yugoslavia was still intact, the elections were held under the old Yugoslavian law, but the results demonstrate that the Yugoslav state was only a frail umbrella for the new emerging countries.

Two prominent, former Communist leaders were elected to the presidencies: Milan Kučan in Slovenia and Kiro Gligorov in Macedonia. Kučan formed a coalition with young, forward-looking politicians from different parties, and the result was a government generally supportive of democracy. Gligorov, too, formed a reasonably open and independent Macedonia, despite formidable Greek opponents. In Bosnia and Herzegovina the collective presidency was formed by Moslems, Croats, and Serbs, headed by Alija Izetbegović, but from the beginning it was obvious that shared governance here was an artificial solution.

Serbia elected Slobodan Milošević, and in Montenegro, voters put in office Milošević followers Milan Bulajić and Milo Đukanović. The results of the election in the Yugoslavian republics demonstrated clear voter support for politicians who favored independence and had no designs for the maintenance of the old Yugoslav collective.

The election in Croatia swept Dr. Franjo Tuđman and his HDZ party into office with large majorities. Professor Vesna Pusić explains Tuđman's victory this way:

A majority of Croatian voters concluded that it would take Croat-nationalist hard-liners to defend Croatia against Milošević and his Serb-nationalist hard-liners. Thus the first free, multiparty elections in the Yugoslav republic of Croatia, held in April and May 1990, produced a victory for Franjo Tuđman's nationalist Croatian Democratic Union (HDZ). . . . Like his Serbian counterpart, Tuđman (who had been a Yugoslav army general under Tito) was a communist turned nationalist.[1]

Slaven Letica, who was Tuđman's advisor then, explained the results of the election:

The conflicts in the former Yugoslavia after the eighties were about the understanding of the fundamental political and constitutional principles upon which the post-communist "Yugoslavia" was to be based.

While Slovenia and Croatia aimed for freedom, federalism, human rights, a multiparty system, and a market economy, the movement that simultaneously emerged in Serbia and the JNA (Yugoslav People's Army) leadership aimed for the negation of these ideas and principles.

Nationalist and secessionist movements in Slovenia, Croatia and Bosnia were therefore not the cause . . . but the inevitable consequence of the pan-Serbian National-Socialist and racist movement.[2]

How could the Yugoslavian crisis be solved? The presidents of the six republics tried to answer this difficult question and resolve this extraordinarily complex matter by holding meetings—one per week in each of the republics.

It was a spectacular media show that made for good public relations but bore no results. At one point, participants even proposed a Slovenian and Croatian confederation, but that was doomed from the start. As for other arrangements, the Yugoslavian state was to share a common foreign policy, and its republics were to enjoy autonomous economies. The military command and control was not so easily settled, however. The Yugoslav People's Army (JNA) was not happy with the proposal to share a common air and naval force, while running independent infantries in each republic. The JNA generals, mostly Serbs and Montenegrins, rejected the plan with the realization that they would lose supreme command over the Yugoslav infantry and, consequently, yield control over all of Yugoslavia.

After the six presidents' tour, the crisis became deeper. It all started to unravel when the Serbs in Croatia showed their disagreement with the newly elected Croatian government, the Croatian state symbol, such as the flag and the official seal, and purification of the language.

Things came to a head in August 1990. It was then that Serbs from Croatia protested openly against the Croatian government in an action called "*balvan-revolucija*" (the Beam Revolution). In the middle of the tourist season, the Serbs blockaded the main coastline road and stopped traffic from the rest of the country, an action that was not only unanticipated but came as a shock to most of the country. Foreign tourists quickly left, their rapid departure causing traffic jams and panic on the roads to Italy. The Croatian prime minister[3] called out the police, but President Tuđman rescinded this action. Many armed Serbs forcefully stopped Croatian journalists from reporting on the "*balvan-revolucija*." The Serbs also organized a referendum, scheduled for August 20, that called for autonomy in an area later referred to as Srpska Krajina.

One of the authors of this book, spending his summer holiday at a seaside town, planned to report on the voting taking place in Obrovac, a small town on the Zrmanja River. He left with a two-member crew from *Vjesnik* (Ivica Marijačić) and *Večernji list* (Ana Dobrović) on that hot Sunday morning. Just the day before, on a bridge over the Zrmanja, Serbs had shot at journalists from *Slobodna Dalmacija*. Nevertheless, three reporters entered the city where the narrow streets were crowded with men. Not a woman was in sight. The men immediately recognized the intruders and told them that they were not welcome. The reporters pressed on, although they thought better of visiting the Orthodox church where the referendum was being held. Instead, they visited city hall, where they asked local government officials for information about the referendum and about "*balvan-revolucija.*" After the official turned them down, they sought out a local police station for information. While walking to the station house, they saw a group of young men crossing the Zrmanja bridge and coming toward them. The Serbian men surrounded the journalists and shouted threats at them, saying they would be killed and thrown in the river if they stayed around. Claiming that Croatian journalist had unfairly reported on Serbian issues and regularly maligned Serbian president Milošević, the angry group even accused the journalists of being Ustasha, a Nazi-like hate group often associated with Croatian nationalism.

The reporters tried to explain that they were simply trying to cover the referendum and the boycott, but they were shouted down by the crowd and again accused of anti-Serb reporting. One man expressed his particular hatred for a reporter he had never seen, Ivica Marijačić, threatening to kill him, not realizing that at the moment Marijačić stood before him.

Finally, the men were satisfied with threats alone and let the journalists go. The three reporters quickly exited, none happier to leave than Marijačić who was trembling but happy that no one recognized him. On their way home, they passed through the nearby Croatian village of Kruševo, where a large Croatian flag was flying and many people were sitting in restaurants eating roasted lamb and drinking travarica.[4] None was aware of the drama that had just taken place a few miles away.

Croatia spent the period between the 1990 elections and start of the war in 1991 forming the state, creating the government, reviving traditional institutions, and enjoying the "Big Croatian Attributes," which are patriotic performances and symbols such as singing traditional nationalistic songs and creating and raising new flags and emblems.

Implementation of a new political system and the significant changes in other institutions that took place after the elections dramatically influenced the Croatian population. Mammoth publishing companies, such as Vjesnik, were broken up. Most of the chief editors from the former regime resigned or were replaced. In some newsrooms, the journalists elected new chief editors as they did in the *Večernji list*—but in most of the media, the government or a managing board appointed new top management.

Management and editorial changes were important in the coverage of news, but the most significant outcome of the elections was a change in media ownership. "Workers' self-management," the great invention of the late President Tito, slipped into history, as the new Croatian government allowed private ownership of the press. During the transitional period, the media were owned by the government (Croatian Radio and Television), stockholders (the majority holders were state-run health and pension funds), and private hands.

Privatization of the media, like the privatization of other market segments, caused problems then and continues to cause problems today. Some of the publishing companies were privatized under strange circumstances and scandals, as was the privatization of *Slobodna Dalmacija*, one of the best-edited dailies. Some of the media were owned by individual shareholders, as is *Novi list* from Rijeka. The daily newspaper *Vjesnik* changed owners twice—the actual owner today is one of the biggest banks in Croatia (Privredna banka).[5]

Media privatization has a democratic ring, but put to practice in Croatia, it came with a lot of political baggage. The ruling party, HDZ, would not easily yield control of the particularly influential media, and neither management nor journalists were in a position to resist their control. Before long, using different means of acquisition, the HDZ controlled Croatian Radio and Television, *Vjesnik, Večernji list, Slobodna Dalmacija,* and *Glas Slavonije*. It obtained the radio and television operation through the legal system and parliamentary votes. It took *Večernji list* from the inside by encouraging journalists loyal to the party to assume control. *Slobodna Dalmacija* was all but a government give-away to Miroslav Kutle, a media mogul who later caused many problems. *Glas Slavonije* was taken from the hands of Drago Hedl, the old editor in chief, who was forced to leave his newsroom with Kalashnikov rifles pointed at his head.

Several new entrepreneurs who showed interest in starting up media operations discovered the difficulties confronting would-be broadcasters, so most turned to print, where the laws were less harsh. New editions quickly poured into an overcrowded market. The new daily *Zapad* (West) went bankrupt after two months; the legendary *Hrvatski tjednik* (Croatian Weekly), which had published for years in England, returned to Croatia but failed after only two issues. The weekly *Dom* (one of the authors of this book was editor in chief), owned by the publishing company Revije, went belly up after the third issue. Overnight, about 20 well-edited magazines and revues went bust, putting nearly 170 seasoned journalists on the street.

While many publications failed, some of them made it. For instance, *Slobodni tjednik*, a weekly tabloid owned and edited by Marinko Božić, and *Globus*, owned by private shareholders, mostly journalists, and edited by Denis Kuljiš, found a market and long-term success.

The turbulent politics of this period was ideal for the tabloids, which thrived on gossip and planted information. From week to week they pursued sensational stories that spun ever larger webs of scandal and accusation. Like many supermarket tabloids in the United States, the veracity of a story printed in the Croatian tabs was less important than the capacity of a headline to grab the reader. Marinko Božić, a capable but shameless journalist, gathered small teams of young reporters and many prominent public figures, including members of the government and presidential advisors, for special features. The temperature of a story and the notoriety of its author had more to do with its value to the paper than its accuracy and its truth.

Globus, by contrast, attempted a more serious journalistic product, but it, too, often came close to the supermarket papers. Editorial decisions, hard-driven by market forces, reflected the public's indifference toward serious political journalism and its preference for easy-going stories, scandals, political gossip, and urban legend fantasies.

The Croatian government had no trust in Tanjug, the former Yugoslav official news agency, and established its own news agency called HINA (Croatian Informative News Agency). But this government, like the previous one, made the mistake of creating an organ that was immediately seen as a public relations tool of the government and the party. From its first day in operation, HINA enjoyed little credibility within the journalistic community and the public.

The Catholic Church soon became unhappy with its treatment by HINA, so it founded the IKA (Informative Catholic Agency). Consequently, within a very short period of time, Croatia had two news agencies, several tabloids and weekly newspapers, and dozens of magazines, although most were under the firm control of the ruling party.

At this time—in 1990 and the beginning of 1991—Croatia was still a part of Yugoslavia, so newsstands regularly stocked papers from Belgrade, Ljubljana,

Sarajevo, and other Yugoslav capitals. The availability of news from these republics, along with the infusion of new media in Croatia, set up conditions for a heated battle within the press. The powerful Milošević propaganda machinery aggressively spread news about the Greater Serbian Plan.

Fighting fire with fire, so to speak, journalists on both sides fought propaganda with propaganda. The media quickly became the battleground for a harsh war of words, but it was a battle not observed by most readers, because average citizens were exposed only to their national media and saw the issues from just one point of view. Very soon, the truth had yielded to provincial interpretations of regional issues, and ordinary citizens became hopelessly lost in the web of political misinformation.

An example of this propaganda war was the publication of a transcript (made from an audio tape) of a meeting between Franjo Tuđman and Jovan Rašković in the weekly news magazine *Danas* on July 31, 1990. Rašković was the leader of the Serbs in Croatia, and his meeting with Tuđman was of great public interest, especially because no one except Slaven Letica, Tuđman's advisor, was present. The secrecy of that meeting was broken by Rašković, who told the Belgrade media about the content of the negotiation. Since Rašković spilled the beans, Tuđman decided to give *Danas* the tapes recorded at the meeting. This caused quite a stir in the public, because both politicians spoke openly about the political situation. They discussed a possible Serbian mutiny, Croatian statehood, Serbian rights and autonomy, Serbian sovereignty in Croatia, and other topics of intense interest to both sides. The discussion was candid and sometimes rough and not meant for public consumption. For instance, the tapes recorded Rašković saying that the Serbs in Croatia "are insane people. They are extremely well armed. These people are armed like commandos."

The next day, in an interview with the Belgrade daily *Politika*, Rašković denied saying the things published in *Danas*. He claimed, "It was a dirty misuse of the conversation I initiated." Rašković said that he was taped without his knowledge and that the transcripts were published without his permission, both acts showing the low dealings of the Croatian government.

This was not the only scandal of this type. On January 27, 1991, Croatian TV broadcast a special show called "Falsified: yes or no?" The show presented a short film by Zastava Film, a JNA movie production company, about Croatia arms-dealing and the role of the former JNA general, Martin Špegelj, now the Croatian minister of defense. The accusation was extremely serious because it suggested Croatia's complicity in violent acts. Špegelj was shown smuggling arms to Croatia, engaging the Ustasha as collaborators, and organizing armed mutiny against the JNA and the Serb population.

Croatian television invited some of the president's advisors to analyze the movie. Their comments about the movie were a total surprise to the Croatian public. Slaven Letica said that there were three possible explanations for the movie. First, it was an authentic and professionally produced documentary; second, it was a forgery; and third, it was a well-done illusion fashioned by Špegelj himself, who played a double role and fooled the JNA secret service.

Ante Barišić, the president's security advisor, said that the documentary was authentic, a part of the wider counter-espionage strategy in Yugoslavia's cold war. Doubtless, the television show provoked a scandal, but it was only a prelude to a growing conflict that would soon evolve into war.

For their part, the Belgrade media orchestrated a Zastava Film documentary, which included secret records about HDZ paramilitary operations. It claimed that special armed units of the HDZ engaged professional Croatian warriors and promoted other hostile activities.

Serbia's *Politika* published the headline "80,000 HDZ members are armed to the teeth." The scandal developed an international angle when Zastava Film accused Špegelj of smuggling arms from Hungary. All the former Yugoslavian media reporting the story took predictable sides, each discovering new secret details that bolstered its particular point of view. Zvonko Ostojić, from Borovo Naselje near Vukovar, killed himself because he was recognized in the movie accusing prominent HDZ politicians of being the extreme hard-liners and claiming that they maintained secret death-lists for political enemies.

Three advisors of the president published a special edition of a book called *The Špegelj Case: War against Croatia*. It explained how the movie was part of a planned army coup. Referring to a story in the Yugoslav news agency, *The Times* (of London) reported that the Croatian minister of defense called the army a "brutal Stalinist organization of the KGB."[6]

The reporters Richard Basset and Desa Trevisan wrote that the war of nerves against Croatia was fostered by Yugoslav president Borisav Jović who accused Croats of not keeping their word about demobilization of reserve militia forces. Jović said, according to *The Times*, that the Yugoslav Army (80 percent of the JNA officers are Serbs) considers the situation to be very serious.

The situation became more dangerous and Špegelj, the Croatian minister of defense, went into hiding. Meanwhile, JNA security forces arrested Špegelj's collaborators and prosecuted them in Zagreb for being Croatian nationalists and mutineers. What an amusing paradox. JNA was in town prosecuting Croats for their advance toward independence at the same time the Croatian Parliament across town was declaring independence.

This bizarre sight, confusing for anyone outside, was a typical spectacle during this turbulent period of Yugoslavia's history. The media were misused to send political messages, to test the other side, to misinform the public, and to confuse political leaders about the real agendas of the opposition. Some of the media played this game with pleasure, enjoying their role in a high-stakes political contest. Others were coerced into participation and given no chance to opt out of dishonest, damaging schemes concocted by the political elite. Confusion among the readers and viewers was also classic.

The Špegelj case was one of many signs that the countries were inching closer to war. On Easter Day 1991, on the Plitvice lakes, 150 kilometers south of Zagreb, the first serious fire fight broke out between local Serbs and Croatian police forces. A policeman, Franko Lisica, was killed, making him the first victim of the war. The police operation in Plitvice was well covered by journalists, and photos taken by Croatian photojournalists were published all over the world.

The Plitvice episode was the first serious war experience for most journalists, who had never before reported under fire or found themselves in the sights of a rifle. Only a handful had covered the Kosovo riots, and a few others had reported on the war in Slovenia in June 1990, where they had witnessed air attacks and tank assaults.

Professor Vesna Pusić explained the beginning of the war between Croatia and Serbia:

Croatia's declaration of independence (timed to coincide with Slovenia's) came on June 25, 1991. Unlike its neighbor to the west, however, Croatia was ill prepared, materially and institutionally, for sovereign statehood. It had no army and no arms to speak of, while facing a stiff Serbian challenge to its independence. Croatia embraced independence as a *fait accompli*: The Slovene's decision to leave the Yugoslav federation had dashed hopes for a looser confederate arrangement, and there seemed to be no way short of independence to fend off the Serbian domination that Milošević was planning.

That summer, Croatia came under direct attack from the Yugoslav (effectively the Serbian) army, which had been arming and training extremist ethnic-Serbian militiamen in Croatia for some time. Serbian warplanes and rocket launchers bombarded Croatian towns and villages while the Croatian police led the resistance. There is no doubt that at this time, with their country the target of unexpectedly heavy attacks, that vast majority of Croatians backed independence and stood ready to fight for it."[7]

Journalists were rushed to the front lines to cover a war that was fought with such brutality and high casualties that it surprised even seasoned war veterans. The war also attracted more international journalists than any battle since the Gulf War. Rather than enjoying some degree of immunity as noncombatants, the press, along with Red Cross workers, became easy targets for eager sharpshooters.[8]

Božo Novak, doyen of Croatian journalists, wrote: "Croatian journalists were part of the people's resistance to Yugo-Serbian aggression toward Croatia. Journalism served a role in the fight against aggression and in that fight they expressed the unity of the nation. Journalists were present on all battlefields, where many were injured. Among the 30 journalists killed in the Homeland war, one-third were Croatian. Some of them are still listed as missing persons."[9]

Figures about journalists killed in the line of duty are a reminder of the inherent dangers of the profession. The count started in 1991 and ended in 1996. All together, during the five years of war fought in Slovenia, Croatia, and Bosnia and Herzegovina, fifty-four journalists died. The worst year was 1991, when twenty-three journalists were killed in Croatia and two in Slovenia; in Bosnia and Herzegovina, twenty-two were killed. These figures have been confirmed by several independent sources, including Božo Novak and Freedom Forum, which conducted a rigorous investigation. See the appendix for a listing and brief statement about each of the journalists whose lives were lost during the war.

BITTER EXPERIENCES

Dr. Sherry Ricchiardi, a professor at the Indiana University School of Journalism and a reporter in the war in the former Yugoslavia, wrote in 1992:

Carol Byrne and three other journalists traveling through Croatia last summer could hear machine-gun fire crackling in the hills as they approached a roadblock manned by Serbian soldiers.

"We tried to explain who we were," recalls Byrne, a reporter for the *Minneapolis/ St. Paul Star Tribune*, "but they searched the car and threw our luggage on the side of the road."

Moments later, as the sun slipped behind western Yugoslavia's mountainous terrain, Byrne, freelance photographer Duane Hall, photographer Rita Reed of the *Star Tribune* and Croatian radio reporter Boris Gložinić found themselves surrounded by uniformed men armed with Kalashnikov assault rifles.

"They kept their guns cocked and pointed at us. They repeatedly told Boris that he was going to be shot," Byrne says. "We were terrified they would kill him. They accused us of having forged passports. . . . The leader was abusive and militaristic."[10]

The group was lucky. The reporters were held overnight and released after the intervention of the U.S. Consulate. Reed saved her film from confiscation by hiding it in her underwear.

The fate of other reporters caught in similar situations was grimmer. By the middle of December, eighteen journalists had been killed in Yugoslavia's six-month-old civil war, according to the Foreign Press Bureau in Zagreb. Two Soviet journalists were presumed dead. Dozens more had been wounded or abused at the hands of captors, and at least a dozen had lost limbs or been critically wounded by mortar fire, grenades, land mines, and snipers.

The international press was placed in the Foreign Press Bureau in the Hotel Intercontinental in Zagreb. Dragan Lozančić, head of the bureau, gathered a group of young U.S. and Canadian citizens of Croatian origin with a good command of English and Croatian. They were placed at the disposal of the journalists to provide translation and research, as language was a problem. The Foreign Press Bureau was a headquarters for the journalists, a center for information, drivers, translators, and contacts. Because of the building's height, it was an ideal place to install television equipment, satellite links, transmitters, and other electronic equipment.

The hotel's atmosphere was unique. Journalists, diplomats, UN officials, high-ranking officers, and a few tourists crowded corridors of the large building. At the same time, the first displaced persons, mostly from Vukovar, were there, adding to the chaos. In addition to the confusion created by the press and diplomatic corps, the Vukovar children ran around and played in the lobby, all only thirty kilometers from the war raging in the south portion of Zagreb.

It was a strange war. No direct, army-to-army combat took place, and there was no real front line or no man's land separating the armies. Very often, journalists came to Zagreb, checked into the Hotel Intercontinental, paid a visit to the Press Bureau, found an interpreter, rented a car, and drove south of the city to get a fix on the action.

It was tough to predict what they might discover. One German reporter got a mortar shell in his lap while driving. Some reporters met snipers eager to shoot at press symbols or ran into Serbian paramilitary troops known to set ambushes for soldiers and civilians alike. The outcomes of these excursions to the south of Zagreb could range from enjoying a pleasant road trip to facing death.

The situation was similar from Vukovar on the eastern frontier, several thousand kilometers south, to Dubrovnik. Croissant-shaped Croatia was virtually cut in two pieces near Karlovac, where the free territory was only a few dozen kilometers wide.

Hundreds of foreign journalists reported from Croatia, and their personal stories were hair-raising. Professor Ricchiardi wrote:

In a scathing report on press conditions in Yugoslavia since hostilities broke out, committee (CPJ) researcher, Allison Jernew, detailed numerous incidents of journalists detained or killed. "In early August," she writes, "correspondents from two Spanish and five Italian newspapers were stopped on the way to a scheduled interview with a Serbian commander. They were accused of spying for Croatia. . . . While the Yugoslav Army officers watched, the Serbs lined up the journalists before a firing squad, raised their rifles, and then, at the last moment, decided to let them go."[11]

Experienced international reporters often compared the war in Croatia with the Vietnam War, some arguing that the Croatian war was even more dangerous for them. Robert Menard, Reporters sans Frontiers general secretary, explained why:

I think the reason Vietnam was different was because journalists were not specially targeted. Obviously a bullet is not going to distinguish between a military person and a journalist, and if you are in the trajectory of a bullet you are going to be hit, but journalists were not specifically targeted. That was not the case in former Yugoslavia. There was a team that wanted to show images that one of the groups involved in the conflict did not want them to show. And they were targeted. In that kind of situation how can you protect yourself? Because we are not just talking about the risk of the job, but about a situation where you yourself are targeted. In that kind of situation, equipment such as flak jackets, armored cars and training no longer helps. On the contrary, it helps to identify the target people want to aim at.[12]

Sherry Ricchiardi has been trying to find answers to this hostility against journalists: "When journalists gather over beer in Zagreb to trade war stories, they search for explanations of the violence directed at the press. Many believe that Serbians view the Western press as sympathetic to Croatia's struggle for independence from Belgrade, making reporters and photographers fair game for attacks."[13] The same hostility was evident in the war in Bosnia and Herzegovina and finally culminated during the Kosovo crisis. In all locations, foreign reporters were at risk.[14]

Many tragic war stories have been reported from the hundreds of journalists and dozens of news companies involved in producing news under fire. The *Glas Slavonije* newsroom was practically on the first front line, but the paper never stopped publishing. Stjepan Penić, correspondent from Vukovar, was captured, tortured, and finally decapitated by the Serbs. Mario Filipi was injured by a mortar shell on the road to Vukovar. Photographer Zoran Jajčinović was shot by dum-dum bullets. The journalist Nevenka Špoljarić was heavily wounded in the stomach. Photojournalist Lidija Livodić was shot in the head. Drago Dečetak was killed when the village of Laslovo was occupied. Zdenko Midžić was seriously wounded.

Allison Jernow told the tragic story about the death of Stjepan Penić. He said: "Serbian rebels abducted Croatian newspaper correspondent Stjepan Penić from his home (and) smashed his typewriter before beating and killing him. To (his) colleagues . . . the message was obvious."[15]

Similar intrusions into the newsroom happened at *Dubrovački vjesnik, Karlovački tjednik, Slobodna Dalmacija*, and other newspapers. Reporters from Croatian Radio in Vukovar became heroic journalistic figures in the war. This was especially so for Siniša Glavašević, a young reporter and poet, whose voice unforgettably told stories from towns under siege.

Marijana Grbeša and Domagoj Bebić report that "Siniša and his team improvised a small studio that daily reported on civilian casualties who couldn't leave the ring of death. In each and every one of his reports, he would finish with the words: 'Vukovar will never surrender!' "[16] During the occupation of Vukovar, Serbian soldiers took men from the hospital, including Glavašević, to Ovčara and killed them all. Their bodies were found several years later in a mass grave; they were identified and properly buried in 1997.

Given the deaths and injuries inflicted on Croatian journalists, often intentionally, the question arises about the capacity of the Croatian press corps to maintain its objectivity in reporting the war. What was the role of the press during that war? Was it to report the facts from a third-party viewpoint or to interpret them in a way that abetted the Croatian war effort? Credible analysts have taken both sides. Reporters at the *Feral Tribune*, for instance, accuse the Croatian media of serving as a propaganda tool of the government while assuming the role of a partial observer.

Most Croatian journalists, though, are not so critical. They see that the reporters' neutrality is often tested against other pressures that build when the reporters' homeland is endangered, their families are jeopardized, their own lives are at risk. Defenders of the journalists' coverage argue that it takes superhuman strength to sustain dispassionate objectivity in the face of events that challenge core personal values. The horrors of war, after all, become intensely personal to the journalist whose country is under siege.

The Croatian media were not prepared to cover that war. As we noted earlier, this was the first time most reporters covered anything more combative than a city council meeting, so for them, donning the hat of war correspondent was something brand new. This corps of novices had to feel their way through the reporting process the way a soldier feels his way through a mine field. Slowly, cautiously, sometimes fatally.

In addition to a lack of experience, these journalists approached their first war-reporting assignments without prior training, even without familiarity of the Geneva Convention provisions and the rights afforded to journalists fulfilling their duties as noncombatant observers. For the most part, management in print and broadcast sent their correspondents (mostly young) into the field without the slightest preparation for the extraordinary conditions they would confront.

The first attacks of JNA warplanes were aimed at the radio and television transmitters. Severing communication links has always been an early objective of war, and this was especially true in the battles directed from Belgrade. More-over, the disruption of ground transportation all but halted regular newspaper distribution, so the population suffered another severed communications link. In reaction to these disruptions, media management turned to makeshift methods. For instance, local radio stations formed into an ad hoc network where one station sent a signal to another station, which, in turn, sent that signal to yet another station, daisy-chain style, until nearly the entire country was covered by the news. It was clumsy and flawed, but it also had an elegance of function that offered a testament to inventiveness under duress.

Not all journalists, of course, were war reporters. The battle front would have looked like a scene from the *Keystone Cops* if all the reporters in Croatia rushed into combat looking for a story. Nearly all journalists operated under stressful conditions imposed by war, but only a handful can claim personal experience in reporting the battles.

While a corps of journalists, photojournalists, cameramen, and technicians honed their professional skills at the front, another group of journalists, mostly correspondents in regional centers, were drafted and participated in activities of the Crisis Headquarters (Krizni štabovi). Some journalists joined the defense units and spent the war as soldiers, not journalists.

The media environment became even more complicated when the government assumed control of the media. Like journalists, government officials had no war experience, so they, too, were uncertain about how to use public communication and the media to their public relations advantage. The only model available during the early days came from Slovenia, and this country's experience did not transfer well, largely because their war lasted only a few days. During that brief conflict, Jelko Kacin, the Slovenian minister for information, became famous for holding daily press conferences at which he updated the foreign and domestic press on this interpretation of battlefield events. All the while he played the press like a well-tuned fiddle, dispensing propaganda and winning friends for his country through his apparent reasonableness and amiable style.

The Croatian government took a page from Slovenia's book, but it did not have an appropriate spokesperson, and its attempts at press manipulation were often heavy-handed and inept. At times, its attempts went overboard, and Croatian press liaisons gave away more information about the war than was prudent. The press conferences also sent practicing reporters the wrong message, suggesting to them the policy of unbridled openness. For example, radio reporters often joyfully described how the enemy's fire was missing a specific target, not realizing that they were actually correcting the enemy's aim.

Journalists faced many ethical dilemmas about what to publish and what to withhold. Should they report battles won and battles lost, and how should they approach that news? Should it be news down the middle or news with an eye toward the home team?

One of the biggest problems was how to handle the photos of massacres. When the first bodies turned up in a village near Sisak, a town 50 kilometers south of Zagreb, editors were jolted by the brutality of the pictures and kept them out of the papers for fear of the impact they might have on their audience. Several foreign television stations and newspapers made the same decision. But when the massacres became frequent, Croatian editors changed their minds and published hardcore photos of war brutalities.

After the early war experiences, President Tuđman and the Croatian Parliament announced new regulations on reporting news about the war (*Uredba o informativnoj djelatnosti za vrijeme ratnog stanja ili u slučaju neposredne ugroženosti neovisnosti i jedinstvenosti Republike Hrvatske* [Ordinance on Information Service during the State of War or in Case of the Immediate Endangering of the Independence and Sovereignty of the Republic of Croatia]). The main purpose was to stop the information leaks about Croatian Army positions, the number and types of weapons in use, and other military information of practical use to the enemy, but, in fact, the regulations imposed censorship on the media. The regulations established the Information Headquarters of the Republic of Croatia to supervise all mass media activities. The Information Headquarters was given broad powers, and it could even replace editors in chief of private or government-owned media. Most of the media activities were regulated, and violators could be punished with up to five years in prison. How did the government explain such a decision?

"During the Homeland War, the Croatian public was exposed to a real flood of false news which was put out there to provoke panic and force people to leave their homes, thus enabling enemy forces to conquer land without a fight [Ilok example]," said Vesna Škare-Ožbolt, the president's spokeswoman.[17]

The regulation also applied to information released by government offices and employees; it mandated what information had to be published and stipulated information that could not be published. Similarly, the media could run combat-related articles only after the story was first cleared by military field command-ers. Of course, airing or publishing of military secrets was strictly forbidden by the regulation.

The regulation influenced war reporting. News filtered through Krizni štabovi (Crisis Headquarters) was less accurate, and stories from the battlefields were stripped of details after they met the censor's red pencil. Even word about the fall of Vukovar was not published when it happened. Reports of celebrated journalists like Siniša Glavaševic were censored.

Effects of the regulation were most visible on broadcast programs. Antun Vrdoljak, general manager of Croatian Radio and Television (HRTV), was a prominent movie director, former journalist, and movie actor whose iron grip on the television operation was especially visible. Almost overnight he had re-placed dozens of experienced journalist with young beginners in an effort to change the face of the television service.[18] It worked. Very soon, television developed a completely new image. The young reporters operated under difficult conditions. They didn't have the professional skills necessary to practice objec-tive reporting and often simply ran official press releases as legitimate news.

The main source of information in Croatia was (and remains so today) Cro-atian television and radio. In the beginning, television regularly aired an open news program, where it reported events of the conflict almost as they happened. Later, however, after the news was filtered, the information was delayed and doctored. The public, always looking for subtle cues in the media, found a way to know what was really happening. Popular Croatian singers produced several patriotic songs, full of emotions, that became very popular. Whenever television played one of these songs, the public knew that something went badly on the battlefield.

The regulation's "kill" feature was implemented only once, and it created a major scandal. Branko Salaj, minister of information of the Croatian govern-ment, prohibited, on January 8, 1992, the distribution of the *Slobodni tjednik* because of an article headlined "Shorthand notes on Jastreb's conversations from Vinkovci." The story published "information on armed forces and defenses which were military secrets and harmful to the country's defense."[19]

Those notes were damaging because Jastreb was the code name of Mile De-daković, defense commander of Vukovar, the hero who became a symbol of the defense against the JNA forces. Dedaković, a former JNA officer, almost single-handedly organized the defense that resisted the JNA. Vukovar was completely destroyed and finally occupied and remains the biggest symbol of the Croatian soldiers' courage.

Dedaković, a.k.a. Jastreb, was controversial. Before the war, he commanded the Zagreb army airport, but at the beginning of the war, he deserted and vol-unteered in the Croatian Army for a post in Vukovar. Under his command, Vukovar's defenses were well organized, and Dedaković managed to stop the assaults of the numerically superior JNA army. Vukovar became the graveyard of destroyed JNA tanks. But Dedaković was never approved of by the HDZ members running army headquarters. He had constant problems getting arms, munitions, supplies, and other support. Once, in the middle of the siege of Vukovar, he came crawling through cornfields to Zagreb, because it was the only way to enter the embattled city. He asked for support but without success. Angry and impulsive as usual, he gave an interview to Croatian television, the contents of which shocked the public. The journalist he spoke with, Luka Mitrović, was soon replaced and put "on ice" for several years. Nor did the Croatian Army forgive Dedaković: He was immediately kicked upstairs as the commander in Vinkovci, a town in the vicinity of Vukovar. A promotion on paper, it was a convenient way to relieve him of his Vukovar command.

After the fall of Vukovar, Dedaković was arrested and accused of stealing money earmarked for the defense. Although the military police brutally beat him, they found no evidence of a crime. He was retired from the army and became a farmer but, several years later, was reactivated as a politician supporting, ironically, the HDZ—the same party whose members had imprisoned him.

His story is not all that unusual, although the publication of his notes about the conversation with the president proved to be a big media and political scandal. *Slobodni tjednik* published notes from Dedaković's conversation with several high-ranking officials, including General Anton Tus, chief of Croatian army headquarters; General Karlo Gorinšek; Robert Travaš, the president's advisor; and Gojko Šušak, the minister of defense.

The sensational headline read, "First Real Truth: Secret of the Vukovar's Tragedy!" The text was even more shocking. Dedaković was shown desperately asking for support without success. The biggest surprise to readers was the government's indifferent and bureaucratic reaction, especially that of Minister Šušak. The story ended with a sentence printed in small letters: "Continued in the next issue."

A week later, *Slobodni tjednik* (*ST*), in the best tradition of the tabloid press, printed the second installment of the shorthand notes under the headline "Tanks entered Vukovar, Mister President!" The subtitle in this remarkable frame was, "The *ST* Team of Lawyers chose to publish these notes in defiance of the Regulation on reporting in war conditions."

The text started with a conversation between Dedaković and Hrvoje Šarinić, the powerful chief of the president's office. Dedaković wanted to speak with the president but was denied. Finally, Šarinić promised him that the president would call him the next morning. Dedaković didn't wait; he called the president first thing in the morning.

Dedaković asked the president if he was informed about the situation in Vukovar and his answer was, "I do not know what you have in mind."

Dedaković said, "Listen, eight tanks entered the town along with a large infantry."

Tuđman said, "Yes, yes."

Dedaković desperately described the military situation, saying that he was unable to conduct the battle without quick military help. Tuđman answered with one or two words, saying, "Yes . . . , well . . . , good . . . , I have to check, . . . You will have to talk with Gorinšek . . ."

No help arrived, and Dedaković again asked Šušak and Tuđman for help, explaining how the hospital was endangered by JNA forces. As before, Tuđman's answers were short, void of facts, hinting at general promises, but offering nothing concrete. Tuđman then said, "We shall fix everything."

Dedaković almost cried, "But we have to do it today, Mister President!" Tuđman's final sentence was, "Well, well, goodbye, long live!"

Nothing ever happened. No help arrived and Vukovar was occupied. Moreover, no news about the tragic loss of Vukovar appeared in the Croatian media. A few months later, when *Slobodni tjednik* published the content of the conversation, the Croatian public was shocked. As a result of the episode, *Slobodni tjednik* was prohibited from publishing. Coverage of the Vukovar story offered a significant lesson about the government's view of where to draw the line for media freedom.

The war surged after the fall of Vukovar, as JNA troops pounded the Croatian countryside. Finally, the international community awoke to the badly deteriorating situation, and on December 2, 1991, the European community dropped arms sanctions against all of the republics except Serbia and Montenegro. A day later, German chancellor Helmuth Kohl announced that Germany would formally recognize Slovenia, and on December 5, Kohl told Tuđman that Germany would recognize Croatia by Christmas. Diplomatic activities were underway as the battles continued, and on January 2, 1992, UN Special Envoy Cyrus R. Vance orchestrated a cease-fire. In March of that year, UN peacekeeping troops arrived in Croatia. Croatia then entered what turned out to be a three-year limbo, a time of no real war, no real peace. That would last until August 1995, when the country was finally liberated in the Storm operation.

Vesna Pusić wrote, in the *Journal of Democracy*, that "Croatia's suffering was terrible. Thousands were killed and wounded, hundreds of thousands became refugees. The country underwent psychical devastation and lost a third of its territory to Serbian arms as it struggled to build an army while fighting off invaders and their insurgent allies. The hardships imposed by this struggle for national survival were great: so was the degree of national unity that Croatians summoned in order to bear them."[20]

The Regulation was lifted from the Croatian media on April 15, 1992. Rigid censorship was replaced by the media controls that existed before the onset of war. They would continue for another five years. While the war with Serbia was over, battles against the Moslems in Bosnia and Herzegovina raged on, so journalists were not yet freed of the obligations to report on combat. But coverage of this war posed its own ethical problems because of the cruelty sometimes committed by the troops and the consequent dilemmas faced by the press. Croatian forces, for instance, imprisoned Moslems in camps, and some soldiers, like those at Ahmići, committed war crimes. The media did not cover these episodes properly, with the detail and prominence that they merited. Only a handful of reports in the independent media told about this and similar sad episodes involving Croatian fighters.

Since the cease fire in 1992, especially after the Storm operation in 1995, Croatian journalists have spent a lot of time discussing their own role during the war, with a special concern about ethical matters. After carefully examining the role of the media during the 1991–1992 war, the Croatian Journalists' Association adopted a strong new code of ethics in 1993. The Association of Catholic Journalists, organized in 1994, conducted an analysis of the "Responsibility of the Journalist in War." In May 1998, that organization held a journalism workshop for members of the Croatian Journalists' Association. Local reporters, along with prominent international journalists and media theorists, discussed "Professionalism and War Reporting." Croatian journalists, so many of whom have been on the front lines, have become sensitive to the ethical dimensions of reporting battles in which one's own country is not only engaged but also vulnerable to aggression.

When all is said and done, the arguments always come down to two basic approaches to war reporting. One is advocacy of the official government position, expressed by Dunja Ujević, a *Večernji list* reporter. She said in 1993, "War in this [Croatia] country should be a reason for implementing censorship, and it is up to the individual conscience and a reporter's sensibility to judge which information should jeopardize Croatian interests and then, keep silent. I am personally always ready to do this." Later, her words were turned into a slogan: "I am ready to lie for Croatia!" This became the rallying cry of "patriotic" journalists.

The other approach to war reporting focuses on the journalists' obligation to objectivity, without regard for the outcome of placing the information in the public's hands. This view is argued by the journalists of *Feral Tribune*. Nothing is sacred, they say, and all news should be published.

Most journalists come in somewhere between these two extremes. They try not to harm the homeland in crucial battles while trying not to be used as an instrument of government propaganda. That's a wonderful position in theory, but how practical is it when put to the test? All war correspondents confront the problem. Christiane Amanpour, a CNN foreign correspondent, said about her experience of war in Bosnia and Herzegovina, "With this war, it was not possible for a human being to be neutral."[21]

In the aftermath of the war, the Croatian media have investigated war events, especially war crimes committed by Croatian soldiers. Their general observations were that the extraordinary conditions imposed by war led to cruelties that the Croatian public was not ready to face. Reports issued during the conflict sketched white and black images with such clarity. Croatian soldiers—the good, the strong, the just—fought against the bad, dirty Serbian aggressors. The government encouraged such an image, in fact mandated it by the regulation, underscoring the innocence of Croatian soldiers. Milan Vuković, Supreme Court president, publicly declared that, in defense of his own country, a soldier could not commit a war crime. The jurist's proclamation came close to declaring blanket amnesty for war criminals.

Consequently, Croatian authorities prosecuted a handful of criminal cases, but none of the men on trial was ever found guilty, even after the media disclosed some egregious cases such as the prison camps and the torture of imprisoned Serbs in Pakračka poljana, a small village in northern Croatia. While the Croatian government sat on his hands, the Croatian Helsinki Committee was active in protecting the rights of minorities and individuals. Some independent media published stories about crimes and atrocities, but their influence was not great.

The breakpoint came after the Storm operation in August 1995, when the entire country was finally liberated in a quick and effective military operation that cleared the territory in three days. The result was not only a free Croatia but also the exodus of over 180,000 Serbs who fled the country in front of the Croatian Army. While the country celebrated its great victory, some within the population looted, killed, and tortured the remaining Serbs, mostly elderly people, who stayed in their homes. The Storm operation was unquestionably justified, but the war crimes associated with that action were a matter of shame.

The role of the media in reporting war crimes committed during the Storm operation was different from its role in the war of 1991. The media now were more independent, and the privately owned media could not be coerced into withholding secrets.

The public remained silent no longer. NGOs, the church, and private citizens all stood up against the war crimes. Unfortunately, this is still not a majority of the citizens or even the majority of journalists. Most are under the influence of state-controlled media and still are not ready for the truth. Someday Croatia must face the awful truth of its homeland war.

NOTES

1. Vesna Pusić, "Croatia at the Crossroads," *Journal of Democracy* 9, no. 1 (January 1998): 11.

2. Slaven Letica, "The Last or Lost American Ambassador?" *Croatian International Relations Review* 2, no. 2 (1996): 22.

3. It was Stipe Mesić, elected in 2000 as the Croatian president.

4. Travarica is the local herb brandy.

5. Stjepan Malović, "Media in Croatia," lecture in conference *Making War and Peace in the Balkans: The Role of the Media*, University of Michigan, Ann Arbor, October 19–20, 1995.

6. *Tanjug Bulletin on Foreign Press*, February 6, 1991. The text published in this edition was quoted from *The Times* (London), February 4, 1991.

7. Pusić, "Croatia at the Crossroads."

8. The Committee to Protect Journalists (CPJ) reported that between 1987 and 1996, 474 journalists around the world were killed while performing their professional duties.

For the journalists killed in wars, the most dangerous countries were Algeria (60 killed), Columbia (41), the Philippines (30), Russia (29), Tajikistan (29), Croatia (26), Bosnia and Herzegovina (21), and Turkey (20).

9. Božo Novak, *Almanac of Croatian Printing Business, Publishing, Journalism, and Library Science* (Zagreb: Horizon Press and Kratis, 1997), 211.

10. Sherry Ricchiardi, "Kill the Reporters!," *Washington Journalism Review* (January/ February 1992):33.

11. Ibid., 34.

12. Marijana Grbeša and Domagoj Bebić, "War Reporting in Croatia," *International Crossroads* (1999), 35. *International Crossroads* is a magazine published at Missouri Southern State College—once in hard copy and online, now online only. Funded in part by the U.S. Department of Education, it publishes stories submitted by students from several dozen countries around the world. Menard is quoted in this article.

13. Ricchiardi, "Kill the Reporters!," 34.

14. The Croatian Journalists' Association paid a tribute to all journalists and technicians killed during the war when, in 1994, it placed a memorial tablet on the Journalists' Home in Zagreb.

15. Quoted in Ricchiardi, "Kill the Reporters!," 34.

16. Grbeša and Bebić, "War Reporting in Croatia," 35.

17. Vesna Škare-Ožbolt was Tuđman's spokeswoman and later became a high-ranking official in the president's office.

18. Many of the seasoned journalists lost their jobs simply because of their Serbian backgrounds.

19. Vesna Škare-Ožbolt, "Countries in the State of War and Freedom of Information," in *Proceedings of the Journalists' Responsibility in the State of War Conference* (Zagreb: Croatian Catholic Journalists' Association, 1994), 48.

20. Pusić, "Croatia at the Crossroads," 9.

21. Quoted in Sherry Ricchiardi, "Over the Line," *American Journalism Review* (September 1996).

10

The Postwar Years

GENERAL OVERVIEW

The worst of the war years were over, but peace was not yet fully at hand. One-third of the Croatian territory was occupied by Serbs, and UN peacekeeping forces (UNPROFOR) implemented the peace agreement and ran security in UN protected areas (UNPA). The main roads crossing into protected regions were blockaded by UNPROFOR, which stopped and checked each passing vehicle. It was a strange time, when the signs and symbols of war were everywhere even though the combat had ended.[1]

In neighboring Bosnia and Herzegovina, combat persisted. Ethnic cleansing proceeded with a vengeance, and mass movements of refugees and displaced persons were evident everywhere. Almost 500,000 homeless people were placed in Croatia. They were sent to private homes, collective centers, hotels, former JNA barracks, and just about anywhere else people could be warehoused until plans for them had been arranged. The refugees presented the Croatian government with the enormous problem of how to accommodate and care for so many people with so few resources. Clearly, Croatia needed international humanitarian assistance, but the problems went beyond money. The refugees from Bosnia and Herzegovina and the indigenous Croatian population had just come through extraordinarily difficult times, and tensions remained high at the personal, public, and political levels.

The Croatian government also faced its own postwar problems, including a damaged transportation and utilities infrastructure, collapsing industries, and a lack of income. In addition, it faced rising unemployment (especially of former soldiers) and a rapidly deteriorating economic base that resulted from scandalous privatization.

How did the Croatian government and the ruling party, HDZ, handle the rising tide? The fact is, they didn't do much—for the country that is—although they exploited all opportunities for political gain. Vesna Pusić stated in the *Journal of Democracy*: "The HDZ increasingly treats Croatia as a party-state. . . . President Tuđman continues to pour contempt on the opposition, calling it a herd of 'grazing cattle' in a 1995 speech. Both he and his party have been high-handed and autocratic enough to alienate a large portion of the populace."[2]

The country was a patchwork quilt of organizations with authority and responsibilities. It started with the enormous presence of the international community, including the European Monitoring Commission, the UN, the European Union (EU), and all the other abbreviations and acronyms that policed and monitored. Add to this the Red Cross, humanitarian organizations and NGOs, and diplomats from all over the world. These well-meaning souls wanted to help rebuilt Croatia and its economy and to develop democracy. Many Croats, especially the young ones with a good command of foreign languages, were engaged in these activities.

On the other side, the authoritarian government and xenophobic HDZ were not yet ready to open the country's doors widely. The HDZ could not turn away the international community, but it could sabotage its operations by making it widely known that cooperation with these organizations could be seen as non-patriotic and even subversive.

During this period, it became apparent that Croatia was returning to the double morals and double standards that existed under communism. Juan Linz et al. wrote, "The current regime in Croatia is authoritarian rather than totalitarian: it tolerates limited political pluralism, religious freedom, and a degree of social and economic pluralism."[3] The halfway measures made it tough to praise Croatia for its openness or to condemn it for its absolutism. This confused the international community, which often was unable to settle on a response to the actions of the Croatian government.

Marvin Stone, an expert on Croatian media, said to one of the authors of this book, "A couple of years ago, after a cursory study of the press in the Balkans, I wrote that Croatia was the 'last fascist state in Europe.' But I had second thoughts and now have deleted that reference. I was right to do that. Croatia is not a fascist state. However, President Tuđman has instincts that are, by definition, uncomfortably close to fascism. He is antidemocratic, powerful, authoritarian and, in a distinct sense, fascistic."[4]

Tuđman gave his critics plenty of ammunition. In one minute, he was ready to sign agreements and pacts proposed by the international community, and the next minute, he would attack them with charges that they were interfering in Croatian politics. Tuđman said in his speech at a meeting of HDZ on December 7, 1996:

In addition to the direct political activity of the varied components of the domestic and foreign anti-HDZ team, there is even a stronger effort in the humanitarian, cultural and publishing/media circles to change the image of Croatia on its policies of human rights and general freedoms. They have pervaded all of our society through Soros's Open Society, the Helsinki Committee and other human rights organizations. Soros registered with the Ministry of the Economy of the Republic of Croatia on March 5, 1993, and obtained agreement for the collection and distribution of humanitarian aid. How has this humanitarian aid been dealt with? I must self-critically admit that I had quite a clear idea as to what kind of humanitarian aid this has been, but I was also aware that our position with respect to Soros and others, as well as with respect to the behavior of diplomats, had to be more indulgent at a time when we struggled for good relations both with European States and with the leading global superpower.[5]

Under such difficult circumstances, the Croatian media came out of a hard, complicated, and extremely sensitive war period and started a new march on the long road to a free press.

The legal framework for media freedom was the so-called Christmas Constitution Law, adopted by the Parliament on December 22, 1990. Article 38, which became the foundation of free media fights later in the nineties, guarantees freedom of thought and expression. The constitution says: "Freedom of expression includes especially freedom of the press and other means of information dissemination. Censorship is forbidden. Journalists have the right to freedom of expression and access to information. The right for correction is guaranteed to everybody whose Constitutional right was jeopardized." The Croatian Parliament adopted the new law very soon after war ended, on April 9, 1992.

Božo Novak, who analyzed the legal framework of the media at that time, wrote:

This law was a big step toward press freedom. It advanced independent, pluralistic and private media, but it also came with some minuses. The responsibility of the Government concerning media freedom was not clearly mentioned, and the possibility of organizing private electronic media was left for some future, better time. Also, Articles 30 and 31, which regulate the damage to citizens caused by false information, are a possible threat to publishers and journalists and they practically suggest self-censorship. This Law did not deal with electronic media, setting up a state monopoly for HRTV.[6]

In 1992, Croatia had an odd collection of controlled, semicontrolled, and almost free media. Radio and television were firmly under governmental control, with no possibility of private broadcast start-ups. On the other hand, the press had a relatively easy time at setting up papers under private ownership, and consequently, almost overnight newsstands were filled with new publications. These new and generally inexperienced publishers, however, were quick to learn the brutality of a free media market. Competition as a concept is remarkable;

as a market force, it can be cruel. Many papers suffered the consequences of an oversaturated media marketplace.

Three monopolies still existed in newspaper production: printing, layout and design, and distribution. In communist times, the state controlled the process from the newsroom to the printing plant to the newsstands. Now, thanks to new information technologies, the first monopoly—preparation of the manuscripts for printing—was in private hands. Desktop publishing (DTP) facilities enabled small, private publishers to produce their newspapers literally at home. Low cost production and full control of the product were extraordinary advantages. The new kids on the block, armed with DTP gear, cranked out papers by the hundreds.

The second monopoly was not so easily avoided. A printing plant is a big investment and an elaborate process from start to finish. Croatia had many small, private printing plants, but they were not capable of producing serious newspapers. They were adequate for small press runs of slim editions, but they had no capacity for daily papers with circulations of 50,000 copies in three or four editions.

The first new daily newspaper, *Zapad*, did not succeed because of an insufficient capacity at the Vjesnik printing plant. *Vjesnik* and *Večernji list* squeezed *Zapad* out by denying the paper access to the presses. When *Večernji list*, in cooperation with *Glas koncila*, bought a new printing plant, the situation changed drastically. The plant had the capacity to print *Jutarnji list*, the first really new daily newspaper on the Croatian market—but that didn't happen until 1998. It was easier to start up a weekly or monthly magazine because of adequate printing capacity in private printing plants that allowed full color production.

The third monopoly, distribution and sales, remained a remarkably efficient means of control over publishers. Croissant-shaped Croatia presents a difficult distribution problem for daily newspapers. The significant distances between cities means that for daily paper in Zagreb to be in Dubrovnik at 7 A.M., it must start printing in the evening of the previous day. That, in turn, means the reporters' deadline bears down around 3 P.M., and with that, the news arrives stale the next morning in Dubrovnik. The Zagreb paper's competition in Split, only several hours from Dubrovnik, has the geographic advantage and, thus, the leverage of fresher news.

So distribution became the trigger domino; when it fell, everything else in the chain was effected. Vjesnik, a government-controlled publishing company, realized this in the 1970s. Getting the paper into the hands of readers was the key to success and, thus, a powerful means of controlling print media. Vjesnik then developed a national distribution operation, which, under the name Tisak, had monopoly control over distribution for all major papers in Croatia. Because this company was a force to reckon with for any major publisher, Tisak became a powerful tool of politicians.

This distribution monopoly was crucial for more than just getting a paper into

Table 10.1
The Number of Newspapers and Magazines Sold in Croatia, 1989–1993

Year	Newspapers	Magazines
1989	163,136,000	50,458,000
1990	174,841,000	70,290,000
1991	115,457,000	58,035,000
1992	64,935,000	21,450,000
1993	63,230,262	20,895,337

Source: Croatian Governmental Institute for Statistics, 1995.

a reader's hands. Newspapers in Croatia earned nearly 80 percent of their income from the sale of papers; only 20 percent came from advertisers. They live or die, therefore, by the steady stream of income derived from over-the-counter sales. Tisak, by monopoly mandate, collected all the sales revenue and, in theory, transferred it back to the papers. In practice, though, the distributor withheld payment to papers that published stories disagreeable to the party. It was blackmail, pure and simple. Small publishers, known for their hand-to-mouth operations, had little tolerance for a delay in their income stream. They were in no position to cross the chiefs at Tisak, and that was how this big distributor made itself an indispensable link in the media chain.

The postwar period was extremely hard for newspaper publishers because of the rapid drop in market potential. The Yugoslavian market, especially in Bosnia and Herzegovina, where Croatian newspapers once sold very well, was now beyond the reach of Croatian papers. Moreover, one-third of the Croatian market dried up because of the occupied territory.

The results were obvious. Circulation dropped like a stone, costs skyrocketed, and public interest for magazines, opinion extras, television listings, and specialty sections simply dried up. Table 10.1 illustrates the fall of the newspaper market during the war years.

Smaller markets were not the only cause of economic problems for the press. At the same time, the Croatian economy was in a deep crisis, and impoverished citizens had little disposable income for papers. Not only were people short of cash, but the newsstand price of a paper was expensive, even by American standards. The average cost of a Croatian paper was around fifty cents, and the average magazine ranged from $1.50 to $5.00. The cost of a prewar basket of Croatian papers could run as high as $90.[7]

In fact, Croatian readers drastically cut their consumption of newspapers and magazines. A typical reader would buy only ten daily papers, a weekly magazine, including the TV listings, a comic book, and a crossword booklet per month. The total cost of this postwar basket was 119 kuna or $24. But even this stripped-down basket is expensive for cash-strapped citizens, a point made more obvious when the basket price is compared to television fees, which ran $7 for a monthly subscription.[8] That seven dollars bought not only news and information on several channels, but also entertainment that ran through the day. Dollar for dollar (or kuna for kuna), that looked like quite a bargain, so large numbers of people followed their wallets and shifted their media preferences toward television.

Those economic cross pressures resulted in the near monopoly of television news. Polls were in wide agreement that nearly nine in ten (87%) Croatian citizens got news primarily from television, and less than one in ten (8%) was informed by newspapers. Such statistics explain how the press had escaped significant government control, while broadcast had fallen under complete government domination. The rationale was clear: What papers print was of little practical consequence, while stories reported on television became embedded in the public consciousness simply because of the popularity of the medium.[9] This was a significant factor in understanding the relationship between the media and government, and it will play in our subsequent analyses.

It was in such an environment that the media started its postwar period, hoping that the difficulties could be overtaken and freedom achieved sooner or later. Thus started the struggle for a free press—a long, hard, high-cost battle without certain success.

MEDIA OWNERSHIP

In the old Yugoslavia, only a few publishers used the so-called Marković law (which laid out the legal procedures) to privatize their newspapers. Over the years, the most successful paper, without a doubt, has been *Novi list*, the daily from Rijeka, which has become one of the best-edited, open-minded papers in Croatia. Although a handful of papers ran as private ventures, most of them were publicly owned, a euphemism for state-run, and like just about everything the state ran in old Yugoslavia, they were inefficient and unprofitable.

When the new Croatian government in 1991 proclaimed Croatia a democracy, it provided for a free market economy and the withdrawal of state support from public media. But, at the same time, the government, thinking like the old communists, was not keen to give up its influence on the media companies. The result was the "Law on Transforming Public Property Companies," which Parliament adopted in April 1991.

"Implementation of this Law caused many problems among newspaper publishing companies," said Božo Novak. "Government had no clear vision of the concept of media pluralism and the media role in a democratic society. The government was not able to foresee the subtleties of this transformation. Especially they could not consider the interests of the journalists, not only as coproprietors of the media, but also as representatives of public interests."[10]

Several models were used by the new government to transform the companies, but in general, the idea was to keep control over the most influential newspapers such as *Vjesnik, Večernji list*, and *Slobodna Dalmacija*. In these "controlled" papers, employees had the right to buy shares up to a total value of 20,000 deutsche marks per person, but laws prevented them from ever becoming majority owners of their own newspapers.

The significance of this provision becomes evident in light of how employees during the socialist, self-management system of old Yugoslavia actually owned their companies, while the managers where under a kind of worker control. At least each month, the management was obliged to inform employees about business results. Some newspapers, like *Večernji list*, had no financial support from the government, so its business operations were under the direct control of workers. This included the control of investments in new technologies and equipment and decisions about publishing new editions and other operational features of the paper. Of course, all this was accomplished under the strict control of the Communist Party, which kept the media under party influence in order to serve party objectives.

With this image in mind, workers figured they could ensure their continuity of management when the government offered them the opportunity to buy shares. That turned out to be a disappointing illusion, because the new government never planned to yield control of the media. So the majority shareholders were actually government-directed organs such as the Pension Fund and the Privatization Fund. These new majority owners established a board of managers and a supervising board, which ran every aspect of the media operation, including the appointment of editors and managers. Journalists of *Večernji list* and other papers no longer had the opportunity to elect their editor in chief or to ask managers about business decisions. Managers could fire anyone with impunity; that was just not possible before. Workers' rights were gone.

Similar conditions were imposed on industries throughout the Croatian economy, and while the transformations were hard on industries and workers everywhere, their imposition on the media was particularly dangerous. Journalists felt threatened and frightened by their loss of control. The new management was under the government's thumb, and of course, this meant journalists could not criticize the government or the ruling party in any of their writings. These conditions incubated self-censorship, and they formed journalists into two groups: supporters of the ruling party, the so-called "*državotvorni novinari*" (nationally constructive journalists), and the silent majority.

The elements were now in place for the government to execute an extraordinary plan to transfer the country's industries into the hands of a few chosen families. The scenario, also underway in other former Communist countries, went something like this. After transformation, the ruling party controlled all the important companies through the supervising boards. Soon after gaining control, the companies were pushed into deep financial trouble, usually through deliberate mismanagement and the adoption of foolish policies that were certain to fail. They failed so spectacularly—or succeeded from the government's point of view—that they brought down even the strongest companies. When the company's value dropped to the bottom and default was imminent, the workers were fired and the Privatization Fund would sell off the company to a waiting member of the ruling party, HDZ. All in all, a beautiful scam!

President Tuđman once declared publicly that 100 families should own all of Croatia's property, and his plans for the transformation and privatization of the economy were his means to that end. This outrageous scheme did not collapse after Tuđman's death. One of the greatest tests of the new president and the new Parliament will be how they deal with these matters: Will they continue to turn over the economy to the political elite, or will they preserve it for the Croatian people? Will they take back what was stolen?

Most transformations in the media business followed the pattern of other industries, but for some media, the government employed a second transformation model that was even more egregious. The case of Slobodna Dalmacija provides a good example.

When the Privatization Fund announced the transformation of this celebrated publishing company from Split, few papers in the country were as financially strong or as successful at turning out a top quality news product every day. By most standards, it was the best paper in the country. Miroslav Kutle, a private businessman and prominent HDZ member, bought a controlling share of the company under strange circumstances never fully disclosed for public examination. The turnover became a scandal. Workers went on strike, and competitors appealed to the courts to halt transformation. None of it was successful. Kutle, now the majority shareowner, turned *Slobodna Dalmacija* into a mouthpiece for the HDZ, and, at the same time, he used his new power to construct a huge media empire. By 1998, he owned several media companies, newspapers, radio and television stations, printing plants, advertising agencies, and—the biggest prize—Tisak, the monopoly distribution company. Kutle was the paradigmatic example of how HDZ seized control of the media.

But he did not stop with the media. Kutle applied this model to other industries, and before long, he became one of the most influential HDZ tycoons, controlling a vast array of industries, including several local banks. Remarkably, all of these takeovers—the factories, the banks, the industries—were accomplished without a single penny from Kutle's pocket. His plan never provided for fresh money to stimulate the economy. Instead, he sucked out anything of value in a company, then discarded the remains when nothing was left. The sad finale is that Slobodna Dalmacija suffered this fate and now, as at the beginning of the 1990s, is owned by the government, which must subsidize the company with taxpayers' money.

Ten years of such persistent and corrosive policies have destroyed the Croatian economy. Once a bright light among the former socialist economies, it has become a poor and struggling state.

The condition of the media in Croatia after the war is easy to summarize: All influential media were state-controlled or privatized under the direction of a party boss. Croatian radio and television were state-owned and regulated by law and the whim of the party. All daily newspapers, except *Novi list*, were controlled by the HDZ. All major printing plants were the property of the HDZ or controlled by it. The all-important advertising companies were under party control. And, most important, the only distribution company was firmly in the hands of the HDZ.

Under the new Law on Information, entrepreneurs were allowed to start up private newspapers, but, in the beginning, most of these papers were too fragile to jeopardize the large, existing media. Consequently, they slipped beneath the radar of government observers who kept watch on media influence on the Croatian people.

The international community realized after a few years that the media were being absorbed by the government, and that provoked protests. Mindful of this concern from the outside, the ruling party, in 1996, changed its strategy to a more elegant means of media control that would be more palatable to citizens and the international community.

One new approach was to turn over public property to private hands. The owners would not be known HDZ members, such as Kutle. In fact, they should be strangers. And so the chase was on for new owners. In one case, Kutle negotiated selling a majority of his company to the famous Ivana Trump. He even offered her the chance to write a regular column! That turned out to be a dry well for Kutle, because Trump flatly turned down his offer.

The next approach to solving the media ownership problem was more successful, as shown in the case of *Večernji list*, Croatia's most popular paper. It had the largest circulation, a well-received international edition printed in Frankfurt, a new printing plant, a well-developed advertising company, and almost 300 professional journalists. The Pension Fund was the majority shareowner, and when it ran into financial problems, management decided to sell the paper for 20 million deutsche marks, a grossly undervalued asking price. Despite the bargain, few local businesses made acceptable offers, so the Pension Fund decided to sell the company to the Caritas Limited Fund, an outfit located in the Virgin Islands. Without any public discussion or information about this offshore company, Croatia's best-selling daily newspaper changed hands. When pushed for answers, officials answered in their typical laconic style, saying that in modern capitalism the origin of business owners is not important and, furthermore, that the Croatian public is not entitled to information about the new owners. Even today, secrecy surrounds this company, but officials just wave their hands and say "Zna se."[11] Yes, we know.

The Law on Information allowed the establishment of new private newspapers, printing plants, sales and advertising companies, and many entrepreneurs jumped into the business. Most were small "Mom and Pop" operations, but it didn't take long for several large outfits to step up to the plate. Ninoslav Pavić and Uroš Šoškić became respectable media moguls and their companies began producing profit-making papers. Šoškić, once the celebrated editor of the Vjesnik publishing company, started up magazines like *My Secret, My Destiny,* and similar publications and sold over 200,000 copies. His magazines have no political dimension, which explains why the international community doesn't even mention this remarkable production.

Ninoslav Pavić became the first real Croatian media mogul in his own right. This former *Vjesnik* journalist joined Denis Kuljiš and Zdravko Jurak in 1990 to found the weekly magazine *Globus*, which quickly became one of the most influential papers in the country. Like the tabloid press but not as extreme as *Slobodni tjednik, Globus* customarily runs sensational stories dealing with government and politics.

Pavić bought all the shares of *Globus* held by his partners, Jurak and Kuljiš, and, thus, became sole owner of the paper. In addition, he soon started up or bought several magazines, advertising companies, radio stations, a television production company, and a daily newspaper, *Jutarnji list*. In 1999, Pavić sold 50 percent (minus one share) of his company to Europapress Holding Company (EPH) and West Allgemaine Zeitung (WAZ), the huge German media company known for its business activities in the former Soviet states. WAZ invested 50 million deutsche marks and became the first serious foreign investor in the Croatian media. Because of its substantial holdings in *Jutarnji list* and its aggressive approach to the media business, this company poses a real challenge to other Croatian media. WAZ is known to invest a lot of money in its local holdings and to drop prices at the newsstands in order to drive out the competition. Although Pavić retains control with one share, the German partners decide the investment strategy. Already there are signs that EPH has designs on Slobodna Dalmacija and Tisak.

One thing became clear to journalists during the tumultuous period of the 1990s, and that is that their jobs were never secure, whether the media were held by private owners or the government. While journalists in no country have iron-clad guarantees of continued employment, journalists in Croatia working for government-owned media were particularly vulnerable. Tuđjamn used to take a great interest in the press, often imposing his own demands on management, deciding who would be editor in chief and general manager. He fired managers when he grew dissatisfied with editorial policy or unhappy with the tone of a story. From 1990 until the end of the decade, Tuđman influenced the appointment of five HRTV general managers, each of whom ran HRTV as the "great leader himself had wished."[12]

Private publishers produced many of the papers that filled Croatian newsstands, and most of them, to avoid confrontations with government, steered clear of politics altogether. These often well-edited, colorful, and professionally produced publications cover all topics. As in any information marketplace, some of these magazines have failed, but a large number of them have attracted large and steady audiences. *Bebe* magazine, for instance, started in 1992, offers young parents advice on child rearing and other subjects specific to newborns. Two young journalists, Vesna and Robert Šipek, expecting their first child, came up with the idea that has proven to be a raging success.

Table 10.2
Overview of Media Owners and Publishers in Croatia, May 1999

Owner	Daily	Weekly	Monthly	TV
Europapress holding (Ninoslav Pavić and WAZ)	*Jutarnji list*	*Globus* *Gloria* *Mila* *Arena* *Auto klub*	*Astro magazin* *Cosmopolitan* *Doktor u kući* *Playboy* *OK* *Cicero*	EPP—Europa Press Produkcija
Revije (Uroš Šoškić)		*Tena*	*Moja sudbina* *Moja tajna* *Moja romanca* *Istinite sudbine* *Auto blic* *Teen* *Teen sport* *Sve o tebi* *Stvarni život* *Posteri i prijatelji* *Horoskop* *Tajne kuhinje*	
Večernji list (Caritas Fund International)	*Večernji list*	*Obzor*		
Slobodna Dalmacija (state owned)	*Slobodna Dalmacija*	*Nedjeljna Dalmacija*	*Elita*	
Glas Istre (shareholders company)	*Glas Istre*			
Novi list (shareholders company)	*Novi list*	*Križaljke*		
Glas Slavonije (shareholders company)	*Glas Slavonije*			

Table 10.2 (*continued*)

Owner	Daily	Weekly	Monthly	TV
HIT PRESS & KIOSK (Vlasnici Milivoj Pašiček i Ivan Hađina			*Moja ispovijed* *Istinite priče* *Erotica* *Sex klub* *Romeo i Julijaljubavni romani* *Vikend ljubani roman* *Erotski roman* *Western roman*	
ANKH Centar (**Centar za poboljšanje kvalitete života-Zagreb**) Vlasnik: Osama Shreim			*Vaš astrolog* *Stella* *Dossier UFO*	
Owner: Nela Barbarić-Puharić			*Svijet* *Dom i vrt*	
BORGIS **private**			*Pet-šest vrsta porno magazina*	
EDAC Morana Paliković Gruden			*Zaposlena*	
Ministry of defense		*Velebit*	*Hrvatski vojnik*	
Ministry of interior			*Halo 92*	
Matica Hrvatske (**NGO**)			*Vijenac* (*dvotjednik*)	
Croatian Writers Society		*Hrvatsko slovo*		
Druga strana **private**			*Zarez* (*dvotjednik*)	

Table 10.2 (*continued*)

Owner	Daily	Weekly	Monthly	TV
Meridijan Owner: Branko Gretić			*VITA*	
FEBRA Owner: Braslav Karlić			*MORE*	
BUG private			*Bug* *Mreža*	
Janus Press private			*HACKER* *PSX*	
3-media private			*Computerworld*	
private			*VIDI*	
Monitor **informatika** private			*Internet* *MONITOR*	
A1 Video private			*PC CHIP*	
MediaPress private			*NACIONAL*	
Feral Tribune private			*Feral Tribune*	
Košarka private			*Košarka*	
K2 (Owner: Tomislav Ivir)			*Automania* *Vjenčanje*	
VEDIS private			*Hollywood*	
M 14 private			*Jet Set*	

Data collected and edited by Gordana Vilović.

Table 10.3
Croatian Mass Media: Ownership Overview, May 1999

Owner	Dailies and News Agencies	Weeklies and Magazines	TV	Radio	Printing Plants	Transmitters	Advertising Agencies	Distribution & Selling
State *including majority of shares owned by funds and banks	Vjesnik, Glas Slavonije, Slobodna Dalmacija, HINA	Halo 92, Velebit, Hrvatsko slovo, Hrvatski vojnik, Nedjeljna Dalmacija, periodicals, comics and cartoons by Slobodna Dalmacija	HTV: First, Second and Third channel	Croatian Radio: First, Second and Third Channels and Regional centers and stations	Hrvatska tiskara, Tiskara Slobodna Dalmacija	RO Odašiljači i veze HRTVa (Croatian RTV transmitters network)	Slobodna Dalmacija	Tisak, Glas Slavonije, Trgoplasman, Slobodna Dalmacija
Catholic Church	IKA	Glas Koncila, MAK, Kana and others	Video production	Katolički radio (national frequency)		Transmitters for za Katolički radio		in the Churches
Europapress holding (Ninoslav Pavić+ WAZ)	Jutarnji list	Globus, Gloria, Cosmopolitan, Playboy, Arena, OK, Studio, Astro	EPH				Direkcija marketinga i promocije Europress holdinga	
Večernji list Caritas Fund International	Večernji list	Obzor			VEKON		EP 64	
Small shareholders and private owners	Novi list, Glas Istre, Zadarski list, Karlovački list	Nacional, Vita Zarez, Moja tajna, Svijet	OTV, TV Moslavina Zadar, Nova, RITV	Radio 101 KL, Obiteljski, Otvoreni, Narodni, Maestral and others	Edit, Radin and others small printing plants		Jadran-McKenna-Erikson	Novi list, Glas Istre, Distri Press

Computers have captured markets in Croatia, as they have around the world, and this fascination with information technologies has propagated a growing audience. The first copyright edition in Croatia of a serious computer magazine was *Byte* in 1992.[13]

Computer magazines, along with most publications about technology, hobbies, and special interests, were generally free of government interference as long as editors walked a wide circle around political matters, especially the politics of the leading party. These popular, apolitical publications have, over the years, provided many journalists with a safe hiding place, far away from politics and the pains that involvement can inflict.

We close this chapter with a catalog of media ownership as of May 1999 (see Tables 10.2 and 10.3). Even this partial list demonstrates the active media market serving a population of little more than four million people.

NOTES

1. The war with the Federal Republic of Yugoslavia ended in February 1992, but a great part of the Croatian occupied territory was liberated in August 1995. Our term "The Post-War Years" includes the period after February 1992.

2. Vesna Pusić, "Croatia at the Crossroads," *Journal of Democracy* 9, no. 1 (January 1998): 12.

3. Juan Linz, Alfred Stepan, and Richard Gunter, "Democratic Transition and Consolidation in Southern Europe, with Reflections on Latin America and Eastern Europe" in Richard Gunther, P. Nikiforos Diamandouros and Hans-Jurgen Puhle, eds., *The Politics of Democratic Consolidation: Southern Europe in Comparative Perspective* (Baltimore: Johns Hopkins University Press, 1995), 82, quoted in Pusić, "Croatia at the Crossroads."

4. Comment offered to Stjepan Malović on November 1996.

5. The text of Franjo Tuđman's speech was provided by HINA, the official Croatian news service. It was translated into English by the authors.

6. Božo Novak, "Croatian Journalism in the Independent and Democratic Republic of Croatia," in *Almanac of Croatian Printing Business, Publishing, Journalism, and Library Science* (Zagreb: Horizon Press and Kratis, 1997), 210.

7. A normal prewar basket consists of one daily newspaper, one weekly newsmagazine, weekly TV guide, women's biweekly magazine, monthly magazine for men (like Playboy), computer, auto or any other hobby magazine, comics for kids, love story or crime short stories or novels, crosswords. The total cost of this basket in 1995 would be 445 kuna or $89. Note that the average monthly salary in 1995 was around 2000 kuna; that's around $400.

8. Unlike in the United States, where over-the-air television is free, in many European countries, including Croatia, viewers are assessed a monthly subscription fee for each television set in their house. Americans confronted the concept of paying for TV only after the introduction of cable and satellite television, but that is paid to private companies. In the European system, the revenue goes to the government; it is, therefore, a tax.

9. In all fairness, the tighter regulations on broadcast v. print are not unique to

Croatia. Even in the United States, laws make a clear distinction between the two, granting print near autonomy, while keeping tighter restraints on broadcasters. Simply put, the First Amendment shields publishers for all but the most extreme content while "public ownership of the airwaves" leverages government regulation over broadcast. Granted, all media controls in the United States are far less restrictive than they are in Croatia, but the differential treatment of the two forms is common in most countries.

10. Novak, "Croatian Journalism in the Independent and Democratic Republic of Croatia," 212.

11. "We know" is the slogan of the HDZ, the Croatian ruling party.

12. The five HRTV managers are Hrvoje Hitrec, Anton Vrdoljak, Ivan Parać, Ivica Mudrinić, and Ivica Vrkić.

13. *Byte* (Croatian edition) publisher was Neven Prašnikar, editor in chief was Stjepan Malović, and president of the Publisher's Board was Ruđer Jenny.

PART V

PUBLIC INPUT AND GLOBALIZATION IN CROATIA'S FUTURE

Professionalism and Ethics of Croatian Journalists

"Croatian media were for the government or against the government. There was nothing in between," said Slavko Goldstein, a noted independent journalist, speaking at a scientific workshop at the Faculty of Political Science at Zagreb University.

Goldstein's observation was short but sharp. The majority of the Croatian media were progovernment for the simple fact that government[1] owned most of them or, in some way, directly influenced or controlled them. No surprise that these media packed in all the favorable government news that fits in print—or broadcast.

On the other side lay a small group of independent media, which were, for the most part, quite opposed to the government. These media attacked government and the leading party at every chance and presented government activities in the worst possible light. Only antigovernment stories found space in these media.

And where were the balanced, impartial, and fair media? It's hard to say. The outlets that came closest to this were *Novi list*, Radio 101 and *Tjednik*, but even these were generally seen as antigovernment. Still, they often gave the floor to HDZ officials and explained governmental policy with reasonable impartiality, so they came as close as any to being evenhanded.

"Croatia never had a government capable of tolerating public criticism and respecting media independence," said Slavko Goldstein.

Croatian governments, even the most rigorous dictatorships, have alternately squeezed the media and let up on the media [called "liberalization"]. Their controls have been almost rhythmic, alternating in ways that were not often very predictable.

But, in good or bad times, in laps of squeezing and loosening, the most important promoter of the public word in Croatia has been the journalistic profession. . . . In relatively good periods, they establish newspapers, affirming new topics and authors, widen the space for public, free and critical information. And in bad periods, *they will never surrender.*[2]

Similar media conditions now exist where democracy did not take a firm foothold in other former Communist countries. Authoritarian regimes, even in nominally democratic systems, were capable of running a country as it was run under the old party system as long as opposition forces in the parliament remain relatively weak. Feeble opposition has allowed the despotic rules of Tuđman, Milošević, Meciar, Kučma, and Lukashenko.

Experiences in the former Yugoslavian states confirm that authoritarian regimes and a free press were natural enemies. Leaders in these systems cannot thrive in an environment of open information; they require a complaint press that promotes their views and supports their policies. Criticisms, complaints, and challenges of official policy become a significant threat because that policy can rarely withstand the test of public scrutiny. The media exist in authoritarian regimes to promote official policy, and renegades who struck off on their own were viewed as enemies. As we have seen in previous chapters, the consequences have been isolation, harassment, economic assaults, and even imprisonment.

The late American journalist Marvin Stone, a well-informed student of the Croatian media, once noted to the authors that "Tuđman runs Croatia with all the fervor of a man summoned by history to rule as an overlord. His doctrinaire decisions were felt by businessmen, bankers, professors, taxpayers and the courts. He was pompous, thin-skinned and imperious, and an enigma to many. . . . The tragedy of Croatia's press was not only the immediate damage that it had suffered. Current ownership schemes, mergers and other invidious strategies threaten to imbed this damage for years to come."[3]

The influence of government on the media was enormous. "Repression of freedom and irresponsible reporting were not the same things," explains Dr. Ivo Žanić, Croatian journalist and media expert. "Inaccurate, incomplete or distorted and idealized reporting is basically bad journalism. Government limitations of the public word, on the other hand, is simply un-democratic, unprofessional journalism is simply bad journalism. But, repressive governments are simply dictatorships."[4]

These circumstances make it easier to understand the state-controlled media. Journalists in Croatia during Tuđman's rule had been in almost the same situation as they were in the days of communism. They were well informed about editorial policy; they knew the taboos, and they knew exactly how far their criticism could go. They knew what lines could not be crossed, so they served as their own worst censors. As a consequence, reports were one-sided, always in favor of the government and the HDZ. Their news agendas were set by official protocol and not the news-value standard used by Western, free media. You can't find a better example than the lead story of the prime-time news, which each evening featured President Tuđman, whether or not his day held anything more exciting than how the cook fried his eggs that morning. Items in the rest of the newscast were also selected according to their political value to the HDZ. It has been common for the first twenty-one minutes of a thirty-minute news program to be devoted to party news. Similar news judgments guided the selection of news for most radio programs and party-controlled daily newspapers.

Most of the well-known journalists who would not buy into this system of news selection would be fired or voluntarily leave media because they couldn't tolerate the low professional standards driving the news. At the same time, surprisingly, journalism became a popular profession among young people. Many had become interested in starting their careers in even these poorly run media. Editors and managers, whose task it was to carry out the promotional and propaganda role of the media, had no problem signing up new, unschooled journalists, then inculcating them with the corrupted editorial policies.

Rookie journalists were not aware that they were being trained as agents of the state, and, even if they were, their novice status denied them any possibility of confronting the powerful editors and managers. So the state-controlled media produced a new generation of young journalists who were incapable of realizing the propaganda role of the Croatian media and could not trace the roots of these media operations directly to the communist period.

Journalists who chose not to be part of this propaganda machine found themselves in a difficult position. It was particularly difficult for the experienced journalists, who had learned their trade during communism. For most, it was a matter of expectations. While under that oppressive system for so many years, most had resigned themselves to the inevitability of the control, the propaganda, the limitations on a free press. During periods of liberalization, they inched the journalistic freedoms forward, but they always knew the risk and anticipated the probability of a rapid return to the old controls. When communism finally ended and the new government declared democracy, most of these journalists expected the riches of a free press, but it didn't take long for them to realize that the new regime was not playing by democratic rules. At that point, many simply gave up the fight. Their betrayed expectations were so defeating, large numbers of the old journalists walked away. Some found jobs in nongovernmental media. Some started their own newspapers, although most of these quickly went bankrupt. Some got jobs in international media and other organizations, and journalists in this group were quickly labeled as spies or traitors.

The international community had been monitoring the suppression of Croatia's media as it observed the country's political developments. These outside observations were especially important during the electoral campaigns at the end of 1999 and the beginning of 2000, where the media played such a crucial role in the thumping defeat of the HDZ.

Conditions for the opposition media were quite different. Their fight was in the economic marketplace, where they had daily battles to sell enough papers and recruit enough advertisers to meet payroll at the end of each month. Journalists writing for the independent media were denied the kind of access to the official news sources enjoyed by their government-media colleagues. They often found it difficult to obtain government-issued credentials for important political events, and it was all but impossible for them to interview the president. They were second-class citizens in the eyes of the government, and that status kept them at arm's length from government sources and information, a limitation that put them at a real disadvantage on the newsstand.

But the independent journalists were better trained, and out of necessity, they cultivated their own discrete information sources. These, it turns out, were often their disgruntled counterparts in government: officials, trampled by the party, who were eager to expose the government's dirty laundry. The opposition, or independent, media, thus, became their allies in the fight against the authoritarian regime. Governmental media, even if they got such information, could never publish it. The disenfranchised media were only too eager.

Journalists writing for opposition papers practiced a journalism similar to their colleagues in the controlled press. They offered one-sided stories and looked for a chance to attack the ruling party by investigating their misdeads, scandals, and failed decisions. You could not find many examples of balanced, impartial, and fair reporting in these papers any more than you could in a controlled press. Even when some media tried to practice evenhanded journalism, as *Tjednik* did, their stories often came across as biased, because they introduced issues that were not a usual part of the government agenda.

There was a simple explanation for the heavy-handed style of the opposition media. First, the official information was already published and broadcast by the government-controlled media, especially HRTV, so there was little news value in repeating a line by this time so well known. Second, the public was not looking for balanced stories. They bought *Nacional, Feral,* or *Globus* to be shocked by the latest government blunder or scandal by the HDZ. The last thing they wanted was a dispassionate, evenhanded analysis, a balance of pros and cons. They wanted to hear the other side of the story, and they wanted that news to be stark and hard-hitting.

The most influential and important independent newspaper was *Novi list* from Rijeka. This daily has a long and impressive history, but during communism it was a small, well-edited regional daily that often influenced events in the Rijeka region and occasionally impacted national-level politics. At the time of Croatia's independence, Rijeka's political life was moderate, balanced, and not at all nationalistic. This coastal city offered a healthy environment that encouraged balanced and impartial journalism. Veljko Vičević, *Novi list*'s young editor in chief, opened the paper to all independent writers and intellectuals who were expelled from newsrooms elsewhere or had nowhere else to publish their articles. He also promoted fair reporting, trying to present all important events in the country without regard to political implications.

As a result, *Novi list* quickly evolved from a small regional newspaper to the leading daily in Croatia. *Novi list*'s editorial policies, based on an objective evaluation of real news value, fostered good writing and reporting by some of the most respected names in Croatian journalism. Vičević's charismatic personality, which smoothed the path for his exceptional editorial policies, proved to be essential in guiding his paper during a time when balanced journalism was missing in Croatia. Vičević died of a heart attack in 1997, brought about in part, some people believe, by his exhausting work to build a credible paper. His death was a great loss for media freedom in Croatia. *Novi list* today continues the same editorial policies, even without the charismatic force that set the paper apart from all others in Croatia.

Special licensing requirements gave government greater leverage over broadcasters, so the electronic media had a tougher time at balanced reporting. On anyone's list of success stories, though, Radio 101 was always at the top. The station, which started during the communist period, was the first to open its microphones to opposition politicians, including Franjo Tuđman. It continued its liberal policies after the communists left and became known as a standard-bearer for fresh, popular journalism that combined news and information with modern music. The station ran interesting and memorable jingles, open interviews, and listener call-ins, all impossible features on official radio stations.

The *101 Parliament Show* was a kind of democracy school where listeners asked questions and Radio 101 aired the answers from high-ranking officials. Ten years ago, no other media had anything similar. Very soon, the *101 Parliament Show* became one of the most popular and influential shows on radio. The *101 Weekly Report* was also one of the station's open-minded, evenhanded news shows. Each Saturday afternoon this show told audiences what really happened during the week, and it used interesting features, such as inventive jingles, to hold the audience and to get the story across.

Radio 101 was at the top of its form when the governmental board responsible for issuing frequency licenses summarily banned the station from the air by pulling its operating license. Like most other government agencies in Croatia, the board expected its decision to be followed quietly and absolutely, but no one could have predicted what actually took place. Over 100,000 Croatian citizens rallied in Zagreb's central square in support of 101. As a direct result of the public protest, the government withdrew its licensing order and granted Radio 101 permission to operate. The station won the battle, but it seems to have lost the war. The incident initiated the decline of Radio 101's long and brilliant role in Croatia's evolution of free radio. Soon after this episode, the station faced significant problems among its journalists, announcers, and management. A group of its most celebrated journalists left for independent careers, and those remaining continued their work with little enthusiasm. Radio 101 remains on the air today and still enforces the same open-minded editorial policy, but the charisma is gone. Nonetheless, the Radio 101 episode marks an extraordinary event in Croatia. For the first time in recent memory, the people took to the streets to protest a government action, and the real news was that the people won.

The Croatian medium best known to international audiences was *Feral Tribune*, the weekly from Split. It was founded as an independent paper in 1993, although its history goes back much further, to when it was a satirical supplement in *Nedjeljina Dalmacija* and *Slobodna Dalmacija*. *Feral Tribune* was truly a unique product, an almost impossible but highly effective combination of satire and opinion. *Feral*'s best known characteristic was its uncompromising fight against any ruling party.

Three journalists created and now run *Feral*: Viktor Ivančić, Boris Dežulović, and Predrag Lucić. This nucleus started back in the 1980s to form *Feral* into a weekly magazine that had a strong presence in Zagreb. The paper hired young, aggressive, and talented journalists to keep a watch on government and to report the stories that all the others were missing.

During the communist period, Ivančić, Dežulović, and Lucić themselves were Communists; in the new Croatian state, they became ardent foes of the HDZ. Their not-so-subtle motto was "Criticism of the Government," and since this motto does not specify a particular government, it was reasonable to assume that *Feral* would keep close watch on the new government and launch criticism when they judge its actions to be contrary to the best interests of the country.

Over the past decade, the international community heaped praise and money on the paper. The Soros Open Society has been particularly generous. Moreover, Croatian readers supported the paper in spirit and patronage, and this popularity infuriated the ruling party and President Tuđman, who was one of the paper's most common targets. It was hard to evaluate *Feral Tribune* as a newspaper, because its satirical section was unique among Croatian papers, and that was what achieved the fame. *Feral*'s so-called serious parts, the newsmagazine and opinion section, were nothing extraordinary and rarely drew much attention. When *Feral Tribune* is remembered in history, it will be acclaimed for its excellent headlines, its satirical column titled "Diary of Robi K," its effective photomontage work, and its "Greatest Shits," the selection of stupidities published in other Croatian media.

Croatian papers have never been known for their grabbing headlines, especially compared to Belgrade's daily papers. *Feral* started the trend toward short, inventive, and aggressive headlines, which it ran in both the satirical and straight news sections of the weekly. This was an important point because at about the same time, journalists in *Globus* and *Nacional* initiated the style of very long and usually scandalous and sensational headlines, which often had little to do with the text. Unfortunately, this drawn-out style, rather than *Feral*'s punchy style, was adopted by most of the Croatian press.

Viktor Ivančić was the editor in chief and also writer of "Diary of Robi K," a satirical column that became a paradigm for sharp and inventive criticism of the government. As we noted, *Feral* was also known for its photomontage, the fusion of several photos into one. Perhaps the most celebrated example was a montage of Tuđman and Milošević lying naked and embraced in bed over the headline. "Is that what we have been fighting for?" Such an image, even in Western media, would have created quite a stir. In Croatia it became an icon for both friends and foes of the HDZ. Tuđman was one of *Feral*'s most popular subjects of these photomontages. *Feral* sometimes crossed the limits of normal decency, even by liberal standards, when it criticized the government with extremely strong metaphors. Its excesses were attacked and prosecuted by state attorneys and sometimes criticized by colleagues.

The "Greatest Shits" were selected stupidities from all the other media in Croatia, print and broadcast, and in the last few years the paper included media from Yugoslavia and Bosnia and Herzegovina. Each year it awarded the person who offered the biggest stupidity. Its mocking style provided a means of flagging foolish government and media policies without itself being accused of gross excesses. After all, *Feral* was simply reprinting the words of its victims.

Feral journalists came under enormous pressure in 1993, when they first published their weekly magazine. Now, after a long period as the leading opposition newspaper, they are losing some of their steam and, along with it, public appeal and international attention. Just before Tuđman's death, many papers joined the attack on government policies, and *Feral* no longer was unique with this bold, aggressive approach. How the paper will position itself with the new government is uncertain at the time of this writing.

In the late 1990s, *Nacional*, a private weekly magazine from Zagreb, took over the leadership role in criticism of the government. Its mixture of experienced journalists (six former editors in chief started *Nacional*) and young, aggressive investigative rookies make it the best informed weekly about political life in Croatia. But the paper has paid a high price by suffering government taping, phone taps, secret police stakeouts, and charges leveled by the party and government officials.[5]

The two extremes—unyieldingly for and adamantly against the government—of the Croatian media changed in 1998 with the influence of new media or through fresh ideas presented in the existing media. For instance, the first five-minute news programs were offered by Mreža, a television production company. Up to this time, most news shows lasted a full thirty minutes or longer. The short programs were developed by a small group of professional journalists who were equipped with only two cameras and who produced the shows in a modest studio. Despite the austerity of their operation, their product became the most interesting news show on television and a model for other small, independent television companies. Croatian TV—the big and powerful kid on the block—didn't like the competition, and eventually it put an end to the Mreža's news show. Despite its demise, the program will be noted for its leadership in a new and effective form of broadcast journalism that since has influenced other stations.

Radio 101 also influenced other media. About a dozen regional radio stations retransmitted 101's most interesting shows, thus spreading the Zagreb station's influence beyond the capital city. In addition, these smaller stations emulated the 101 news shows, practiced an open-minded editorial policy, and opened the air to all voices. Today, listeners all around the country can find good independent news shows on local radio stations. Although their influence is small, their success is encouraging.

The most important news product has been *Jutarnji list*, the relatively new daily paper published by Nino Pavić's Europapress Holding Company. Pavić, an experienced journalist, knew the power of the independent press, and it was his long-time dream to start up his own daily paper. *Jutarnji list* is a modern newspaper with all the features expected of a successful daily today. It is an aggressive investigative tabloid filled with human interest stories and independent of political agendas. It offers tight, well-written stories augmented with attractive headlines and lots of photos. *Jutarnji list* publishes crime stories, sensations, and scandals. It prints graphic photos of dead bodies and other carnage. But it provides the missing link in the Croatian media chain.

Jutarnji list, at first, caused panic among the established daily press, where the old ways governed story selection and treatment. Journalists of *Večernji list* were particularly threatened by this new competition. As a result of concerns about the new, flashier, bolder journalism, a media war broke out for the readers' attention. The outcome has been a line-up of papers (even state-controlled papers) that today look and read better than ever before.

These small but crucial changes in the media were reflected in the training of young journalists. Michael Foley, an Irish journalist and media professor, participated twice in a workshop of the Croatian Journalists' Association—before and after *Jutarnji list* appeared on the market. One of Foley's training methods was to write on the whiteboard a dozen news headlines, such as "Tuđman Visited the Milk Factory," "Two Murdered on the Central Square in Zagreb," "Government Discussed New Law on Health," "Hospitals were without Blood," and "New Gasoline Prices." The students were to assume the following: You were the front-page editor of a Zagreb daily newspaper. Select the most important headline. First-time students nearly always selected the official, political headline, usually about Tuđman or some other government official, and overlooked the murder on the central square. Foley was surprised and said, "Wait for some competition in the market, then you will scramble to attract buyers." That happened sooner than anyone expected. In Foley's session the following year—after *Jutarnji list* hit the streets—the students had a different take on the selection of headlines. Without exception, each chose headlines that reported the murder, new prices, or a similar human interest story that was relevant to people's lives.

Sometimes the poor editorial judgments were based on a lack of good sense; sometimes they were driven by poor ethics. For all the problems raised by unethical calls, they sometimes yielded a humorous outcome. Take traffic reports, for instance. Several times each day, the Croatian Automobile Club

(HAK) issues reports on traffic, flagging traffic jams and issuing estimates of delays at border crossings and ferry landings. Even these simple, verifiable accounts were often distorted to create the public image that Croatia's roadways were better run and more efficient than was actually the case. Two-hour waits were reported to be ten-minute ones, border crossings with fifty-minute backups were said to be clear and open. Although the expectation of government officials was that "optimistic" reports will yield better public perceptions of government efficiency, in fact, these easy-to-verify distortions create disbelief throughout the country, not only for traffic reports, but for everything reported in the press. Trust and the lack of trust spread broadly across all reports, whether the topic was traffic jams or government policies. In the end, government and a compliant press erode their own credibility, and for what? To try to fool people into believing that they can cross a bridge more quickly than they know to be the case.

This cheerleading role for media creates problems for professional and responsible journalists who revile such practices and who lose self-respect because of their own forced participation. It's not easy for an honest reporter to twist a story, to alter the truth, to withhold the facts in order to protect governmental officials who disdain media freedom and public scrutiny. Practicing make-no-waves journalism was even more difficult if colleagues in the neighboring newsroom were putting out more honest accounts of the same events.

How should journalists solve ethical problems? How can they keep professional independence and fair and balanced reporting and, at the same time, keep their jobs? That's difficult in many places, and it was almost impossible for broadcasters such as those working for HRTV, where the ruling party's iron grip held a censor's pen that struck any line not in direct support of official policy.

There were many cases where journalists reported fair, impartial, and balanced news, but editors, prodded by government bosses, altered their work. Editors became the party's surrogates, maintaining the official line at the operational end of reporting. Journalists who didn't play such games had to quit and find a job at another news organization. This was tough, because there weren't many media that could accommodate reporters unwilling to play the game. If they could not keep silent, they would be forced into some inconsequential section of the paper, or be forced to quit journalism entirely.

This was difficult for seasoned journalists who have been on the job for a lifetime. Many of them faced personal crises, which often led to alcoholism. Newsrooms of government-controlled media were crowded with such old-timers, who were biding their time for retirement, living all the while with the stress and fear.

Young journalists faced different dilemmas. Most came to the newsroom with idealism about the power of their profession. Their first experiences with the restrictive system were often painful. Some were ready to pay any price. They were welcomed by co-opted editors who spotlighted them on the front page or on the evening newscast. The public liked new faces, because they believed they might offer a fresh perspective on the news. But the public was almost always disappointed.

Some young journalists could not play along, and they quit the profession entirely. The independent media simply could not hire all the journalists booted from controlled outlets. Then, too, media opposing the government often employed the same coercive methods to swing audiences to their point of view. Their perspectives were different, but their tactics were the same. Like so much else in Croatia, opportunities for the media and the craft of journalism depended on the will of the people, the decisions of the government, and the resolve of professionals in their own ranks.

NOTES

1. Government basically means ruling party, HDZ, because all decisions were made by the president, presidential office, or similar organizations or bodies, which were run by the president himself or HDZ executives.

2. Slavko Goldstein, "Public Word in Croatia," *Erasmus, Review for Culture of Democracy* (Erasmus Guild, Zagreb) (1996): 3.

3. Stone analyzed Croatian media in November 1996.

4. Ivo Zanić, "Press, radio and television," *Erasmus, Review for Culture of Democracy* (Erasmus Guild Zagreb) (1996): 10.

5. *Nacional*'s role in investigating secret service activities is described in chapter 6.

12

The Public View of Democracy and the Press

In the United States, freedom of the press is not a gift from the heaven. It is constant struggle for the right to freely express facts and opinions. Journalists all over the world are fighting for media freedom.

Jayme Sirotsky, President of the World Association of Newspapers

"The founding fathers of the World Association of Newspapers [WAN], or FIEJ as it was once called, set defense and promotion of press freedom as the principal objective of our organization," said WAN president Jayme Sirotsky, speaking of the organization's beginnings in 1948. "This mission remains at the heart of our activities, even though our programs now embrace many other fields, most notably professional support to newspaper companies trying to improve their operating practices and decide their publishing strategies."

Today, as in 1948, freedom of the press is a scarce commodity in several regions of the world, including the Croatia of the nineties.[1] As we mentioned earlier, the laws are liberal enough. Article 38 of the Croatian constitution gives complete media freedom, and the Law on Information (adopted on October 2, 1996[2]) was passed under the watchful eye of the international community. The modification and amendments of the Penal Code in spring of 1966, however, gave the government the authority to pressure the media and the journalists.

Legal conditions in the nineties created a hostile environment in which to develop and sustain independent media. Further, they worked against fair and accurate reporting and a balanced presentation of news. Investigations of government activities were often quickly declared as acts against the young Croatian state and listed as enemy activities equal to treason or subversion of Croatian democracy. When these charges failed to instill fear among journalists and failed their purpose, the ruling party used other legal prods, such as lawsuits against the press, confiscation of income, limitations on advertiser patronage, restricted licenses, and monopoly advantage of governmental companies.

Each step in overcoming these restrictions on media freedom was burdened by the formidable competition with state-controlled media that enjoyed a range of economic and political advantages, including easy access to official information sources. The race against state-backed media was tough in the tight Croatian market, which was barely strong enough to support the independent press. The low incomes of average citizens allowed only 10 percent of the people to purchase a daily paper, and very few, indeed, could buy more than one paper. Most people had been driven to television for their diet of news, and, of course, the government had an airtight lock on that.

How did the independents fight against the strong state? How could they practice free speech if they could not survive economically? How could they investigate the ruling party and the government if the ruling party and the government controlled the legal system and used it like a bludgeon against the independents?

The most visible means used by the government to intimidate the independent media was the free-wheeling application of the legal system. At the end of the nineties, there were over 1,000 law cases pending against Croatian journalists, with a total damage of over 100 million deutsche marks requested. The late President Tuđman, members of his family, HDZ politicians, party-blessed businessmen, and other political insiders sued journalists on the frailest of charges. At one point, in an almost comedic episode, the entire government pressed charges against journalist Davor Butković. The prime minister, deputies of the prime minister, and twenty-two eminent ministers arrived at the courthouse several times to testify against one journalist. Why? *Globus* published a report by an American company, which emphasized the risk of investing in Croatia due to serious levels of corruption within the government. The government pile-on said it better than any story in *Globus* ever could.

Višnja Bojanić, Croatian Helsinki Committee analyst, explains the legal maneuvers to control Croatia's press:

In cases of insults, the official concerned no longer needed to request prosecution through the Public Attorney, but could simply give written consent for legal actions to be undertaken by the Public Prosecutor. This reform has clearly shown that the idea was to facilitate the prosecution of journalists to the Public Prosecutor. Immediately after this reform the first lawsuits have been filed against the *Feral Tribune* journalists Viktor Ivančić and Marinko Čulić. Soon after, Nevenka Tuđman, the daughter of President Tuđman, sued the three independent weeklies *Feral Tribune, Globus* and *Nacional* at the same time. The ruling party members and high governmental officials have filed a series of suits. The Ministry of Defense had sued Davor Butković, the then editor-in-chief of *Globus* for publishing an article stating that Ivica Rajić indicted for war crimes and sought by the ICTY [International Criminal Tribunal for the Former Yugoslavia] resided in the territory of the Republic of Croatia. A photograph published with the article showed Rajić in the town in the south of Croatia.[3]

Vesna Alaburić, a well-known attorney and media expert, became well known for promoting media freedoms and defending journalists in court. She received an American Bar Association award for her important contribution to the promotion of human rights and the rule of law. Vesna Alaburić comments on her unusual law practice:

In Ex-Yugoslavia, compensation claims against publishers were practically non-existing. In the Former Yugoslavia the media were also controlled but in a different way. Publishing an article, which might harm a politician or other public person, was generally prevented from the start. Therefore, lawsuits against journalists were extremely rare.

In Croatia, the legal proceedings against publishers and journalists have become almost the only way in which the Public Prosecutor reacts to published information. This could be—only partly—due to the commonly accepted opinion that not filing a suit means admitting the verity of the information published. Still, the huge number of lawsuits, enormously high compensation claims and simultaneous criminal proceedings against journalists undoubtedly confirm the ruling party intent to 'discipline' the media by means of legal proceedings. The purpose of these proceedings is to cause bankruptcy to publishers and strengthen self-censorship of journalists. Today, the biggest fight for freedom of the media in Croatia is being fought in courts.[4]

Publishers were in a bind. In 1998, the weekly paper *Globus* was facing a total of $5.9 million in claims by over 100 lawsuits. *Feral Tribune* faced $2.5 million in claims, *Nacional* was charged with $2.8 million, and the daily *Novi list* faced 53 compensation claims totaling $1.5 million.

Of course, publishers, living hand-to-mouth, could never have paid these claims. Luckily, court procedures are painfully slow and take years to resolve, often at the Croatian Supreme Court level. Only after this sentence could a publisher appeal to the international court for human rights. The Croatian legal system did not push quickly for decisions, because resolution was not a primary aim. The main reason for the lawsuits in the first place was to keep publishers under pressure, to keep them burdened with the endless hectoring of the legal system. Some publishers resorted to tricks when obliged to pay compensation. *Nacional*, for instance, was obliged to pay Patter Ante Baković[5] compensation, which would have bankrupted the publishing company. Overnight, the publishers shifted ownership to another publishing company and did not pay. It was a dirty trick, yes, but Croatian law allowed it, not with *Nacional* in mind, but to accommodate financial manipulations of the local tycoons.

Lawsuits harassed, but they also were a financial burden to publishers. To ease the pain, the United States Information Service (USIS) office in Zagreb established a $100,000 foundation to help targeted publishers. Each publisher could ask for legal protection, and the lawyers were paid from the fund.

Like so many government excesses in Croatia, some lawsuits had a comical side. Some distinguished officials of the ruling party asked for enormous sums to compensate them for "emotional distress." In the Croatian language, the word for it is *duševna bol*. But the term *duševni bolesnici* means "mental illness." So many people seized the chance to poke fun at party leaders who they claimed were asking for compensation from newspapers because they were mentally ill!

The satirical weekly, *Feral Tribune*, was the subject of several spectacular lawsuits. The most celebrated was when President Tuđman, in 1996, sued editor in chief Viktor Ivančić, and reporter Marinko Čulić. Ivančić was sued because he was said to be responsible for publishing the sentence "President Tuđman is declared a follower of generalissimus Franco." Čulić was dragged to court by Tuđman because he wrote an article bearing the headline "Bonds in mixer."[6] The first trial in a local Zagreb court ended with a surprise decision by Judge Marin Mrčela, who declared the pair not guilty of personal insult. Not bound by double-jeopardy protections found in the United States, the state prosecutor appealed the not guilty verdict. The entire process restarted in 1997 and is continuing, years later, at the time of this writing.

Oddly enough, legal problems were not limited to the independent media. *Večernji list*, for instance, which is close to the government, has approximately eighty lawsuits pending at the time of this writing. But, in all fairness, the origin of their suits was quite different from those of the independents. In the case of government-allied media, compensation claims were almost always made by private persons, small companies, and other small organizations. Eminent politicians and members of the ruling party didn't sue papers such as *Večernji list* or other state-controlled media. They could if they wished, but it was hardly necessary, when these papers, censored in advance, rarely published anything that depicted officials in a negative light.

One pressure imposed by the lawsuits was the need for journalists to provide scrupulous background research, including triple confirmation of every fact, in case they should need to defend their story later. Accuracy is a journalist's obligation, of course, but the level of confirmation had ratcheted up so high that many stories just couldn't meet the "lawsuit" test and were scrubbed. Furthermore, much of the information needed for political stories could be found only in government records or other government sources, and these had been sealed off from the independents. Stories that could otherwise be confirmed and published often lacked that critical government citation. The government-controlled media, of course, even with open access to officials, were unlikely to touch a story that could generate official discontent. The result? Many stories that would make it to the streets in other countries never saw the light of day in Croatia.

The economics of ownership are another way to control the media. Almost every influential medium in Croatia was owned by the government or by members or friends of the ruling party. It was an efficient means of control.

Members of the managing or supervising boards of all the leading media were loyal HDZ members, and their role was to implement HDZ politics. This system has been in place for many years and began with the former publishing house Vjesnik, comprised of several dozen smaller companies. The consortium was still the biggest media operation in the Balkans.

In the early 1990s, several strong member papers, such as *Večernji list* and *Sportske novosti*, wanted to become independent companies. This had been their long-standing hope, even during the communist period. But the new government stopped their independence by establishing five-person managing boards for each of the companies. Four of the members had government affiliations; the fifth was changeable and represented the company. Of course, the company representative was greatly outnumbered and had little influence on any significant decision. The president of all managing boards was a government man, Ivica Gaži, who was there to implement HDZ policy.

The most efficient means of managing board control was the appointment of a loyal editor in chief. Sometimes the selection went awry because the journalists found ways to circumvent the editor's rule, and the media control failed. But, in these cases, the state appointed a new editor and, eventually, found a loyal editor in chief who strictly obeyed the party policy and laid down the gospel to the staff. Under these conditions, the media did not need strong-arm tactics or censorship. The role of the state-controlled media was to tell the state story on all issues. It's a philosophy that throws back to the communist days.

Governmental control over the media created new media moguls. While the managing board took care of media content, the government found people who could run the media business. One boss, Miroslav Kutle, an unknown businessman and once a middle-ranking official of the Pension Fund, was allowed to buy Slobodna Dalmacija publishing, printing, and selling company in Split. Slobodna Dalmacija was a well-managed and profitable company with vast control over the Dalmatian market. Slobodna Dalmacija was the first major company to be adopted into the privatization plan for the Croatian economy.

Overnight, Kutle and his partners became the biggest media owners in Croatia, but their empire was not limited to media. Company by company, they added banking, trading, and other business opportunities to form a huge empire that reached into nearly every corner of Croatian life.

On July 1, 1998, *Nacional* published a series of articles that listed Kutle's media holdings. It said:

Miroslav Kutle ownership: *Večernji list, Slobodna Dalmacija, Nedjeljna Dalmacija, Penthouse, Imperijal*, Mreža [TV producing company]. Obiteljski radio [Family Radio], Narodni radio (People's Radio), Radio Cibona. Radio Dalmacija, TV Marijana, Tisak and print company.

Ownership of M. Kutle's partners are: *Jutarnji list, Globus, Playboy, Arena*.

The HDZ right-wing ownership is HRTV [Croatian radio and television], *Vjesnik*.

Not under the control of M. Kutle: *Novi list, Feral Tribune*, Radio 101 and *Nacional*.

Nacional was the first to write that Kutle owned *Večernji list*. Officially, the real owner was unknown and nobody, including the prime minister, wanted to announce the name of the owner of the country's largest daily paper.

Very soon, Kutle tampered with media freedoms. First, he played musical editors in chief, changing editors who did not please him or who did not toe the party line. *Slobodna Dalmacija*, for instance, experienced several editors in chief in a short period of time, and like the editors, beat reporters who stepped out of line were quick to be fired. No one could be sure how long his job would last. News quickly narrowed to propaganda, and some new media, like Obiteljski and Narodni Radio, shifted formats from news to entertainment, from discussions of politics to play-lists of pop music.

Kutle's empire collapsed in 1999, when he was caught in a scandal involving the Dubrovačka Bank. In fact, many officials were involved in that affair, but for reasons not entirely clear, Kutle was the chosen scapegoat. He was dethroned as business king and thrown out of the HDZ in a public display to save face for the party. Many observers believe that Kutle remains a key figure behind the scenes. At the time of this writing, Kutle is in jail awaiting trail.

The state still owns the Croatian Radio and Television Company, the most important source of information for nearly 90 percent of the Croatian people. Media analyst Marvin Stone described the HRTV situation: "Rather than open the air he had pledged in 1990, Tuđman started to rein in its all independent tendencies. Croatian television and radio are run by a Council of 35 people. Directors of the state enterprise are chosen by parliament. In virtually all cases, the Council is formed of members of Tuđman's party. To start with, this environment lends itself to manipulation by the HDZ."

What kind of manipulation? In mid-November 1996, while Tuđman was being treated for cancer at Walter Reed Hospital in what was said to be "very serious condition," HRTV was initially under orders to report that Tuđman had a digestive problem and would be back in Zagreb soon to play tennis with his pals.

Officially, HRTV was public television, and it acted under special laws adopted by the Parliament. Parliament decided who would be general manager, and the general manager proposed to the HRTV council the candidates for editors in chief of radio and television. Citizens who owned a television or radio receiver were (and still are) obliged to pay monthly subscription fees of 45 kuna (about $7). The state fully controlled three national television channels and three national radio channels. Because of frequency licensing, competition was almost impossible. Journalists worked under heavy control, and they could not be independent. If journalists, editors, or administrators tried to practice balanced journalism, they were very soon replaced or fired.

The payoff was a broadcast operation totally committed to support of the ruling party. In 1999, popular television journalist Goran Milić said on *The Freedom Forum Newshour* in Zagreb, that "no Croatian Television journalist ever criticized President Tuđman in any HRTV show." Imagine any truly democratic nation making such a claim.

Frequency licenses efficiently controlled the electronic media. The law entitled the Board of Telecommunication to issue frequency licenses according to criteria that have never been publicly disclosed. The board regularly announced free frequencies and invited all interested companies to send their bids. The bids were opened in public sessions of the board, and members decided the allocations through a vote.

The problems for anyone outside the circle of party-favored bidders started with members of the board, most of whom were either close to the ruling party or were members of it. Even before the meeting, they already knew the candidates with the best references, which means the most party-supportive editorial policies, so the outcomes are hardly a surprise. The process was a ruse, but it served the party well in directing licenses to private, "independent" local radio or TV stations that supported official policy. If license recipients were to step out of line, the board had the power to selectively raise the frequency license fee to punishing levels.

The final control of the media was powerful Tisak, the monopolistic distribution and sales company. Simply put, Tisak sold your papers for you or they didn't get sold at all, so small, independent papers could fold if Tisak blocked distribution or withheld income. Tisak was an enormously wealthy company, with over a thousand distribution points all over Croatia. In addition to newspapers, it sold cigarettes, candies, postcards, and a variety of other common consumer goods. Whoever controlled Tisak was the king of the newspaper market in Croatia.

Controls on the media severely restricted the kinds of information that could hit the streets in Croatia, and even when the independents sometimes got at the truth, their voices were rarely heard. Largely because of newspaper costs, as we noted earlier, almost 90 percent of the people got their information from Croatian television. The best-selling *Večernji list* held a significant portion of the print market. Together, both media set a public agenda that could not be much altered by competing outlets.

It was no surprise when the Freedom House report on media freedom in the world placed Croatia near the bottom of the list, along with Yugoslavia and Bosnia and Herzegovina. Freedom House explained that Croatia practiced a more artful form of censorship than it did in the late 1980s. Leonard Sussman, head of the Freedom House research team, said that Croatia's media environment received a negative evaluation largely because of legal and economic restrictions.

In general, there was a consensus among independent media experts in Croatia and experts from international agencies. In a phrase, they concluded that the media were not free. That view was not shared, however, by some public representatives, university professors, media experts, and journalists close to the government. They concluded that the greatest problem of the Croatian media was the misuse of freedom granted them by the state. Journalists, they say, failed to respect objectivity, accuracy, and the convention to confirm all facts of a story. They also faulted independent media for insulting public officials.

President Tuđman was one of the biggest media critics. In his speech at a meeting of HDZ on December 7, 1996, he attacked the independent Croatian press:

In creating a situation for the change of the actual Government and circumstances in Croatia, for gaining the control over all spheres of life, the media and culture require the greatest influence and the strongest action. This is what they are repeating and all their meetings and all their written documents. Soros's mission to help the media has also engaged other foreign, European and American foundations, and even diplomatic missions. For this purpose financial assistance is provided to *Feral, Arkin, Vijenac, Novi list, Bumerang, Otok-Ivanić, Dan, Metro, Start nove generacije*, Radio Baranja, Radio Labin. And the levels at which they are operating are evident from the fact that they attach particular importance to a *Feral Tribune*, in the media sphere, as one of their most successful projects in the free world in general. In addition to *Feral*, and Radio 101, they also include in the list of their successful projects a *Bumerang* in Osijek and an *Otok* in Ivanićgrad where they succeeded—as they have reported themselves—in initiating the relief of the mayor and of the director of the medical center, and stir up in the defense office.[7]

President Tuđman did not stop at criticizing the foreign influence to the Croatian media, but he also stressed the difficulties faced by the media supporting HDZ policy.

In contrast to this, neither the Croatian Democratic Union nor the democratic Croatian government has been able to ensure normal financial conditions even for the publication of a daily like *Vjesnik*, a solution has barely been found for the *Obzor* weekly, but not yet completely for the literary weekly *Hrvatsko slovo*. While we, who have had to provide for the defense and development of the State, lack funds, those that plot against the State have the money and the time. Certain conclusions are obviously self-evident.[8]

These extracts from Tuđman's speeches suggest how difficult it was to practice free journalism and how firmly the ruling party gripped the media. On several occasions, the Croatian public had expressed its dissatisfaction with media freedoms in the country.

When the state was first formed, there was no public reaction to harassment of the press, no matter how severely the government came down. For instance, in 1991, Anton Vrdoljak, HRTV general manager, made a list each morning of the television and radio journalists who would be allowed into the building that day. Those not on the list were turned away at the door. Vrdoljak was not obliged to explain his admission decisions, even though this gatekeeper power had an extraordinary effect on the outcome of a newscast. It drew no public reaction, because little was known about the practice.

Occasionally, when restrictive government practices did become known, officials explained that their efforts were merely a precaution because of the war or because they were attempting to prevent disruptive measures to preserve the new and fragile democracy. Little by little, when other government misdeeds became visible, sometimes through the independent press, the public grew discontented. Groups held public meetings, roundtables, and seminars to support media freedoms, and they supported several journalists who challenged the system. Occasionally, these journalists even won a small legal battle, and in these cases, supporters were buoyed by their rare prize.

Given the outcome of the turn-of-the-century elections in Croatia, it could be argued that through the 1990s, the actions of the ruling party toward the press and other institutions, have had a cumulative effect on the public. Perhaps people were quietly recording the events of government abuses, economic corruption, press control, and perhaps, little by little, people grew dissatisfied with the ruling party and government, because with each election cycle, the ruling party won by smaller margins, and people turned out to the polls in smaller numbers. Later in the nineties, workers protested more often. Even high school teachers took regularly to the streets to demand better pay and better conditions. In such an environment, on November 21, 1996, the Radio 101 protest took place, in what was Croatia's most celebrated strike. What a magnificent example of public disobedience.

Another significant event was the formation of Forum 21, a movement organized by journalists from Croatian Radio and Television proposing to change HRTV from state-controlled to public TV. Forum 21 was founded by 23 broadcast journalists, but very soon membership grew to 200. Although the organization had popular appeal—among many journalists and the public—it was unable to bring about much change. Nonetheless, it was an orchestrated effort to improve the deteriorating media conditions in the country, and that was a significant demonstration that the broadcast journalists were neither all-compliant nor willing to go along silently with the oppressive conditions imposed on their profession. Had Croatia's political conditions not changed markedly at the end of the decade, Forum 21 may have matured into a more forceful institution. For now, at least, Forum 21, like so many other institutions, has adopted a wait-and-see attitude toward the new government. The next move depends on the evolving media-government relationship.

NOTES

1. "1998: A Year for Press Freedom," *Newsletter of World Association of Newspapers* (Paris) (1998): 1.

2. The Law on Information was adopted by the House of the Representatives of the Croatian Parliament and officially published on October 8, 1996.

3. Vesna Alaburić quoted in Visnja Bojanić, "Freedom of the Media in Croatia," HHO [Croatian Helsinki Committee for Human Rights] report, July 18, 1998, 3.

4. Ibid.

5. Patter Ante Baković, controversial Catholic priest and HDZ supporter, founded a movement for increasing the Croatian population, asking married couples to have more than three children because it is "their patriotic duty."

6. Tuđman's idea of peace among all Croatian warriors was similar to Franco's idea. He wanted all the factions to join in harmony and peace, the Partisans and the Ustasha to be one friendly group. At the end, they would all be behind the president as Tuđman's new warriors.

7. *Vjesnik*'s "difficult" situation was that it survived by selling fewer than 20,000 copies daily, which is much below the profitable minimum. Also, difficulties arose when *Hrvatsko slovo* became identified for its hate speech and anti-Semitism.

8. Tuđman speech, December 7, 1996.

13

Role of the International Community

INTRODUCTION

Free speech is the DNA of democracy. Whatever form free speech may take—writing, e-mailing, gossiping over the back fence, or, more broadly, communicating through a medium such as radio, television, newspaper, or the Internet—it is the double helix of democratic government. Without free speech, democracy remains an unworkable laboratory concept.

A happy offspring of free speech is a free press. The freedom of reporters to dig out the truth as they see it and publish it locally by newspaper or internationally by satellite is the very heartbeat of politics in a participatory democracy. Without those "truth snoopers," whether fair-minded or brassy, balanced or skewed, you can be sure that somebody in government (also somebody in business, somebody in university, somebody in religion) would be doing something they wouldn't be doing if they knew it might appear on the front page or the six o'clock news. A free press is the backbone of a thriving democracy.

This integral role of the press accounts for the global outrage when news is censored. For professionals in the press and for everyone who cherishes civil rights, the fist whiff of censorship is cause for immediate alarm, because it strikes at the roots of human well-being. Modern history shows that censoring the press is the first step on the slippery slope from freedom to tyranny. Jail a reporter for nailing corporate corruption or embarrassing the government, or in the case of Croatia, persecute journalists for causing "mental anguish" to government officials, and you start down the path that leads to the dismantling of democracy.

That, in a word, is why Croatia has been given such a hard time by "outsiders," those regarded by party professionals as hypercritical meddlers—the international press organizations, democratic governments, nongovernmental organizations (NGOs) like Soros's Open Society Institute, Amnesty International, Reporters sans-Frontiers, and business and labor groups.

In this chapter, we look at free speech and press control in Croatia up to 2000 through the eyes of those concerned outsiders. They react to some of the episodes we have treated in previous chapters (e.g., the jailing of reporters, the repression of publishers or broadcasters, the corruption among party leaders) from different perspectives, depending upon their variety of interests. All of them, predictably, deplored the government's meddling in press business. They differed, however, in their recipes for treatment. Should it be carrot and stick? More or fewer millions in aid? Walk away and declare a fiasco or hang in and hope for the best?

What happened in Tuđman's Croatia was a laboratory proving the efficacy of international pressure in the ongoing battle for basic access to the public mind. As we shall see in detail, HDZ craved all the benefits of Western benevolence, including trading partnership in the European Union and transatlantic alliances, without reforming its repressive, corrupt, and censorial policies.

A CONFLICTED NATION AND THE REFORM PRESSURE FROM THE WEST

Croatia, like many countries emerging from the shadow of Communism, held conflicting views of itself. The Tuđman government promoted a desperate nationalism while longing for the embrace of Western governments. It touted the country's ability to go it alone economically and politically but was keen for partners in commerce and for membership in world councils. It was a country torn between the predictable paternalism of its communist past and the chancy promises of Western democracies for an uncertain future.

Geographically, Croatia is a buffer between the affluent West and the impoverished East, but it fits comfortably into neither world. These very uncertainties contribute to an uneasiness among Western observers.

Free press groups worldwide, for example, objected strongly to Croatia's policies toward the press in Tuđman's time. They chided public officials for filing hundreds of lawsuits against publishers who have offended them, and they criticized the laws, unique in Europe, that put journalists in jail for "insulting" government officials or causing officials "mental anguish." They fiercely objected to the arrest of publishers who report on government corruption, and they railed against government-affiliated companies that robbed publishers of their rightful payments.

Similarly, human rights watchers complained about the unfair treatment of some ethnic groups, particularly the Serb minorities. They often quoted from the speeches of Croatia's President Tuđman as evidence of discriminatory policies that violated not only human decency but also official treaties. They also made a compelling case against elections that were not fair in their conduct or their outcomes, trumping any hope of truly democratic rule.

In light of these practices, Western governments were wary of closer relations with Croatia. The European Union did not see Croatia as a candidate ready for membership any time soon. The U.S. government chills to the notion of broader relations, citing Croatia's treatment of the press, its running of elections, its treatment of minorities, its economic, social, and environmental policies. Unlike Slovenia, its neighbor to the north, which is entering the fold of Western democracies, Croatian progress was too slow. With HDZ defeat at the polls in 1999 and 2000, however, Western governments on both sides of the Atlantic are likely to speed up improved relations with Croatia.

Since the breakup of Yugoslavia,[1] countries in the West have offered financial and technical support to move Croatia more quickly through its transition. "Assistance," of course, is a slippery concept. Too little assistance deprives the target country of needed resources; too much, usually in the form of gratuitous advice and heavy instruction, builds resentment against the contributor.

Frustrations with the economy are sometimes presented in the press as a chicken-and-egg story: If Croatia's economy would only improve, outside investors would become more involved. If outside investors would only become more involved, Croatia's economy would improve. The truth is more complicated. An anemic economy, weakened by the sell-off of state properties and corruption, has frightened away corporate investors. Instability and resistance to reform has discouraged more substantial international assistance. The root cause of economic depression has been the arrogance of the Tuđman government itself. You just can't sell off major state assets, drain the country's banks, and then hope the economy will thrive.

Meanwhile, Western governments and nongovernmental organizations were generous with other kinds of assistance. They contributed food and temporary housing, power stations, water treatment facilities, communication systems, and other hardware during and right after the war in the early and mid-nineties. Western governments sent in peacekeeping forces and even temporary civil governments to maintain stability in the most volatile regions while the Croatian authorities assembled the resources necessary to ensure order and rebuild the society.

Early in the nineties, NGOs such as Soros's Open Society Institute and the Red Cross—by some counts more than forty-four foreign organizations in all—brought in staffs and resources to assist the government, professional guilds, schools, and businesses.[2] Many NGOs have stayed the course, but many of these well-meaning groups have left. Some have moved to other global hot spots,[3] while some, by design, are short-lived. Most of the larger, institutional outfits, with deeper pockets and greater staying power, continue their efforts to improve the conditions which can further promote a free society.

This chapter traces the involvement of these outsiders as they enhanced the efforts of those who must today create an open society in Croatia—the Croatians themselves. We have argued from the beginning that the people must be the engine of change. No outsider can help them maintain an independent press, a free society, or an open government if they are not hungry for this new and difficult way of life.

Crucial building blocks of democracy are missing from Croatia's history, and that leaves the people at a disadvantage. Vaclav Havel said that you must feel democracy in your soul. In Croatia, as in many other former Communist countries getting off to a slow start, the people have not had time to imbue their own souls with a sense of democracy. People forget that Tito was as cruelly controlling as Stalin but escaped much of the denunciations by the free world because he fell out with the Soviet tyrant. The lessons from those years do not advance the concept of self-rule. The HDZ party government that followed put every roadblock in the path of independent new organizations.

The United States should remind itself that the lust for freedom is not innate. Just leaf through the history of civil rights in America. After emancipation, it took 100 years before African American leaders were able to galvanize their own people, much less persuade the mass of whites. A slave mentality (intensified by means both subtle and vicious by whites at every level) kept the masses from demanding "freedom now."

Like any habit, principles of an open society must be learned; there is nothing genetic about them. This is where other governments and NGOs must come in. They can provide the new Croatia the expertise, the encouragement, and the resources. They can offer guidance, talent, and moral support. They can make the arguments for better approaches and point the way to concrete applications. But that's about all they can do. The rest is up to the people of Croatia, their government, and their home-grown institutions.

A VIEW FROM THE OUTSIDE: A BRIEF HISTORY OF THE PRESSURES PUT UPON THE TUÐMAN GOVERNMENT BY THE WEST

News out of Croatia during the nineties was not good. In the earliest part of that decade, as the Berlin Wall fell, hopes soared everywhere for a quick redemption from Communism in all the countries of Central and Eastern Europe. For the six Yugoslavian countries, expectations were particularly high after Slovenia had such an easy time at independence. Optimists saw that painless separation as a model for the other five countries, but, of course, that was not to be. Croatia's war was much longer and bloodier, and the government, which took firm hold, proved more resistant to democratic reforms.

As the decade progressed, news from Croatia turned from war to the aftermath of war, and that news, too, was disheartening. Reintegration of the Serbs driven from their homes during the fighting grabbed the headlines. That story shared space in the world media with reports of Croatia's faltering economy, a stubborn president, and a fragile democracy that appeared strong but withered from within. Reports out of Croatia were somber.

Only travel writers offered a favorable look at Croatia as they described the marvels of the Adriatic coast, the blue waters, abundant seafood, and cozy coast-side villas. This complimentary press was good for the seacoast, but it was never enough to pump up the country's economy or to turn around the outsider's broad view of the country. Even at the end of the decade, just as tourism was picking up, the country became tarred by the bombing in Kosovo—in which it played no part—a tragic event that offset several successful years of tourism building. The summer of 1999 was a economic disaster on the Dalmatian coast, as fearful visitors steered a wide circle around it. How sad that the progress in this region was so quickly and so unfairly blunted.

The Press

The brotherhood of reporters in other countries kept close watch on the media in Croatia, and those observations have been relentlessly negative. They typi-cally charge the government with subtle but disturbingly effective control of the media through economic and legal devices. The subtlety lay in the existence of opposition media and alternative communications, which gave the illusion of press freedom while keeping opposition voices to a whisper. Knowledgeable journalists objected to the cozy relationship between the leading party (HDZ) and the owners of the country's major newspapers. Of course, the largest broad-cast stations were run by the state.

A newspaper has value only if it lands in the hands of its readers, so outside press organizations smelled a rat when they observed that Tisak, the newspaper distribution monopoly, held back legitimate payments to publishers and mis-delivered their papers when they offended the government. Press observers be-come irate when state security forces tapped publishers' phones and searched their offices.

The laws inhibiting nonparty media drew heavy fire. While declaring free expression and an open exchange of public information, the Croatian constitu-tion also mandates "corrections" when the press violates the rights of the wrong people, meaning the party members. The devil is in the details, of course: Who determines a violation of rights? Which rights? Who decides the nature of the correction? Recent history has shown that government insiders play that role to the max, their intent antidemocratic, their pretense democratic.

Furthermore, press organizations pointed out that Croatia was the only country in Europe that imprisoned journalists for "insulting" certain government offi-cials—the "Sacred Five," the president of the republic, the speaker of the Par-liament, the prime minister, the presidents of the Supreme and Constitutional Court.

And then there were the statutes that allowed lawsuits when a story "generated concern in the majority of the population" or caused government officials "mental anguish." Earlier we noted that more than 900 journalists and publishers had been under prosecution for such offenses during the 1990s. And if these laws were not pernicious enough, prosecutors had the right to appeal acquittals, thus subjecting defendants to double jeopardy.

A long list of free press organizations, human rights groups, and foreign governments cried foul.

- Reporters sans Frontiers (RSF), a Paris-based group that investigates abuses of the press worldwide reported that, in June 1999, the Croatian weekly *Nacional*, an independent newspaper, published a story that charged the Croatian secret services with pressuring soccer officials. *Nacional* backed up its story with copies of police reports and eyewitnesses. Soon after the story hit the streets, police from the antiterrorist unit searched *Nacional*'s editorial offices, then moved on to search the homes of the editor and reporter who broke the story. What they found, if anything, is uncertain, but the boorish assault on the journalists sent a signal to would-be investigative reporters throughout the country: Report something that offends the state and pay the price. RSF expressed its anger at such treatment and broadcast details of the event as widely as possible.[4]

- In the spring of 1998, the International Federation of Journalists (IFJ) issued a report on a lawsuit against Davor Butković, the former editor in chief of the weekly newspaper *Globus*. Butković was being sued for malicious slander by twenty-three government ministers for having run a story in which he quoted an American report critical of the Croatian government ("The Government is corrupted and highly influenced by organized crime").

  The federation's general secretary released this statement: "It is outrageous for individual government ministers to victimize or penalize a journalist who is reporting on matters of the highest public interest. . . . For the government to attempt to stifle 'bad news' not only offends the profession of journalism, it flies in the face of Croatia's duty to freedom of expression and opinion." The IFJ reported that on the court dockets were more than 1,000 libel suits against journalists, worth a total of nearly $13 million in fines.[5] Faced with this treatment, even the most resilient journalist can hardly resist such coercive tactics.

- Early in 1999, journalist Orlanda Obad from the daily newspaper *Jutarnji list* was indicted for covering a story about large bank deposits by Ankica Tuđman, the Croatian president's wife. The story, using information provided by four bank employees (who were also indicted), said that Mrs. Tuđman deposited nearly 500,000 deutsche marks in various accounts but failed to declare them as required by law. The International Press Institute (IPI) in Vienna protested the indictment, saying the president's finances were a matter of "overriding public interest" and a valid concern of the country's media. The IPI recommended that journalists' organizations and others send appeals to President Tuđman, urging him to ensure that the indictment of Obad be withdrawn immediately and that journalists be allowed to report freely and without harassment in his country.[6]

- The Committee to Protect Journalists (CPJ) runs an annual survey of press conditions throughout Europe. Radio Free Europe reporter Julie Moffett summarizes the CPJ findings in 1997: "In Croatia . . . President Franjo Tuđman was able to consolidate his control over the media after landslide presidential elections in June ensured his party's control over the appointment of executives and editors in the state-dominated media. . . . Tuđman exerted pressure on the independent media by permitting hundreds of libel suits to be filed against journalists."[7]

- The Organization for Security and Cooperation in Europe reported, in 1998, that censorship in Croatia was an "indirect structural repression." The report said that the government hindered the press through its close alliance with Tisak, which, in turn, had a lock on the distribution of newspapers. The government kept up pressure on the independent media by instituting law suites against publishers and imposing suffocating rules against broadcasters. Officials in the media section of OSCE put Croatia in the same category as Belarus, Slovakia, and Turkey, where, the report said, media freedoms are endangered.[8]

- The 1999 annual report of the International Helsinki Federation for Human Rights strongly criticized media conditions in the country: "In this pre-election year the government showed openly that it did not have any intention of renouncing its monopoly on the most important media; quite the contrary, it even introduced new methods to increase control of and pressure on the independent media."

  The report drew up a long and varied laundry list of government intrusions into press freedoms.[9] A sampling:

  "Charges were filed against journalists from *Jutarnji list* for writing a story about an undeclared bank deposit made by Ankica Tuđman, the president's wife. The journalists were threatened with prison sentences lasting from one to three years."

  "The editor-in-chief of the news and political program, Obrad Kosovac, suspended the editor of the prime time news and a member of Forum 21, Tihomir Ladišić after he had refused to censor the news regarding the presentation of a book on human rights published by the Croatian Helsinki Committee."

  Several "journalists and the editor-in-chief of the *Novi brodski list* received threatening letters signed by the Croatian Patriotic Action, which accused the journal of being anti-Croatian and said that those who work there should be killed. *Novi brodski list* has reported criminal activities taking place in the region of Posavina and Brod county."

  "Soon after threats against *Novi brodski list*, two unknown attackers brutally beat Nenad Hlaca, editor-in-chief of *Karlovacki list*. An anonymous call was made before the attack saying it was 'high time to get rid of Serbs from newspapers."

  "Independent weekly *Nacional* faced 73 court proceedings with the compensation required for 'emotional anguish' in total of 10 million deutsche marks. At the same time, there were 28 criminal proceedings against its editors and journalists."

  "Against weekly *Globus*, there were 170 trials with the compensation required for 'emotional anguish' in total of 12 million deutsche marks. The highest state and party officials, including the entire government, sued the weekly. Its editors and journalists faced a total of 24 criminal proceedings."[10]

- Reporters sans Frontiers, in 1999, issued an action alert through the International Freedom of Expression Exchange Clearing House over actions by Tisak, the newspaper distribution monopoly. The group charged that this state-friendly company was using its position to "choke the last dissenting voices in the run up to the legislative elections expected in 1999. After having been harassed, threatened and dragged through the courts, media which are critical of the government risk economic asphyxiation today."[11]

Reporters sans Frontiers, the International Federation of Journalists, the International Press Institute, the International Helsinki Federation for Human Rights, and many other press watch groups issued alerts and reported the difficult conditions that existed for journalists in the Croatia of Tuđman. No doubt, stories critical of the government must have looked threatening to officials who have had no experience with an aggressive press. It must have been especially threatening to those insiders who have cashed in on their government positions and now wish to avoid any public disclosure of favoritism, if not outright fraud.

The reaction of the majority party was predictable at the time. Here is Croatia, a tiny country emerging from Communism, recovering from a blistering war, striving to find its footing in a notoriously unstable region, and now it gets picked on by do-gooders who don't understand the harm that a nosy press could inflict on the present government. What mischief journalists might stir if they were given access to government records and a free rein to attack legislation, the president, economic policies, and other pillars of a fragile society.

Did this argument hold water? Not in our opinion. Could it be used today to steal back state power from the new democratic leaders? Our sense is that, far from destabilizing, a free press contributes enormously to Croatia's movement toward an open society. An open press would have challenged the prevailing philosophy that the people are the *subjects* of the government, not the *owners* of it. Press critics from the outside must continue a relentless campaign against new abuses of the media.

In today's interconnected world, foreign governments must carefully monitor press activities and channel objections back to Croatia, directly, in discussions with the country's leaders, and, indirectly, in their formation of policies and business decisions toward the country. A fine example of international pressure working was the case of *Feral Tribune*. That satirical weekly, printed in Split on the Adriatic coast, is one of a kind, but it shows what can be done to resist government pressure that is focused and unyielding.

Feral has a history of offending the government, particularly President Tuđman, and, consequently, often found itself running afoul of the law that prohibits the press from causing insult or mental anguish.[12] In the mid-1990s, *Feral* crossed the line with stories that antagonized the president, his family, and the ruling party. The items were not vicious by Western standards and were so clearly satirical that they would have been overlooked in most countries. But not here. A front-page picture of President Tuđman, digitally stripped of his clothes, became a signature piece of the paper's bad-boy ventures.

In an odd way, *Feral*'s humorous poke worked to Tuđman's advantage because it provided him and his supporters with a convenient, if spurious, example of what happens when the press is given free rein. Unregulated newsmen, they said, naturally resort to their basest instincts and assault the reading public with such offensive images. This argument concludes that it's better to allow the state to make the media behave with decent restraint than to expect reporters to do it on their own.

Feral suffered a second assault when Tisak, the monopoly distributor, withheld more than half a million dollars (3.2 million kuna) of the paper's sales revenue. This was a significant loss to a small town paper, and it may have forced *Feral* to close, were it not for notable international pressure. Free press organizations around the world banded behind the paper with press releases, news stories, and letters to the Croatian government and governments in Western countries. Soros's Open Society and other funding organizations stepped in to subsidize *Feral* in defiance of Tuđman's government.[13] Finally, Western nations applied diplomatic pressure, and, late in 1998, Tisak settled the bill, at least in part.[14]

Does this demonstrate the success of outside pressure? Yes, it does, but it also proves the tenacity of the government to withstand tough pressures and to thumb its nose at standards universally accepted in free societies. *Feral*'s victory was modest and it was limited. The government did not use the *Feral* case as an object lesson from which to rewrite the laws or to extend press freedoms more broadly throughout the country. Sadly, *Feral* was a concession and not a turning point in public policy toward the press.

Radio 101 was also a concession, and, as it turned out, it too failed as a watershed event. A Zagreb-based news and entertainment station, Radio 101 developed a reputation for candid reporting and frank discussion about government misdeeds. In 1996, the government's Telecommunications Council rejected Radio 101's fourth and final appeal for a long-term operating license. The council's action brought a hue and cry from the international community and the Croatian public, and this groundswell of outrage eventually persuaded the council to approve the license, although with harsh provisions: Radio 101 had to reduce its coverage to 50 percent of its Zagreb market.

As expected, outside organizations and governments were not satisfied with the council's conditions and continued their pressure on the Croatian authorities. Finally, after more than 100,000 people protested in the center of Zagreb, the government allowed Radio 101 to broadcast without restrictions. That victory imbued optimists with hopes that this marked a turning point in media freedoms, much as the fall of the Berlin Wall marked the turning point in the freedoms of East Germans. Unfortunately, that was not the case, and those small victories with the Telecommunications Council proved to have little impact beyond Radio 101.

On balance, the Croatian government was not resistant to outside pressures, as long as outsiders were relentless and focused, and more, coming from all quarters: media organizations, nonprofit groups, and governments. Even then, the victories were minimal and confined to specific cases. *Feral*'s marginal success did not extend to all newspapers, and Radio 101's limited victory did not benefit Croatian broadcasters at large. Each incident was isolated, and neither cultivated broader internal support for a free press.

Perhaps the worst news from these two episodes was that they demonstrate the government's ability to weather any but the most powerful outside pressures. Applied to the world beyond Croatia, this is discouraging. Indeed, tenacity works, at least in the short run, because dictators know that a little bit of freedom is a dangerous thing. In Croatia, leaders exhibited their leather-tough resistance, maintained their original policies, and, for all the slings and arrows from an army of pressure groups, gave little ground and seemingly suffered no long-term consequences until the surprising surge of public independence gave the HDZ a very bad dose of democracy. To sum it up, the effectiveness of outsiders to encourage a free press is mixed.

In the following section, we will look at some of the other issues that draw outside attention to Croatia.

Economy, Democracy, and Human Rights

The criticism of human rights abuses leveled at Croatia from world press reports, NGO accounts, and government analyses was so overwhelmingly negative that a researcher's first reaction is disbelief. The charges were severe and wide-ranging; they suggested little progress during the nineties, and worse, they inspired little hope for significant improvement in the days ahead. It was, of course, the dark before the light, but consider these allegations abstracted from Amnesty International's 1999 annual report:

Some critics of the government were prosecuted on criminal charges. Tens of thousands of Croatian Serbs remained exiled; many were prevented from returning because of administrative obstacles; others feared for their safety if they returned. Dozens of houses of Croatian Serbs, possibly more, were deliberately destroyed for political reasons. Political prisoners faced unfair trial procedures. Police ill-treated detainees and at least one person died as a result. Although hundreds of cases of 'disappearance' were resolved, the fate of more than 2,000 people who went missing or had 'disappeared' in previous years remained unclear. There was little progress in resolving hundreds of cases of ethnically motivated killings committed in 1995.[15]

The Amnesty report backed these charges with a convincing array of names, places, and events. This exhaustive report, and others like it, built a hauntingly grim case against Croatia's government and the leading party, the HDZ.

Although this evidence was compelling, one need not become an apologist for government or party officials to feel that the cumulative impact of so many negative reports, one after the other, like box cars in a freight train, may have led to conclusions that were unduly bleak and unfairly fatalistic. Were conditions for democratic institution-building poor? Yes, but hopeful. Were human rights concerns valid? Yes, but a light was in view. Were economic inequities a real threat to Croatian society? Absolutely, but evolving relationships with outside economies were leading to small improvements.[16]

Meanwhile, the following sample of press releases, news accounts, and NGO studies presented some chilling appraisals of democratic elements in Croatian society.

- In 1999, Juri Dienstbier, the United Nations special reporter for human rights on the former Yugoslav federation, "expressed dissatisfaction with the condition of the two-way refugee return, human rights, freedom of the media and democracy in general in Croatia." His remedy was stark: "The only way out is the creation of a [new] civil society." This includes, he said, the establishment of trust among the various ethnic groups and the institution of equal rights for everyone.

  Dienstbier expressed frustration with President Tuđman and senior officials, who, he said, claimed they were unable to control authorities at the local level. Dienstbier responded that if Croatia expects outside assistance and wishes an invitation into the family of Western nations, the government in Zagreb must issue clear instructions to local officials. Dienstbier reflected the frustrations held by many foreign governments and NGOs with Tuđman's duplicity. On matters that serve his political objectives, the president demonstrates a iron grip on the country's institutions and local authorities in all of its cities and towns. On matters of human rights and democratic governance, such as those raised by Dienstbier, Tuđman claims he is unable to exercise control.[17] Tuđman was either unaware of this jarring disparity and its effect on his credibility, or he didn't care what world leaders thought of him and his regime.

- The United Nations' assessment was buttressed by national assessments. Anthony Lloyd, British Minister of State at the Foreign Office, said in July 1999, "Problems which have been burdening, over a number of years, the relations between the international community and Croatia have not yet been removed and the way in which they will be solved is to be of crucial importance for the future of these ties. . . . Concerns which have dominated the relationship between the international community and Croatia over a number of years are still present and Croatia has to address them."

  Lloyd specified the need for reforms of election and media laws, the return of refugees to their homes, and greater cooperation with the International War Crimes Tribunal in The Hague. Lloyd showed special concern for the freedom of media during the upcoming national elections. "The present control of the electronic media, particularly of television, means that there isn't equal access to all political views." With specific reference to the democratic process, Lloyd added that election laws must be amended in order for ordinary Croatians to "exercise their democratic choice so that it is the people who become sovereign in a democratic process."

  Like other foreign government leaders, Lloyd used the lever of Western integration to get the attention of Croatian officials. He made clear that Croatia would remain a pariah as long as it failed to undertake significant steps toward genuine democratic reform.[18]

- The Organization for Security and Cooperation in Europe blasted Croatia's progress toward an open society in a report released in spring 1999. The *New York Times* reports that the OSCE concluded Croatia was "nominally democratic" but "in reality authoritarian." The report's bottom line was this: "There has been no progress in improving respect for human rights, the rights of minorities and the rule of law."

The OSCE also contested the means by which the government was manipulating its own population to accept flawed policies. It pointed out that the government-influenced television station, watched regularly by 90 percent of the people, often contained "hate speech" toward ethnic minorities. This works in direct opposition to reintegration, an inherently difficult task that is doomed without strong public support. Regular doses of "hate speech" are not fitting prescriptions for tolerance and acceptance.

The OSCE was also troubled by the television station's disdainful treatment of Croatia's political opposition. The report said that news accounts are "misleadingly presented, distorted by selection and by prejudicial terminology or comment." The persistent drumming of the political opposition was blatant meddling in electoral politics that effectively poisoned the population against candidates and policies not arising from the HDZ.

Another aspect of HDZ's party line was its vilification of the international tribunal in The Hague. OSCE characterized this as a manipulation of public opinion against outside judicial authority. The government has often used the tribunal to inflame Croatian nationalism and to associate patriotism with the ruling party. This, in turn, has enabled the HDZ to exploit the tribunal as a tool of domestic politics, positioning the HDZ as defenders of Croatian rights.[19]

- The International Helsinki Federation for Human Rights challenged Croatia's human rights record in its 1999 annual report. It said that despite the national government's agreement to implement the return of all refugees, the plan was not carried out at the local level, or it proceeded at a snail's pace. As other observers have noted, Tuđman's unquestioned authority was conspicuously absent from the enactment of reintegration programs. The powers in Zagreb clicked their tongues at the local governments for inaction but said they were powerless to hasten the process. Powerless indeed.

The Helsinki Federation said Croatia broke its promises to settle Croats from Bosnia, Vojvodina, and Kosovo, to return displaced persons, and to return Serb refugees. The report highlighted the planting of mines in Lika, the deaths of ten people, and the serious wounding of twenty-one others in the region. These incidents, the report concludes, were designed to scare off non-Croats and ethnically cleanse the region.[20]

- Outside press reports about Croatia were equally stinging. The *New York Times*, for instance, decried the economic policies in the country as "miserable." Reporter Raymond Bonner said that Tuđman and his political friends have acquired great wealth at the expense of the middle class, which has been driven to economic ruin. Another *New York Times* reporter, John Tagliabue, said that corruption in Croatia is widespread. "Tudjman has sold off nationalized industries, but the businesses have often gone to his cronies. The banking system has been milked to fill his party's coffers."[21]

New York Times reporters explained how the average monthly salary of $400 falls far short of the amount needed to cover family expenses. The shortfall requires people to sharply lower their standards of living, driving them to shop in neighboring countries, where consumer goods cost less than half their cost in Croatia. Ordinary food and clothing items, in fact, often cost more in Croatia than they do in the United States, where salaries are five times higher. The elevated prices are due to heavy taxes (22 percent on most items) and greedy industrialists in league with government officials.[22]

- Press accounts from the streets of Croatia were also filled with gloom. In June 1999, *New York Times* reporter Chris Hedges wrote about police blockades erected to keep workers, angry over unpaid wages, from storming the Parliament building. He reported that, earlier, railway workers and hotel workers walked off the job to protest a lack of pay.

  Hedges clearly believed that the failings of President Tudman and his party were responsible not only for Croatia's economic woes but also for fratricidal nationalism: "The hard-line nationalists are increasingly public. They raised over half a million dollars in an auction of paintings June 18 for 'our Croatian heros' awaiting trial for war crimes in The Hague, Netherlands. The justice minister, Zvonimir Separović, appeared at the airport to embrace one of the convicted Croats. . . ." This certainly is not the reception one would expect for a man found guilty of mass murder.

- Finally, the U.S. Department of State *Report on Human Rights Practices* for 1998 (released in February 1999) painted a bleak picture of Croatia's political environment. "The extensive constitutional powers of the presidency, the overwhelming dominance of the HDZ, its absolute control of television, the continuing concentration of power within the one-party central Government, and government influence that circumscribes and weakens the judiciary combine to make the country's nominally democratic system in reality authoritarian."

As for the economy, the report said that the "market-based, free enterprise system is proceeding slowly." It offered these items in evidence:

"While agriculture is mostly in private hands and family-owned small enterprises are multiplying, industry and media enterprises were largely either still controlled by the state or deliberately were transferred in non-transparent, noncompetitive processes to individuals sympathetic to the ruling party."

"The economy showed underlying weakness throughout the year, especially in the financial sector. Several banks collapsed and illiquidity worsened considerably, squeezing hundreds of thousands of depositors, employees, and small entrepreneurs."

The human rights "record remained poor: although improvement was measurable in certain areas, serious problems continued in others." The report offered these examples:

"Police committed one extrajudicial killing and occasionally beat persons."

"The Government does not always respect due process provisions for arrest and detention."

"Lengthy pretrial detention is a problem."

"The judicial system is subject to executive and political influence, and the court system suffers from such a severe backlog of cases and shortage of judges that the right of citizens to address their concerns in court is seriously impaired."

"Cases of interest to the ruling party are processed expeditiously, while others languish in court, further calling into question the independence of the judiciary."

"The courts sometimes deny citizens fair trials."

As for other civil rights and basic freedoms, the report was similarly discouraging:

"The Government restricted freedom of assembly, and circumscribed freedom of association by a law that prohibited groups from forming or meeting unless expressly authorized to do so my means of an intrusive registration process."

"The Government seriously limited citizens' right to change their government."

"It used the manipulation of laws, harassment, economic pressure, and its almost total control of the electronic media to control the political process."

"Cases of abuse from the 1995 military actions, including the alleged murders of hundreds of civilians by government forces, remain largely unsolved."

"Violence and discrimination against women remained problems."

"Ethnic minorities, including Roma, also faced continued discrimination."

"Although the Government made progress in establishing civil authority in the former occupied areas, and physical violence declined overall, some abuses, such as harassment, threats, and in some instances, even beatings still occurred, particularly in the areas of the former conflict."

It was difficult to reconcile the Croatian government's enthusiasm for membership in Western economic and political alliances with its steadfast disregard for the overwhelmingly negative views reported by Western observers. Perhaps it was a diplomatic anomaly that put Croatia in this exposed position. Repressive governments, like those of China and Iraq, which care not a fig for a free press and make no pretense at democracy, were not loudly rebuked or sanctioned for their censorship. But Croatia opened itself to scrutiny because it insincerely promised freedom and sincerely wanted acceptance among the world's democracies. Croatia may have been slammed for its hypocrisy, or maybe it was slammed because outsiders believed there was hope of change through criticism. Throughout the 1990s, the West responded to these overtures by making conditions for closer cooperation quite clear: open the society, free the press, observe human rights, reform the economy.

Meanwhile, foreign governments had been direct and unambiguous. Official visitors and diplomats posted in Zagreb rarely missed the chance to make the case with Croatian leaders. In a 1997 interview, U.S. ambassador to Croatia Peter Galbraith explained his persistence with the government on media freedoms:

It is a major part of our dialogue with the Croatians. We constantly raise the absence of independent media, particularly independent broadcast media as something that is inconsistent with modern democracy. I do it. I've done it dramatically. . . . This [media freedom] has been raised by the Vice President [Gore] in meetings with President Tuđman and by deputy secretary Talbot. So, up and down the government we have been raising this.[23]

U.S. Secretary of State Madeleine Albright, was forthright with Croatian officials over her dissatisfaction with many policies. During a visit with Croatian journalists in Zagreb, she stressed her determination in appealing to Croatian government leaders.

I can assure you that in my discussions with President Tuđman and with others, I had this right at the top, that is that HRTV [the leading, government-influenced television station] cannot operate this way. What we have done is lay out a roadmap for the government, so that it can become a part of the Euro-Atlantic institutional system and having an open and free media, especially a television that functions freely, is one of the benchmarks of what has to happen. Because we agree with you that there is no way to have an open and free system, if you don't have these things.[24]

No, it cannot be said that outsiders were unclear about the relationship between significant reforms and a welcoming hand by the West. The Croatian government, for reasons of its own, chose a policy of obstinacy, despite the continuing rejection from the West and the obvious and punishing costs to its own people.

During the terrible nineties, press freedoms hardly budged.[25] Elections run by Tuđman at the end of the decade were no more free or open or accommodating to opposition parties than they were immediately after the fall of Communism. It wasn't until Tuđman passed from the scene that Croatia saw significant electoral reforms. Economic conditions grew worse through the years as pals of the HDZ grabbed up the industries and siphoned off cash from the country's banks. The paltry incomes of average people stagnated while taxes and prices climbed. Many workers, denied their low monthly wages by insolvent institutions, were enjoined from street rallies to petition their government.

A lesson for today: When press freedom fails, other rights are quick to follow. Thus, in Croatia, minorities faced discrimination, the accused were denied due process, and refugees were prevented from resettlement. Hate speech that aired on the principal television station inflamed prejudices lying near the surface.

The evident winners, then, from such repressive policies were politicians, those who use their power to grow their bank accounts, along with wealthy industrialists or corporate owners, who harvest ever larger portions of the public holdings. As a result, the gap between the haves and have-nots widened, poverty increased, freedoms decreased, and Croatia slipped further from the embrace of Western countries it appeared to covet.

OUTSIDE ASSISTANCE

However tempted to wash its hands of Croatia or treat that nation like an alcoholic who needs to hit bottom before admitting the problem, the international community tried to help where it could.

U.S. Aid

Croatia's regular supporters came from a wide geographical and organizational spectrum. In a 1999 funding request to the U.S. Congress, the United States International Development Agency (USAID) described the donor base this way:

USAID has been the most important bilateral donor in the areas of reintegration of war-affected areas and democratic transition. Over the past two years, in addition to the UN-funded operation in Eastern Slavonia, the international community led by USAID, the European Union (EU), Norway, Belgium and Italy has pledged over $80 million to support reconstruction and reintegration efforts. Additionally, the Open Society Foundation, the EU and the governments of Norway, Belgium and Sweden have provided significant support for democratization. The UN High Commissioner for Refugees (UNHCR) will remain a major donor and development partner as long as Bosnian refugees and Croatia displaced populations remain in Croatia. In the area of Economic Restructuring, the World Bank, the International Monetary Fund and the European Bank for Reconstruction and Development are providing substantial resources to support structural adjustment and financial and private sector development.[26]

Assistance to Croatia shifted from material support of the population during the postwar years to education and development for long-term political stability. These efforts, aimed at relieving Croatia's population from authoritarian rule and at hastening Croatia's integration into the West, positioned it as an anchor of regional stability.

Croatia is a geographic buffer between two regions very different from each other in culture, politics, and economies. It is on the fault line between two tectonic plates: the affluent, open societies of the West and the distressed, authoritarian societies of the East. By history and recent events, Croatia shares characteristics of each, although its eventual movement toward the East or the West, even now, is not entirely certain. That explains the concern among outside groups to lend continuing support for progress toward democratic ideals and economic strength.

This view was expressed by the USAID when it wrote:

The importance of Croatia to regional stability and the realistic potential for exerting a strong positive influence in favor of systemic change constitute the rationale for continued U.S. engagement in Croatia. The USAID program in Croatia directly supports achievement of U.S. foreign policy objectives in the region to establish a sustainable peace, foster full democratization, and enable newly independent republics to gain full access to European and Trans-Atlantic institutions.[27]

USAID, the lead administrative organization for U.S. assistance to Croatia, followed a blueprint with three strategic objectives (SOs):

1. Return and reintegration of displaced persons and refugees in communities of origin,
2. Increased, better-informed, citizens' participation in political processes and public decision making,
3. More competitive, market-responsive, private financial sector.[28].

The agency packaged several other objectives around each strategic objective. For instance in support of the first SO, the agency

1. encourages municipalities to resettle displaced persons into their original communities,
2. promotes respect for human and civil rights and equal treatment under the law,
3. supports growth of small and medium-small private enterprises to provide jobs for returning populations.

These objectives, in turn, have spawned five programs, funded by USAID but generally operated by local NGOs.[29]

Further, the USAID report provided the names of organizations that were involved in each program, although it did not specify the nature of their involvement, whether it is to fund the programs or to operate them. The following groups were involved in the return and reintegration of refugees:

International Organization for Migration

America's Development Foundation

Opportunity International

Small Enterprise Assistance Fund

Croatian Savings and Loan Cooperative

Parsons Delaware

World Learning

University of Delaware, Firm Level Assistance Group

Urban Institute

UN High Commissioner for Refugees[30]

Between 1997 and 1999, USAID committed around $41 million in assistance to Croatia.[31] This represented direct programmatic assistance and did not include expenditures through other agencies,[32] the military, the Fulbright program, or operating costs for the embassy and other U.S. government facilities.

Other Contributors

The U.S. government has headed the list of contributors, but other governments, NGOs, and philanthropic organizations have played a significant role since the breakup of Communism. We noted earlier that the European Union along with the governments of Norway, Sweden, Belgium, and Italy have brought their own groceries to the table. Other countries have salted the food with money or material, especially during the war and immediately afterwards. As USAID reported, financial institutions such as the World Bank, the International Monetary Fund, and the European Bank for Reconstruction and Development have also made funds available for specific projects, many of them involving the reconstruction of war-damaged facilities.

International philanthropist George Soros has become a legend for his deep-pocketed support in Croatia, as in most of the countries in Central and Eastern Europe. Over the years, his Open Society Institute (OSI) poured millions of dollars into Croatia for education, libraries, Civil Society Creative Centers, media, publishing, and the environment. Working on projects independently as well as with other established NGOs, the OSI has been committed to providing the people with the information and the resources necessary to build a market economy and establish democratic rule. Soros keeps at arm's length from controversial issues and focuses instead on programs that encourage civil rule. The organization has adopted the belief that fundamental reforms must originate from the people and provides the tools needed for the job.

As we discussed before, the work of outside groups to foster democratic reforms is not always warmly welcomed by the Croatian government. After contributing tens of millions of dollars, Soros has regularly been the target of official sanctions. In 1997, for example, two Soros officials went to trial for tax evasion, a charge seen by many observers, including the U.S. government, as politically motivated. The accused received a one-year suspended prison sentence, but not before the U.S. government intervened on their behalf.

THE TUĐMAN REPORT CARD

At the end of October 1999, Transparency International (TI), a multinational research organization, released an exhaustive and damning study. TI found that on a list of ninety-nine countries, Croatia ranked among the lowest 25 percent in perceived corruption. Corruption was defined as "the misuse of public trust or authority for personal gain."[33] On a 1-to-10 scale (1 = a high degree of corruption; 10 = a low degree of corruption), Croatia received an index score of 2.7—more corrupt than Romania, Macedonia and Bulgaria (3.3), Slovakia (3.7) and Poland (4.2) and less corrupt than Moldova and Ukraine (2.6).

This study reflected relative rankings and subjective views, and that made the findings particularly alarming. Two sources of data contributed to this study. First, data were examined from "17 research projects by institutions from 10 countries." Each project was based on "strict scientific research and controls," and the convergence of their results lends support to the credence of their damning conclusions.

The second data source came from personal interviews, conducted by Gallup International, among 34,000 people in the general public, business men and women, and risk analysts. The size and composition of this respondent pool represents a significant cross section of a professional group that is essential to Croatia's long-term economic health: the experts who steer the allocation of commercial investments. These are not bleeding-heart social workers, government bureaucrats, or media cry-babies but a special group of decision makers that distribute global wealth.

The prevailing view of Croatia's corruption came from the combined effects of a thousand blows: the images of Croatia's war in the first half of the nineties, the endless news accounts about a government that hands over the people's treasures to political hacks and strong-arms reporters with lawsuits and surveillance. Perceptions sharpened with news about unfair elections, slow resettlements, unfulfilled promises of economic reform, nationalistic speeches upon the return of convicted war criminals, the government's resistance to reform, and its refusal to overhaul national policies.

The Croatian government complained that it did not receive the financial largesse offered to Poland, yet it did not take the bold steps Poland has taken to fix its economy. Croatian officials griped that their country was denied favors shown to Slovenia, its sister to the north, yet Croatia did not free its media or clean up its electoral process. As Jesse Jackson put it, "They talk the talk, but they don't walk the walk." The complaints continued, and the pessimistic views of outsiders hardened further.

Sadly, the Croatian people were the biggest losers and they suffered twice. First, at the hands of their own government which denied them basic freedoms. Second, from an international community that withheld its favors.

Croatia's move toward democracy was triggered by the death of a dictator. But those reforms would not have surfaced had there not been a lust for freedom. Enough citizens had to want freedom more than security. In an earlier chapter, we likened democracy to a rope that the people must pull for themselves. Outsiders cannot push it on them. To change the metaphor, the best outsiders can do is tease the government with carrots and sticks. At some point, the people must find the collective will for change. They must recognize themselves as the owners of their government, not the subjects of it. The opening of society in Croatia came from Croatians. But preparing the way, perhaps strengthening their will, was the impact of international forces, communities, and nations.

CONCLUSION: CASE FOR CROATIAN LESSONS BEING EFFICACIOUS FOR THE WORLD

Croatia, of course, is not Iraq or Cuba or even Yugoslavia, much less China, which, like the former USSR, is not just huge but also powerful. What did international groups learn in Croatia that might be applied to any or all nations that censor? Many things. Like all autocrats, Tudman and company had "rabbit ears:" They hated criticism, squirmed before satire, and gnashed their teeth in frustration when people rose up in discontent. Finally, the censored public developed a cynicism toward state pronouncements, and when their distrust reached a critical mass, and when the perpetrator of their oppression began to falter, they moved. They were nudged along by a strengthening press and prodded by the international community, encouraged maybe a little by satellite TV and the amazing Internet. Given the chance for free elections and a press to support the democratic process, people said enough is enough and threw the bums out.

For other countries emerging from totalitarian rule, the Croatian experience offers some pointers. For one, it is becoming increasingly difficult to bail against the tide of outside opinion and information. Like it or not, national borders really are becoming more porous and interdependence is surging. Driven by economies, pursued by politics, supported by the unstoppable flow of information, the world is becoming a more hostile place for governments that abuse their people and threaten their neighbors.

Croatia's reconstitution as a full democracy is not entirely certain, but the pieces are falling in place. The press is keeping its own house, the people are enjoying their first breaths of freedom, the political leaders are realizing that they are the caretakers, not the owners, of their offices. Croatia now has the best chance in many generations to sustain its newfound freedoms. The international community has been quick to do its part, but at the end, in Croatia as it is everywhere, it is up to the will of the people and the tenacity of the press to do the job.

NOTES

1. Yugoslavia, today comprised of only Serbia and Montenegro, saw the departure of Bosnia, Croatia, Macedonia, and Slovenia.

2. The number of foreign NGOs is cited by Bandurina & Associates of Falmouth, Virginia. This source also reports 1,178 domestic, national NGOs and 14,000 NGOs operating on the local level. November 24, 1998, on website: <http://www.dalmatia.net/croatia/bandurina/ngos.htm>.

3. Countries or regions in the news have been called "The Flavor of the Month." NGOs, like some press organizations, jump to places that receive the greatest global attention at any given time, to the "Flavor of the Month."

4. Reporters sans Frontiers, Paris. The story was distributed by the International Freedom of Expression Exchange (IFEX) Clearing House. See website: <http://www.ifex.org>.

5. The information and the quotations were obtained from a press release issued by the International Federation of Journalists on April 17, 1998. See website: <http://www.ifj.org/pr/65.html>.

6. This information and the quotations were obtained from an International Press Institute press release distributed on May 7, 1999, by the International Freedom of Expression Exchange. See website: <http://www.ifex.org>.

7. Julie Moffett, "The East: Greater Freedom Has Not Brought A Free Press." Released on Radio Free Europe and Radio Liberty and posted at the following website: <http://www.rferl.org/nca/features/1998/F.RU.98037111722.html>.

8. "Press freedom is still hampered by state controls, says OSCE," Deutsche Presse-Agentur News Service, July 16, 1998.

9. The Helsinki Federation's list of violations against free media goes on for nearly seven pages.

10. Information about International Helsinki Federation for Human Rights obtained form the organization's annual report, 1999, posted at the website: <http:www.ihf-hr.org/reports/ar99/ar99cro.htm>.

11. Information and quotations from Reporters Sans Frontiers press release ("RSF accuses Croatian authorities of increasing pressure on independent media") issued by International Freedom of Expression Exchange Clearing House on January 29, 1999.

12. It's easy to cross that threshold of offenses in Croatia or anywhere else. Imagine how many journalists in the United States and Western Europe would be dragged into court every time they gave someone reason to feel insulted or experience mental anguish. This foolish standard would be a free press killer in any country.

13. Soros's Open Society Institute has contributed several times to *Feral*. In 1999, it donated $30,000 to keep *Feral* on the streets. This was reported by the "BBC Monitoring Media," London, June 18, 1999.

14. To make matters even worse for the troubled *Feral*, local advertisers have avoided the paper because of its antigovernment stance. They fear, and for good reason, that association with *Feral* would instigate government wrath. Consequently, in addition to the other financial troubles *Feral* faces, its advertising revenue has all but dried up.

15. Amnesty International, Annual Report, 1999.

16. Whether exculpatory evidence goes unreported or unrecognized or is too minor to get much notice is hard to say, but our efforts to find reports of noteworthy improvements in Croatia's advance toward an open society have largely come up dry.

17. Information about Juri Dienstbier comes from "UN rapporteur says Croatia needs to be more democratic," BBC Monitoring European, February 16, 1999.

18. Information about Anthony Lloyd's observations came from "Croatia has to address problems in relations with Europe," BBC Monitoring European, July 14, 1999.

19. Information about the OSCE report was obtained from Raymond Bonner, "Croatia Branded as Another Balkans Pariah," *New York Times*, March 3, 1999.

20. International Helsinki Federation for Human Rights, Annual Report, 1999.

21. John Tagliabue, "Four Countries Alive and Ailing in the Balkans," *New York Times*, June 27, 1999.

22. Raymond Bonner, "Croatia Branded as Another Balkans Pariah," *New York Times*, March 3, 1999.

23. Interview conducted with Ambassador Peter Galbraith on November 10, 1997.

24. Secretary of State Madeleine K. Albright in a meeting with independent media representatives at the Hotel Sheraton in Zagreb, Croatia, August 30, 1998. For a full transcript of this session, see Appendix B.

25. International Helsinki Federation for Human Rights, Annual Report, 1999.

26. USAID Congressional Presentation for fiscal year 1999.

27. Ibid.

28. Description of USAID activities in Croatia obtained from website: <http://www.info.usaid.gov>.

29. The programs supporting the first strategic objective are:

The Return Assistance Program (RAP): supports small-scale municipal infrastructure and community development projects in war-affected partner municipalities throughout Croatia to facilitate development and implementation of mutually agreed return strategies and programs.

Civil Rights/Legal Assistance Project: provides training, technical assistance, and grants to local NGOs providing legal services and advice to displaced persons, refugees, and returnees to resolve legal and administrative issues including citizenship, property rights, professional licensing, certification, and access to social benefits.

Private Sector Development: provides consulting services, training, and management support to small- and medium-scale private enterprises and to agricultural and industrial associations to promote economic revitalization and development in war-affected areas throughout Croatia.

Micro-Loan Project: provides loans of between $500 and $10,000 to small-scale private enterprises in the Slavonia region to create jobs and incomes for returning and remaining populations.

Equity Finance Project: provides equity investments of between $50,000 and $350,000 to small- and medium-scale private enterprises to promote economic growth. This project operates nationally, with special emphasis on Slavonia and other war-affected areas.

30. The implementing partners for the two remaining strategic objectives follow. The better-informed citizens effort:

Independent Research Exchange Commission (IREX)

American Center for International Labor Solidarity

National Democratic Institute (NDI)

International Republican Institute (IRI)

American Bar Association (ABA)

World Learning

Delphi International

Croatian Journalists Association

Croatian Judges Association

International Rescue Committee (IRC)

Croatian Trade Unions

Croatian Women Lawyers Association

Academy for Educational Development (AED)

Croatian Law Center

Croatian Bar Association

The private financial sector effort:

KPMG Barents Group

National Bank of Croatia

Financial Sector Volunteer Corps

Croatia Ministry of Finance

U.S. Securities & Exchange Commission

World Bank (IBRD)

World Learning

Croatia Securities and Exchange Commission

Croatia Central Registry/Depository

Croatia Over-the-Counter Market

Croatia Association of Small Shareholders

31. Based on amount received for 1997 and 1998 and the amount requested for 1999. USAID Congressional Presentation for fiscal year 1999.

32. For instance, in July 1999, the U.S. embassy in Zagreb donated $100,000 to Society for the Protection of Journalists. The money was planned to defend journalists on trial in Croatian courts.

33. "International agency concerned about level of corruption in Croatia," BBC Monitoring, October 26, 1999.

14

Technology: Catalyst for Change

INTRODUCTION

We conclude with a look at a new and powerful medium that may change the chemistry of interactions among the people, the press, and politics, not only in Croatia, but in every country. Throughout the earlier chapters we focused on traditional media because, to date, they have been the large vessels of information, the powerful influencers of public opinion. The role of broadcast and print throughout history has been well known and well documented, and their contribution to the recent Croatian experience has been undeniable.

The Internet is new, untested, unknown, undeveloped, and misunderstood, but one thing is certain: It will become a significant force in global communication, and in this capacity, it will change the power alignment among the forces that have preoccupied our discussions.

In this chapter, we speculate—that's all anyone can do at this point—about the possible impact of this new interactive medium. While the Net is sweeping into populations in the United States and other Western nations, it is moving more slowly into Central and Eastern Europe, but it is, nonetheless, growing here as well. Although the Net may have had little, if any, influence on the Croatian elections at the end of the last decade, it will likely become a force to reckon with as the country struggles with its evolution toward a new and more open society.

Just down the road—and closer than many people think—the Internet will sap the power of a state to control the flow of information to the people. Such is the kinship between a free press and democratic polity, that people, sick of official manipulations and newly nourished by the flood of facts only a click away, will demand a libertarian government. That is our prediction wherever and whenever the Internet takes hold.

For as long as there have been centralized media—from mass circulation newspapers to radio and television networks—it has been easy for the few to control the many. Whether led by a supreme leader or an official party, the state simply shuts down a handful of printing plants or throws the switch on a few transmitters to halt the flow of credible news and information by which the public can make electoral judgments. All a ham-fisted bureaucrat has to do is intimidate a few publishers and broadcasters, creating a climate of fear and, thereby, predetermining the way the news is slanted.

The Internet is decentralized, so it defies control. Unlike newspapers and broadcasting, "printing plants" and "transmitters" of the Net can be any one of thousands of computers within or outside the country. Even if the government could locate an offending computer and pull the plug, it would be bailing against the tide. Before the errant image faded from the screen, the information could be back on-line, fed from another location. Remember, this technology was invented to withstand a nuclear holocaust; it will not submit easily to a bully's jack boots.

Moreover, Internet publishers and editors are not as easy to identify as are the chiefs of traditional media. Who is writing the website that challenges government's corruption? Who is creating a site that taunts the leadership? It's tough to know because the writers don't sit around wearing green eye shades in plainly marked building. A site developer could be anyone sitting inconspicuously in his basement, kitchen, or a classroom down the block or 10,000 miles away.

Totalitarian governments, which ensure their power through the control of information, are bound to be frustrated with the emerging Internet technologies. In many developing countries, the Internet is little more than a promise. The equipment is expensive and the infrastructure is undeveloped. But with lowering costs and rising global expectations for the expansion of this technology, every country will join the club sooner or later.

The technology itself is becoming more adaptable, portable, and accessible, putting it further beyond the despot's reach. Big, easy-to-spot desktop equipment, once needed to access the Net, is being supplanted by miniaturized versions that you can hold in your hand and slide in your pocket. You can connect these tiny sets through cell phones—soon through convenient satellites from anyplace on earth.[1] Small, portable, inconspicuous equipment, no longer tethered by a phone cord, will make the technology virtually impossible to control.

The sending and receiving of information will soon be beyond the reach of the state. And that explains how a government inclined to tamper with the press to retain control of the people is likely to run into trouble. None of this can take place yet; after all, the medium is barely a toddler. But already heroic examples forecast a time near at hand when the flow of information will elude state interference and the people will enjoy a reliable source of information.

The Kosovo war in 1999 provided a useful test of the Net's effectiveness in getting out news where other media have failed. The most celebrated case was the Internet use by B-92, an independent radio station in Belgrade with a history of government opposition. The station was shut down at the height of the antigovernment demonstrations in 1996, and its plug was pulled again in 1999, when the broadcasters condemned Serbia's incursion into Kosovo. Both times B-92 turned to the Web to report government activities with a frankness that was not possible in traditional print and broadcast. B-92 denounced Milošević's policies in Kosovo and called for a halt to aggression, but it certainly was no stooge for NATO. The station's website slammed NATO policies as well and called for an unconditional halt to the bombing of civilian and military targets in Serbia.

Sadly, B-92 had almost no domestic audience, so it could have little influence on domestic politics. Tracy Wilkinson, a reporter for the *Los Angeles Times*, said the Internet reports have "raised [B-92's] profile but [did] little for the people living in Yugoslavia."[2] Maybe not this time, because few people in Serbia had Internet access, but it demonstrated to the rest of the world that the Internet was bulletproof and had the capacity to function when other media had been choked by government sanctions. The B-92 feed (through a server operating in Amsterdam) provided a steady flow of opposition news available nowhere else.

News of another kind came in a series of intimate e-mail reports from a Muslim teenage girl, "Adana," hiding in a basement with her family in Kosovo. She sent periodic messages to a student in Berkeley, California, who, in turn, made the correspondence available for public broadcast to National Public Radio.[3] These simple, first-person reports provided gripping accounts of Serbian aggression against the Albanian population in Kosovo. Their telling of the story from the perspective of a victim living through the experience provided a rare poignancy and presence that could never be represented by traditional news media. Void of the customary details about politics and battlefield strategies that often fill reports of war, these intensely personal descriptions showed audiences a side of war rarely seen.[4]

What lies in store for Kosovo may be forecast by the experiments now underway in Croatia. Can the Internet serve the Croatian people in their quest for honest information about their government, their economy, and the public policies that play havoc with their daily lives? At this time, the thought must seem very much like pie in the sky, but it would be a mistake to discount the real possibility that the Net could serve Croatia by filling the information void left by its state-influenced media.

Already Croatians are logging onto the Net from home, work, and school. A study conducted in August 1999 found that 6 percent of Croatians are regular users of the Internet, and 12 percent have gone on-line at least once during the past several years. That may not seem like a lot, but 400,000 Croatian adults can make a difference in a nation of 4.5 million people.[5]

Of the homes with PCs (around one in eight), 60 percent subscribe to a service provider account. These subscribers typically spend nearly five hours on line each week, most (63%) surfing the Net with no particular objective in mind. About half (53%) use it for e-mail and about half (48%) say they read news off the Web.

This use of the Net is not inconsequential when you consider that the "typical Croatian Internet user is educated, wealthy and young."[6] Moreover, the greatest concentration of users resides in Zagreb, the capital city and its surroundings, and along the relatively affluent northern Adriatic coast. The country's opinion leaders (or soon to be opinion leaders) are concentrated among these users, the ones for whom accurate information has the greatest consequence. Through them, information about the government, generated by independent journalists and outside observers, can ripple through the population with a multiplier effect.

Thirty years ago, Everett Rogers's diffusion studies demonstrated the importance of information to opinion leaders and their power to sway the rest of society.[7] The numbers of users may be small, but the impact of their views can be great. Even a small reach of the Net into Croatian society, therefore, can have a significant effect on a broader population.

The country's prominent newspapers have gone on-line, joined by internal and outside news sources, which are reporting news with a candor that has been unfamiliar to Croatian audiences through the nineties.[8] Some of them provide a rare look at domestic politics and openly discuss Croatia's relationship with countries in the rest of Europe. Several sites, for instance, those sponsored by outside free press organizations, assess Croatia's progress toward membership in the European Union, NATO, and other alliances that are both a reward for democratic reforms and a stimulus for economic expansion. Often the websites covering Croatia offer views that you simply could not have found in the country's newspapers or watched on its evening telecasts in recent years. Many of them level charges at the government that would be commonplace in the Western press but had been culled from most Croatian media. With its stinging criticism, documented charges, and unproved allegations, the Web is an immersion in the hurly-burly of a Western-style open press, and there is not much any government can do about it.

As more citizens get more information from more independent sources online, its hard to see how any government can sustain its control of the press and, by extension, its tight grasp on the society. In light of disclosures that people discover on-line, the news presented in a controlled press will be seen increasingly as annoying fiction. Something has to give.

THE INTERNET IN EUROPE

Many media practitioners and analysts in the United States and in Europe are impatient with the Internet. It's not fast enough, they say, not interactive enough, and not generating enough business. Compared with one's phone, radio, or television set, it seems more a hothouse flower than a household appliance. Ironically, these disappointments, which arise from heightened expectations, say more about the success of the medium than they do about its failures.

For perspective, bear in mind that public access to the Internet is a fairly recent phenomenon. The Web, which for most people *is* the Internet, came to life in 1993 with the development of Mosaic, the first publicly available browser.[9] Looking back to the long lag time between the introduction and acceptance of radio, TV, and the telephone, it's truly remarkable to see how quickly the international public has hooked into the Net. The adoption statistics tell the true story.

Consider this research on the phenomenal growth of the Internet in Europe:

- European use of the Internet grew by 91 percent in 1998—that's more than 20 million users just at work.
- Overall, online use in Europe jumped from 17.7 million in 1997 to more than 35 million in 1998.
- Many Nordic countries have attained the 20 percent threshold, which many experts believe is the penetration necessary to reach commercial viability. In Austria, Germany, the Netherlands, Switzerland, and the United Kingdom, Net penetration is nearing that level.
- Germany had the highest number of Internet users in Europe, going from more than 5 million in 1997 to more than 8 million last year.[10]
- The European ISP (Internet Service Provider) market, worth $246 million in 1998, is predicted to reach $13.8 billion by 2005.[11]

Several events stand to fuel even more active growth over the next few years.[12] For one, the deregulation of the European telecommunication industry in 1998 has the enormous potential of lowering phone charges, which, in turn, will lower Internet connection costs. One of the major impediments to a more rapid expansion of Internet use in Europe has been the metered-by-the-minute phone charges that oblige users to keep one eye on the screen and the other on a stopwatch. Eventual adoption of flat-rate phone charges will reduce a significant barrier to wider and more frequent use.[13]

Until the late 1990s, following the telephone model, service providers in Europe charged Internet users by the minute, a practice which burdened users with high costs and limited their use of the Net. In 1998, however, Freeserve, a small upstart company in the UK, began offering free access to the Web. Within a year, it signed up 1.3 million customers in the UK, quickly overtaking the once-dominant AOL. Freeserve's move was the camel's nose in the tent. Its success inspired clones, and by summer of 1999, it forced AOL, once Europe's leading Internet provider, to offer free service. Free Internet access in the UK quickly took hold in the rest of Western Europe, and economic barriers to adoption of the Net began to fade. Obviously, free Internet access and cheaper phone rates will spur the rapid adoption of Internet technology across Europe.[14]

Meanwhile, money talks. Commerce on the Web has increased significantly since big credit card companies and computer firms agreed on secure data transmission standards. Until that happened, online catalogue sales, banking, bill paying, and other financial transactions were hampered by fears of data compromise. That fear still exists, probably with some justification, but after people have more experience with safe transactions, many analysts believe that when the security threats are finally put to rest, the Web will become the hub of financial transactions worldwide.

On the downside, European systems, like systems everywhere, suffer from slow access speeds, regional gridlocks, and occasional system failures. The Internet has been groaning under the weight of popular demand. Designers of the early systems did not anticipate such rapid or widespread adoption, and the result has been an overburdened network. With a Net that is successful to a fault, government and business are now strengthening the infrastructure and preparing the system for heavier anticipated use.

Building on this improving technology is an age factor not unlike that in the United States. Young people, introduced to the Internet in schools, are now beginning to enter the work force. For them, unlike their parents, the Internet is not just a clever innovation but a mainstream resource. They are familiar with its functions and they understand its possibilities. Indeed, many young people would be as lost today without the Web and e-mail as their elders would have been lost without a telephone and daily postal service. Young employees will carry the Internet habit into the workplace, and they will use it for news and personal communication as naturally as previous generations had carried along the quill, read daily papers, and talked on the telephone. Insofar as the permanence of the new medium is concerned, the societal effects outweigh the technological developments—and that's true worldwide.

Finally, the European Union will push Internet growth throughout the continent and beyond. The driving vision behind the EU and the Net is one and the same: commerce. It is the union's good fortune that the Net should have come along just when this fledgling was most in need of a communication tool to unite its members.

English, the voice of Shakespeare, if not love, has become the Net's lingua franca, the language used in 85 percent of websites worldwide. As a metaphor, the Web is a Tower of Babel in reverse. It offers the people of different tongues a common language and provides the tie that binds 300 million members. Possibly the dominance of English will be short-lived because of universal translators now assembling on the Web, but whether users around the world speak

English or a native translation, the Web provides a central meeting place for all members of the new union.

For all the evidence of the Net's capacities to link audiences, it's premature to conclude that technology or anything else can melt away centuries-old barriers formed by language, economies, culture, and philosophy, to say nothing of the riches therein. Even in the context of Internet communication, observers note the continuing need to accommodate regional tastes and customs, to recognize inherent differences among audiences, and to move slowly in attempts to form big happy families at the cost of local color and variety.

Fabiola Arredondo, head of Yahoo's operation in Europe, said that in Europe "You will have to think locally in each of the national markets. . . . We put all our energy into local teams and local partnerships."[15] Arredondo and others raise red flags when large companies and organizations, American and European, attempt to blanket Internet audiences with messages that do not account for regional tastes. They argue that the jump to rapid globalization with the expectation of appealing to traditionally disparate groups is unrealistic and likely to fail.

Recognition of national differences and the need to appeal to local tastes, no doubt, is sound advice, but none of that changes the universal nature of this medium. The Net's inherent reach is global. Any user can access any website and reach any e-mailbox from anyplace on earth. A resident of Zagreb can read the *London Times* or the *New York Times* or listen in to the BBC or CNN. A Croatian student can research free speech sites at Berkeley, and a professor at Rutgers can look in on Zagreb's HRTV. That has never before been possible in practice or in theory.

Some analysts, both social and political, disputed the claim by Net boosters that someday soon the "Electronic Village" of McLuhan will become a reality. They say that television and radio never globalized the world. Regional diversities and native cultures are stronger than ever. Although even that claim is open for debate, those analysts overlook the unique, interactive capabilities of Net audiences. The seemingly unremarkable addition of feedback, in fact, is a revolutionary innovation, one that radically alters the dynamics of traditional media. Interactivity will change global communication and do for McLuhan's vision what television could never do.

Some of these arguments against the globalizing effects of the Internet take for granted that audiences in the future, under the influence of the new media, will act like audiences of the past. The assumption is wrong. Audiences are defined by the reach of their media. Print and broadcast have traditionally been bound to an area by the newspaper deliverer, the drop box, and the transmitter, and their regional reach and regional focus have cultivated regional views.

Nothing limits the global stretch of the Internet, and its audiences accordingly will develop new horizons. Their sense of group will change from a geographic definition to a definition derived from special interests, such as professions and hobbies, and beliefs based on politics, religion, and philosophy. This is due to the reach of the Net and also to its interactive capacities, as we noted above. The world has never known a medium that allows a two-way flow of information, giving users the capacity to form a communication web of their own. Interaction and information exchange on the Net, so essential to the formation of any group, is already giving birth to new communities that never before could have formed. The smart money says an electronic "rapture" is here. The adventists who see the end of the old world and the beginning of a new millennium may be prophetic after all—only the changes may be more electronic than evangelical.

The expansive vision of the Internet is necessary to understand how the Internet will contribute to the integration of countries within the new European Union and, beyond that, how the Net eventually will embrace the countries of Central and Eastern Europe. As the adoption statistics show, Croatian Internet users are already well on their way.

INTERNET BASICS

Centralized and Decentralized Media

To understand the Internet and to recognize its power to impact Croatian society or *any* society, we need to acknowledge the differences between centralized and decentralized media. Simply put, a centralized medium works like a funnel. All the information is gathered into a central location, processed, then dispensed to broad audiences from a single point—a newspaper or broadcast station.

The integral role of the centralized media has been maintained by the size of its technology and the cost of its operation. News organizations use their big printing presses and powerful transmitters to send out their digested information. This machinery has guaranteed publishers and broadcasters their key roles. In years past, you simply could not move information to the masses without the large hardware, an obvious fact that makes centralized media easy to control. Extinguish the signal from a single transmitter and you snuff out the television station. Moreover, the huge investment in technology makes it difficult for new players to get into the game, even when laws permit it. The threshold of entry is just too high for anyone but the wealthiest interests.

A decentralized medium—and the Internet is the first large-scale example— works like a sieve. It allows all sources and all receivers of information to talk directly without the need for a middle man. There is no gathering, processing, and central-point dispensing. There is no central broker to gather, analyze, judge, interpret, and release the information; all that is done at the source.

Information does not channel through a central processing plant, and it does not have to pass muster with the editors, writers, and producers who prepare it for mass distribution. On the Internet, information sources can bypass the filters of news and distribute directly to the people, or more accurately, distribute for the people to access themselves.

Without high-tech presses or transmitters and the support staff needed to operate them, the Internet does not incur the expenses of conventional media ownership. For pocket change, anyone with an idea can set up an information site. The lower threshold opens the medium to anyone interested in taking on the assignment.

What does this decentralized distribution system with its universal access mean to the traditional media structure?

Without a doubt, the old media will have to endure new and truly different competition. We already see alternative news operations forming on the Web, some of them arising from a handful of like-minded people with something to say. Croatia has its share of these renegade operators running websites.[16]

They collect information and disseminate news, they offer more opinion and commentary, they shade the information with their own special bias, and they concentrate on special interests. In other words, they may be more newsletters than newspapers, and their audiences tend to be more targeted than mass. The simple fact is, as these alternative information sources grow, the centralized media will lose their status as the only game in town.

Does this mean that the traditional centralized media will wither and die? No, the same thing happened in the United States before the Web came along. Cable television, with its forty channels, cut deeply into network lineups of news and entertainment, but it didn't kill the networks so much as it chipped away at their supremacy and altered their style. Neither will the Web kill the conventional media, but it will further reduce their dominance and alter their style. It's safe to say that newspapers and networks will not go belly-up, nor will journalists go the way of blacksmiths. Historically, the world has never lost a medium; we have only altered the existing media to accommodate new ones.

When the Internet muscles in, it will challenge the mainstream press, no doubt diminishing the latter's central importance. This will be particularly true in those nations where the mainstream press is exposed as a mouthpiece for the state, and its information, stripped of objectivity, is seen as the official line. Information born on the Internet can lay bare these truths and deprive the mainstream press of credibility and relevance. In societies where the government depends on press to manage public thinking, the Internet can stand as a significant de-stabilizing force.

THE INTERNET AND THE TRADITIONAL MEDIA

The Web Will Impose Changes on Journalists

Despite the affinities, the histories of the traditional media haven't told us much about what to expect during these early days of the Internet. Two hundred years of newspapers and over seventy years with broadcast have hardly prepared us for a new medium that has few barriers to entry, one free of editorial oversight and lacking standards for accuracy and taste. Furthermore, the traditional media have shed no light on what we can expect when information choices number in the hundreds of thousands. How will people find the truth among these sources? How will they arrive at balance in their understanding of a story? How will they respond to the working press when they and reporters share the same access to national events, databases, and other primary sources? There are no precedents and few clues arising from the traditional media.

We do know that the Internet will change the flow of news and information into the public arena and will have some surprising impacts on the traditional media, particularly on the relationship between journalists and audiences every-where.

As prominence of the Web increases, it will likely impose several changes on the reporter's trade. In the United States and many European countries with an aggressive media presence on the Web, reporting techniques already have changed in subtle ways. The pace of news is quickening, and the telling of it is tightening. U.S. journalist Phillip Davis at National Public Radio (in an interview with Gary W. Selnow in December 2000) said that the Web has imposed new time pressures on journalists working in all the other media, especially in broadcasting. "Web news media can update the sites every few minutes. How can you beat that? In time, radio and television reporters will have to assume that audiences are already familiar with news developments and the breaking stories." Reporters will put a stopwatch on hot stories and keep a close eye on key websites.

As for the tightening of a news story, Randy Reddick, director of PCSNET, suggests in an article that traditional story structures don't hold on the Web and that the most effective news reporting requires two kinds of writing. First is the core piece, short and to the point, giving readers the gist of the event but not burdening them with detail. The early evidence is that they just won't read lengthy stories.

Second are background pieces linked to the core story. These are more com-plete and detail-rich, and they usually are less time-sensitive in that they offer historical analysis that does not change by the second. Reddick calls these "ar-chive pieces" and says they can be stored indefinitely and linked to many core stories. As with all news on the Web, archive pieces are increasingly offered in audio and video formats as well as in familiar text.

Describing an interesting outcome of the two-step method, Reddick writes: "Such a story, written in several distinct modules with an eye to an interactive environment, leads to a situation in which the audience takes part in creating the story it reads. Six people reading the same 'core' story could create for themselves six different story packages as they follow different combinations of links."[17]

This process suggests an era of participatory journalism in which the social outcomes are quite different from the those of traditional model, where everyone in the audience each day shares the same information. It's easy to see how people who read the same core story come away with a different view of the underlying issue.

Another change that the Web will likely impose on journalism is a fundamental alteration of the relationship between the reporter and the audience. Andrew Glass, Washington bureau chief for Cox newspapers, and a leading expert in the impact of the Internet on journalism, says that everyone with a computer has access to all the information—the sites, databases, information archives—and, therefore, "Journalists become end users and end users become journalists."

That's an interesting way of putting the shifting roles and the newly forming relationships between journalists and their audiences. With access to the raw information, average users can do much of the job that traditionally fell to professional journalists. When journalists and voters drink from the same pools of information, it alters the traditional hierarchy. Until now, information delivery has always been mostly a two-step process, with journalists at the top serving as the gate keepers and the interpreters of news and everyone else as recipients of the information that results. Most items that people came by first passed through the gate-keeping press. The journalists set the agendas by passing along some information and blocking out other information, but the readers and viewers caught only the items that passed through the filter.

The Internet will change that process by cutting a course around the press, giving users and voters the raw information with which to draw their own conclusions. As gate keeping lessens, interpretation functions of the press will change as well. For instance, in the coverage of politics and, particularly, political campaigns, the peripheral players, which in the past had almost no coverage in the mainstream media, will have direct access to voters, as will the advocates of third-string philosophies, theories, and ideas that often were overlooked in conventional coverage. In the United States, Jesse Ventura, governor of Minnesota, was one of the first political candidates to credit the Internet as a primary information tool. The third-party candidate had little funding and a weak organization, but through the Internet, he raised funds and recruited followers. At the end, with a Web-based campaign, he defeated two established candidates.

Perhaps not yet but in the near future, opposition parties in Croatia, systematically ignored by the mainstream press, will have a forum in which to be heard. Leading party control over the media mean nothing here. Voters may explore and interpret opposition views for themselves and make judgments that the press earlier made for them. As in Glass's comment, voters will become their own journalists.

As users cobble together their own rag-tag collections of sources, they will increasingly need to draw upon the fusion skills of journalists for analysis and context. This will not only keep journalists in the loop, but it also will impose on them heavy obligations to serve as arbiters, judges, historians, and teachers. The credibility of journalists will depend not only on their analyses but also on their abilities to divine the truth, hard enough when they're tearing stories off the AP wire, incredibly difficult when exploring this anarchic medium.

The question for professional Croatian journalists is this: Are they prepared to serve this expanded role? Perhaps more to the point, will the current system permit them the flexibility necessary to engage in the kind of analysis and interpretation of events demanded by the Net? Will the government's grasp loosen enough to allow them to do the job?

The free-for-all nature of the Web mocks a controlled press and exposes the pretenses of state-sponsored journalism. As greater numbers of Croatian people go on-line and see first-hand raw information about their own country and neighboring countries, the dominant media—press and broadcast alike—will be forced to change which stories they cover and how they cover them. If they do not make these changes, they will condemn mainstream Croatian journalism to irrelevancy, leaving the job to upstarts within the country and outsiders who will tell Croatian news from a decidedly un-Croatian point of view.

The Internet as a Research Tool

While altering the style and substance of reporting, the Internet will also offer journalists a host of new tools with which to conduct research and develop stories. Government, businesses, universities, think tanks, and other organizations post a huge amount of information on their sites, presenting reporters with a veritable smorgasbord of easy-to-access information custom-made for a profession that writes to deadlines.

Although Web penetration in Croatia is limited to about 6 percent of the population, already a number of the country's institutions have arrived on-line. The government hosts an elaborate site, which, like governments everywhere, toots its own horn and polishes its own image. One of the more promising moves of the new government, however, has been the installation of a website that contains a wealth of government information. This is in stark contrast to the promotion-only site maintained by the HDZ.

Mainstream Croatian media are on-line, including the dominant television station HRTV and newspapers such as *Vjesnik, Večernji list, Slobodna Dalmacija*, and *Nacional*. The universities in Zagreb, Split, Pula, and Osijek have sites, and so do a host of businesses, such as the Bank of Zagreb and the Hotel Intercontinental. These sites, paper-thin by and large, offer journalists little substance for story development, but they are a start and a confirmation of an institutional commitment in Croatia to the Internet. Their participation in Web-based activities is likely to grow along with the popularity of the Net among the Croatian people.

Internet users in Croatia, as everywhere, will find the on-line information both a blessing and a curse. Joining the "safer" institutional sites are crowds of unverified sources and unreliable sites that make using the Web for research a tricky business. These sites are often well written and nicely displayed; their sponsors' names sound legitimate, and their information looks authentic. They can mislead any user, but when they mislead a reporter, their unreliable information can spread like ripples in a pond. The mainstream press can extend the reach of these sites to larger audiences, and it can bestow on them an undeserved legitimacy, lending credence to the false information they provide. Fortunately, aware of the dangers but unwilling to discount an entire medium because of a few bad apples, reporters today come armed with checks and standards to thin out, if not eliminate, unreliable sources. Verification procedures are used routinely in newsrooms, and they have become staples of journalism education in the United States and abroad.

Every journalism school in the United States of even modest size now offers Web training for its students, including how to use the Web in journalism research and how to guard against the bogus sites. Professional organizations that offer continuation training for working journalists also provide lessons in Web research and source verification. The Poynter Institute, the premier professional journalism center in the United States, has been tracking the applications of the Net for journalists since the Web was developed. Poynter has been a booster of the Net, but it has always kept a wary eye on the medium's potential to sabotage journalists' best research efforts.[18]

Journalism schools and professional journalism organizations in Europe have been equally as aggressive in the use of the Web. For instance, the Danish School of Journalism in Arhus, the School of Journalism and Communications at the Hogeschool van Utrecht, the Netherlands, and the School of Journalism, Media & Cultural Studies at Cardiff University of Wales have formed a training consortium for journalists across Europe.[19] Organizations such as the European Journalism Center Training Program, the Freedom Forum, and the Forum for European Journalism Studies commit resources to training new and mid-career journalists in Eastern and Western Europe.[20] These organizations are designed to train journalists how to write for the Net and how to use it in their research.

Journalist organizations in Croatia have not been asleep at the switch. They, too, have recognized the importance of the Net for internal news consumption as well as for exporting Croatian news to outside news wires and foreign media. The International Center for Education of Journalists, located in Opatija (western Croatia), trains journalists from Central and Eastern European countries along with Croatian journalists.[21] The organization, which receives funding from the Open Society Institute, the European Union, and other supporters, runs monthly workshops that include extensive Web training in the ICEJ's dedicated Internet lab.

The Croatian Journalists' Association provides training and refresher courses specifically for Croatian journalists. It invites professional journalists and academics from around the world to teach journalism ethics, writing techniques, and investigative reporting at its training facility in central Zagreb. In 1997, the association installed a twenty-station Internet lab, which since has served as a training facility for all journalists who pass through the program. Although many newsrooms in Croatia are not yet on-line, the CJA has been preparing young journalists to use the Internet for research and for the distribution of news when the equipment is put in place.

Organizational Initiatives in Media Relations

While journalists are using the Web to research their stories, organizations are using the Web to connect with journalists. The Web has brought about significant changes in Journalism 101 and Public Relations 101, where both sets of students now look at the same resource from a different angle.

For organizations, the Web serves as a significant outreach tool. On their own website, organizations can discuss their values, present their own points of view, and assert their own agendas. They become their own publishers so they can do as they please. Savvy organizations recognize the Internet as a conspicuous link to conventional media, and they are using it to their advantage. Websites can be designed with journalists in mind, a kind of organic library that stocks the organization's resume, its goals and objectives, its point of view on developing issues. By feeding the journalists, this information can make its way into the print or broadcast telling of a story, and it can provide an organizational perspective that may otherwise go unreported.

In an informal study, journalists told researchers that they often turned first to a website for organizational information, for speech text and policy statements, and for reactions to fast changing events.[22] They also used websites as an on-line Rolodex to obtain the names and phone numbers of contacts—whom to call for clarification, whom to call for an interview. Some reporters turned to websites for photographs, which could be downloaded with two clicks of a mouse and the image pasted into a newspaper column or dropped into a newscast. Increasingly, air-quality sound and video clips will be available on the Web for use in radio and television reports.

Websites remain open twenty-four hours a day, so reporters, known to write at odd hours, can access information when they need it, unfettered by the restrictive work schedules of organizations. Websites, furthermore, are everywhere accessible. Reporters can reach them from a hotel room or a bar or, with cellular technology, from a beach. The always open and always reachable qualities increase the chances that reporters can make contact and that the organization's views will be represented in developing stories. Resourceful organizations can profit from these features by stocking their websites with the things that journalists want and need for their work.

E-mail, too, has become a fixture in modern reporting. It's a natural medium for people who are on the road and keep unusual hours. E-mail permits easy responses, it archives the incoming and outgoing messages, and it simplifies the distribution of correspondence to third parties—through "CCs" and forwarding. Reporters can attach documents, and with new graphic facilities, they can send photos, voice files, and formatted program files. The e-mail once looked upon as a simple conveyance of messages has become the U-Haul of cyberspace. Finally, e-mail is inexpensive, even free, and that puts it within reach of all takers, even the small players in the news business. E-mail is a remarkable success at keeping organizations and the press in touch.

CONCLUSION

The story of media involvement in the Web is a web in itself, one of truth and fiction, enlightenment and confusion. Journalists, accustomed to print and broadcast formats, have found a new and highly adaptable medium with which to disseminate their stories. They use it to distribute news, but they also use it to gather facts and information in the preparation of their reports. Meanwhile, organizations, businesses, political candidates, and others use the Web to tell their stories, many with the hope of attracting notice of the journalist who can carry the information into the mainstream press.

All the while, others lie in wait for the unsuspecting visitor—a journalist or not, although the journalist is a prize—with pranks and side shows and off-beat philosophies, hoping to draw someone's notice. From organizational sites, the journalists must cull legitimate news from PR hype, and from everywhere else on the Web, they must spot the jesters who would contaminate news stories with so much fiction. This is a medium of speed, where now is too late, where journalists must make snap judgments about what is real and what is counterfeit, about what is worthy of news and what is sucker's bait.

The United States and Western Europe, with populations of rapid adopters, are hopelessly caught up in this medium, but Croatia and other countries in Central and Eastern Europe are close behind. Chances are almost certain that they, too, will become swept away in the maelstrom, but amid all the negatives and all the silliness of this overheated medium, lies one very positive aspect for their emerging democracies: The Internet will change their staggering, hand-cuffed media. As we noted earlier, the Web's open marketplace of information exposes state-influenced media as the handmaidens of government, and it undermines the media's legitimacy and, so, their influence on the society. In the end, the Net can change the way a government does business with the media, and at long last that will change the government itself.

In countries around the world where the press works under the government's thumb, the Net may emerge as the "propaganda killer" of the third millennium. Ever since 1622, when the "Congregation for the Propagation of the Faith" was established in Rome, the apostles of thought control have been powerful bullies with all the muscle. Almost 400 years later, the media lords held sway. As long as their control of mass media was airtight, their propaganda was almost debate-proof. Who could contend with Goebbels' stranglehold on the German mind during Hitler's regime? Certainly not a few brave souls listening to their crystal sets. What could break Stalin's control of the written word? Not even the mass medium of television.

Now, the Internet—owned by everyone and owned by no one, where all people are senders and all are receivers—introduces into the public arena a communication tool that is truly different from anything we have seen before. The strength of this medium lies in its capacity to shift the power from the few to the many, to let the people talk back to their governments and to talk with each other, to introduce ideas and information into the public debate that before could have been halted with the stroke of a pen or the butt of a rifle.

The Internet was in its infancy at the time of Croatia's change from the rule of Tuđman and his oppressive HDZ to the more moderate government of Stipe Mesić. In the days ahead, as the people wait and watch the moves of the new government, they will not be isolated as they had been under the thumb of Tito or the fist of Tuđman. Now they can access information from internal sources of opposition and outside observers, and they can send their messages beyond their borders and among each other. The Internet holds forth the promise of providing a powerful two-way channel of information, and in this new millennium, that will change the chemistry among the people, the press, and politics in Croatia and other countries around the globe.

NOTES

1. Linda Bridges et al., "High-Tech Rejuvenation: Fifteen Trends in the Computer Industry," *PC Week*, March 1, 1999, 107.

2. Tracy Wilkinson, "Crisis in Yugoslavia; Manipulating the Media is Milošević's MO," *Los Angeles Times*, March 30, 1999, A 20.

3. The Following transcript is excerpted from NPR's *Morning Edition* series, "Letters from Kosovo." This installment is from February 5, 1999. Audio versions are available from: <http://allthingsconsidered.com/programs/morning/kosovo-emails.hmtl>.

BOB EDWARDS, host: Just days after a massacre last month in Kosovo, a teenage girl began e-mailing her experiences of living in the middle of a war zone to a pen pal in Berkeley, California. Excerpts of her messages, under a pseudonym, are presented through a dramatic reading in this report from Youth Radio's Finnegan Hamill.

FINNEGAN HAMILL, reporting: It all started because I had the week off from hockey practice. I went to a meeting of my church youth group. We had a visitor, a peace worker recently back from Kosovo. He brought with him the e-mail address of an Albanian girl my age, 16-year-old Adona. She had access to a computer and wanted to use it to correspond with other teens here in the United States. I decided to write her a letter when I got back from the meeting. The next day, I received the first of what was to be a series of letters from Adona that would change the way I look at the world.

"ADONA," read by BELIA MAYENO CHOY (Narrator): "Hello, Finnegan. I'm glad that you wrote to me so soon. About my English, I have learned it through the movies, school, special classes, etc., but mostly from TV. I can speak Serbian as well, Spanish and understand a bit of Turkish. I love learning languages. But I don't have much time to learn them. You never know what'll happen to you. One night, last week I think, we were all surrounded by police and armed forces. And if it wasn't for the OSCE observers, God knows how many victims would there be. And my flat was surrounded, too. I cannot describe you the fear. Some day before, there was a bomb explosion . . . Hello, Finne. I guess you're OK. Did I tell you that I'm not a practicing Muslim, and do you know why? Because if the Turks didn't force my grand-grandparents to change their religion, I might now have been a Catholic or an Orthodox. And I think religion is a good, clean and pure thing that in a way supports people in their life. Thanks to religion, I think many people are afraid of God, or believe that there is another world after we die, so they don't commit any crimes. Personally, I agree with DesCartes when he says that God is imagined by the human mind."

"Dear Finnegan, how did you pass on your exams? I hope good. About the music, I love listening to Rolling Stones, Sade, Jewel and R.E.M., my favorite. You don't know how I'm longing to go to a party, on a trip or anywhere. I must tell you, it's scary sometimes when the situation here gets really tensed and the whole family comes together and we talk about how and where will we be going in case of emergency, where we can find money. What do we do? Who do we call for help? Where do we keep our passports and other documents? We have also brought warm clothes in case we have to flee our homes and go to the mountains or elsewhere. And we are all prepared for the worst and taught that life goes on, no matter what."

"About the NATO thing, you know, I feel they should come here and protect us. I wish somebody could. I don't even know how many people get killed anymore. You just see them in the memorial pages of newspapers. I really don't want to end up raped, with no parts of body like the massacred ones. I wish nobody in the world, in the whole universe would have to go through what we are. You don't know how lucky you are to have a normal life. We all want to be free and living like you do. Finnegan, I'm telling you how I feel about this war and my friends feel the same. Bye, Adona, Kosovo. P.S., send me some photos of you. I'll be sending some of mine as soon as the scanner gets fixed."

4. Information from CNN Special Report on March 25, 1999, and from NPR reports, various dates in spring 1999.

5. It is difficult to be precise with Croatian population statistics. The last census was conducted in 1991, and conditions since then have altered the population considerably. This figure of 400,000 was calculated by applying a European average adult proportion (71 percent) to a total Croatian population estimate of 4.5 million.

6. *CyberAtlas: The Web Marketer's Guide to Online Facts.* Reporting results of a study conducted by IPSA, a Croatian survey research firm in Zagreb, August 19, 1999. See also <http://cyberatlas.internet.com/big_picture/demographics/article/0,1323,5911_186111,00.html>.

7. E. M. Rogers and F. F. Shoemaker, *Communication of Innovations: A Cross-Cultural Approach*, 2nd ed. (New York: Free Press, 1971).

8. See Croatia.net <http://www.croatia.net> for an extensive list of on-line sources for Croatian news. There are a few examples of websites that provide on-line news about Croatia: HINA (Official Croatian news agency: <http://www.hina.hr/nws-bin/hot.cgi>; Croatian Information Center (Non-profit organization presenting news about the Croatian Diaspora): <http://www.hic.hr>; Croatian Internet News (Independent news organization): <http://www.bosnet.org>; and Info Trend (Business news): <http://www.trend.hr>.

9. Robert Hobbes Zakon in "The Internet: A Timeline." See website: <http://info.isoc.org/guest/zakon/Internet/History/HIT.html>.

10. The previous four points were described in Robert Fox, "European Online Explosion," *Communications of the ACM* 42, no. 8 (August 1999): 9.

11. "ISP market to reach 14 billion," *Computer Weekly*, April 22, 1999.

12. Several of these items have been suggested on <http://www.lsilink.com/why_multi.html>, November 26, 1997, and Business2.0 (on-line magazine), "European Internet Growth" September 22, 2000 <http://www.business2.com/content/research/numbers/2000/09/22/19524>.

13. Some observers are skeptical of the effectiveness of deregulation of the telecommunication industry. They argue that the monopolies are so well entrenched in the marketplace and so well connected politically that they will continue to dominate the industry without significant competitive pressures. If this is so, cost reductions and wider Internet use may remain unrealistic expectations.

14. Sadly, the lowering of impulse charges for phone use, experienced across most of Western Europe, has not occurred in Croatia. Soon after the 1999 separation of the Croatian Post (HP) and Croatian Telecommunication Service (HT), Ivica Mudrinic, chairman of the HT, said there would be no reduction in the impulse costs. He said that these charges were already low enough. This comes from the British Broadcasting Corporation reporting a HINA news agency release, December 30, 1998.

15. Bruno Giussani, "Europe's Internet Lag: An American Fabrication?" *Cbyertimes*, September 14, 1999. See website: <http://www.nytimes.com>.

16. Examples of nonofficial websites providing information about Croatia: CroGuide.com (Tourism Information): <http://ctirs.iii.hr/GB/drzave/cl.asp>; Croatian Music Information Center: <http://www.mic.hr/>; Croatian Information Center (CroNet.com): <http://ns.cronet.com/cic/cic.htm>; Croatian Information Service for Biodiversity: <http://pubwww.srce.hr/botanic/cisb/Edoc/biodataE.html>.

17. Quotation taken from Randy Reddick, *News Backgrounder: A Briefing Paper for Journalists*. Reddick is the director of the Foundation for American Communications, an independent nonprofit educational institution for journalists. The new *Backgrounder* is part of an ongoing series of briefing papers published by the organization.

18. See the Poynter Institute's website: <www.poynter.org>.

19. See <http://www.cf.ac.uk/jomec/post/EuroMA/euroma.html>.

20. See websites: European Journalism Center Training Program <www.ejc.nl>, The Freedom Forum <www.mediastudies.org>, and the Forum for European Journalism Studies <www.djh.dk/fejs>.

21. The ICEJ was established in 1997 under the direction of this book's co-author, Dr. Stjepan Malovic.

22. From informal discussions with American journalists in 1997.

Journalists Killed during the War

Figures about journalists who died in war may be the most convincing way to demonstrate that the profession has its dangers. Several sources report on journalists killed during the war in Slovenia, Croatia, and Bosnia and Herzegovina. The Freedom Forum reports reliable figures, which we present here.

These data cover the period from 1991 to 1996. All together, during the five years of war in the region, fifty-four journalists were killed in hostilities. The worst year was 1991, when twenty-three journalists died in Croatia and two perished in Slovenia. During the five years of war in Croatia, thirty journalists died.

1991

Croatia

1. ZORAN AMIDŽIĆ, BELGRADE TELEVISION, YUGOSLAVIA. Died with three other camera crewmembers on October 9, when their car was hit by a mortar round near Petrinja, south of Zagreb. Belgrade radio blamed the attack on Croat forces.

2. PIERRE BLANCHET, *NOUVEL OBSERVATEUR*, FRANCE. Killed September 19, when the car he and two other journalists were traveling in struck a land mine outside an army barracks near the village of Petrinja, south of Zagreb. He was 47.

3. PETER BRYSKY, FREELANCE. A photographer. He was killed on October 6 by mortar fire in Karlovac.

4. JUSUF ČEHAJIĆ, *VEČERNJE NOVOSTI*, YUGOSLAVIA. Disappeared on October 12 under unknown circumstances in Vukovar. He was a writer for his Belgrade tabloid.

5. SINIŠA GLAVAŠEVIĆ, RADIO VUKOVAR, CROATIA. Killed by Serbian fighters when they captured Vukovar on November 18. His body was one of 200 exhumed from the Ovčara mass grave near Vukovar. At 33, he was Radio Vukovar's most famous reporter. His last report told listeners about a Red Cross convoy. "The agony is over," he said.

6. SRETEN ILIČ, RADIO ŠABAC, YUGOSLAVIA. Died with three camera crew members from Belgrade Television on October 9, when their car came under attack near Petrinja.

7. ŽARKO KAIĆ, CROATIAN TELEVISION, CROATIA. Killed August 28 near Osijek by gunfire from a Yugoslav Federal Army armored vehicle. He was a cameraman.

8. ŽIVKO KRSTIČEVIĆ, WORLDWIDE TELEVISION NEWS (WTN), UNITED KINGDOM. Killed December 30 by a mortar shell explosion in Karlovac near fighting between Croat forces and the federal army. "A mortar shell landed right beside him," said WTN producer Eric Bremmer. "It seems to have been the only shell that landed." Krstičević was 37.

9. GENNADY KURINNOY, SOVIET TELEVISION AND RADIO, RUSSIA. A cameraman-correspondent in Belgrade. He disappeared with a colleague on September 1. He was last seen driving toward Zagreb from Belgrade.

10. GORDAN LEDERER, CROATIAN TELEVISION, CROATIA. Killed August 10 by Serbian militia while filming a battle outside Kostajnica. A cameraman, he was hit first by a sniper and later by a mortar round. The Yugoslav army would not allow a helicopter to take him to Zagreb, and he died en route to the hospital.

11. BODISLAV MARJANOVIĆ, FREELANCE. Killed November 16 in Vukovar. He was 28. No other details of his death are known.

12. DEJAN MILIČEVIĆ, BELGRADE TELEVISION, YUGOSLAVIA. Died with two other camera crew members and a radio reporter on October 9, when their car came under mortar attack near Petrinja, south of Zagreb.

13. VICTOR NOGIN, SOVIET TELEVISION, RUSSIA. The Soviet Television bureau chief in Belgrade. He disappeared with a colleague September 1. He was last seen driving toward Zagreb from Belgrade.

14. STJEPAN PENIĆ, *GLAS SLAVONIJE*, CROATIA. Shot and killed August 4 on a soccer field in Dalj after he was abducted from his home by Serbian militia. His body was left for three days before it was burned by the guerrillas who killed him. He was a Croatian radio producer.

15. BORA PETROVĆ, BELGRADE TELEVISION, YUGOSLAVIA. Died with two other camera crew members and a radio reporter on October 9, when their car came under mortar attack near Petrinja, south of Zagreb.

16. ÐURO PODBOJ, CROATIAN TELEVISION, CROATIA. Killed August 29 in Beli Manastir during an attack by Serbian forces.

17. ZDENKO PURGAR, *BOROVO*, CROATIA. Knifed to death in Borovo on November 25. The Croatian Journalists' Union believes the attack was related to his reporting.

18. DAMIEN RUEDIN, RADIO SUISSE ROMANDE, SWITZERLAND. Killed September 19 by a land mine outside an army barracks near the village of Petrinja.

19. EGON SCOTLAND, *SUDDEUTSCHE ZEITUNG*, GERMANY. Shot in the stomach with a dum-dum bullet on July 26 by Serbian militia while riding in a clearly marked press car. He had been searching for an inexperienced colleague who was late in coming back from the field. A Knight Fellow at Stanford University in 1989–1990, he was carrying a poem at the time of his death. It was written by a resident of the embattled town of Osijek, Croatia, and it urged reporters to remember the people who died in war, "because a number has no name and no stolen future."

20. NIKOLA STOJANAC, CROATIAN TELEVISION, CROATIA. Killed by machine gun fire from Yugoslav Army jets on September 15. He was filming the army warplanes at Gospic when he was slain.

21. PAVO URBAN, FREELANCE. A photographer, he was killed December 6, during the shelling of Dubrovnik. He was 22.

22. MILAN ŽEGARAC, *VEČERNJE NOVOSTI*, YUGOSLAVIA. Killed October 7 in a crossfire in Vukovar.

Slovenia

1. NICK VOGEL, FREELANCE. An Austrian photographer, he was killed June 28, when his car was struck by a missile on the runway of the Ljubljana airport during an attack by the Yugoslav Federal Army. Colleague Norbert Werner died with him.

2. NORBERT WERNER, FREELANCE. Killed June 28 with colleague Nick Vogel, when a missile struck their car at the Ljubljana airport during a Yugoslav Federal Army attack. He was a photographer.

1992

Bosnia-Herzegovina

1. SALKO HONDO, *OSLOBOĐENJE*, BOSNIA-HERZEGOVINA. A photographer for the daily newspaper in Sarajevo, he was killed July 16, when a mortar shell exploded in the city's open-air market.

2. DAVID KAPLAN, ABC, UNITED STATES. A producer. An unidentified sniper shot him August 13, while riding in a convoy taking Serb officials from Sarajevo airport to UN headquarters. The bullet entered the vehicle between the letters "T" and "V" plainly taped to its exterior. A twenty-year veteran with ABC, he died within hours of arriving in the Bosnian capital.

3. KRUNO MARINOVIĆ, CROATIAN RADIO, CROATIA. Disappeared from his home in Foča on April 14. He was believed abducted by the Yogoslav Army or armed Serbs and was never heard from again.

4. JORDIPUJOL PUENTE, *AVUI*, SPAIN. Killed May 17, when a mortar shell exploded in a Sarajevo suburb. A photographer, he was the earliest known journalist killed while covering the war in Bosnia-Herzegovina.

5. KJASIF SMAJLOVIĆ, *OSLOBOĐENJE*, BOSNIA-HERZEGOVINA. Killed in his office by Serbian soldiers on April 19. He was a correspondent in Zvornik for the Sarajevo daily newspaper.

6. IVO STANDEKER, *MLADINA*, SLOVENIA. Died June 16 after being hit in a Serbian mortar attack on the Sarajevo suburb of Dobrinja while working for his magazine. He was trying to help a wounded colleague.

7. TIHOMIR TUNUKOVIĆ, BBC, UNITED KINGDOM. Killed instantly near Travnik on November 1 while on assignment as a cameraman. His armored Land Rover was destroyed by an antiaircraft shell fired from a hilltop by Bosnian Serbs.

Croatia

1. PAUL JENKS, EUROPEAN PRESS-PHOTO AGENCY, GERMANY. Shot January 17 by a sniper near Osijek. A British photographer, he was working for a Frankfurt-based photo agency when he was shot in the back of the neck some 800 yards from Serbian fighting positions. His family believes Jenks was assassinated to stop him from revealing details about the murder of Swiss journalist Christian Wurtenberg. Wurtenberg was strangled after infiltrating the extreme right-wing Croatian International Brigade. Jenks was 29.

2. IVAN MARŠIĆ, RADIO BARANJA-OSIJEK, CROATIA. The details of this journalist's death on June 9 are uncertain.

3. CHRISTIAN WURTENBERG, FREELANCE. Strangled January 6 after having joined and infiltrated the extreme right-wing Croatian International Brigade. He was killed while on guard duty near Osijek. He was a 27-year-old Swiss freelance journalist. Photojournalist colleague Paul Jenks was murdered on January 17 by a sniper in what family members believe was an assassination to keep the details of Wurtenberg's death a mystery.

1993

Bosnia-Herzegovina

1. IBRAHIM GOSKEL, FREELANCE. Shot July 10 at Sarajevo Airport. He carried a British passport.

2. DOMINIQUE LONNEUX, FREELANCE. Died of wounds suffered June 2, when the UN Protection Force convoy in which he was riding came under attack in the western part of the country.

3. TASAR, OMER, FREELANCE. Killed by a sniper June 27, while attending a funeral in Sarajevo for seven young people who had died in shelling the previous day.

4. GUIDO PULETTI, FREELANCE. Shot May 29 with two relief workers during an ambush on a road in central Bosnia by assailants of unknown nationality. The victims may have been slain for relief supplies.

5. ŽELJKO RUŽIČIĆ, RTV BOSNIA AND HERZEGOVINA, BOSNIA-HERZEGOVINA. Died February 3, when a grenade exploded in front of the presidential offices in Sarajevo. He was a Croat.

6. KARMELA STOJANOVIĆ, *OSLOBOĐENJE*, BOSNIA-HERZEGOVINA. Killed by a sniper January 10 at her home in Sarajevo, the third reporter on her newspaper to be killed in two years. Two others disappeared and are presumed dead.

1994

Bosnia-Herzegovina

1. BRYAN BRINTON, FREELANCE. Killed May 1, when the car in which he was riding to Mostar with other journalists struck a land mine. He was on assignment for the Seattle-based Magnolia News. He had contacted Magnolia one week before from Croatia, offering his photos for free in exchange for press credentials.

2. DARIO D'ANGELO, RAI-TV, ITALY. Killed January 28, along with two other Italian TV journalists, when mortar rounds fired by Bosnian Croat forces struck his vehicle. He was entering Mostar to film a documentary about children orphaned by war. He was a cameraman.

3. MARCO LUCHETTA, RAI-TV, ITALY. Killed along with two other Italian TV journalists on January 28. His vehicle was struck by mortar rounds fired by Bosnian Croat forces. He was entering Mostar to film a documentary about children orphaned by war. He was 41 years old.

4. MOHAMMED HUSSEIN NAVAB, *KEYAN*, IRAN. A correspondent for a Tehran daily, he was murdered August 30 near Mostar by unidentified gunmen. His body was found September 5 by Iranian officials who said he had been abducted and killed by Croat militiamen.

5. ALESSANDRO OTA, RAI-TV, ITALY. Killed January 28, along with two other Italian TV journalists, when his vehicle was struck by mortar rounds fired by Bosnian Croat forces. He was entering Mostar to film a documentary about children orphaned by war. He was a 37-year-old technician.

6. FRANCIS TOMASIC, *SPIN*, UNITED STATES. Killed May 1, six miles north of Mostar, when the vehicle in which he and two colleagues were riding hit a land mine. He was a translator and photographer working with William Vollman, a reporter for *Spin* magazine, who was wounded in the incident. Tomasic was 36.

Croatia

1. JOHN HASEK, FREELANCE. Died January 1 in a Prague hospital from injuries suffered June 23, 1993, when his car crashed in the mountains. A retired Canadian paratrooper, he was investigating Canada's peacekeeping operations in the former Yugoslavia. He was 55.

1995

Bosnia-Herzegovina

1. SAŠA KOLEVSKI, BOSNIAN SERB TELEVISION, BOSNIA-HERZEGOVINA. Killed by Bosnian troops September 23, along with his driver, Goran Pejčinović, when they were caught in crossfire during fighting on Mount Ozren. He was a cameraman based in Banja Luka.

2. KARIM ZAIMOVIĆ, *DANI*, BOSNIA-HERZEGOVINA. Died August 15 of injuries suffered two weeks earlier, when he was hit by shrapnel from a rocket-propelled

grenade not far from downtown Sarajevo. He was cultural editor for his weekly magazine. He was 24.

Croatia

1. JOHN SCHOFIELD, BBC, UNITED KINGDOM. Killed August 9 near Vrginmost when Croat forces fired on the radio reporter and his BBC television colleagues as they stopped on the way from Zagreb to Bihać. The TV crew was trying to film houses burning in the battle zone. His widow, Susannah Schofield, gave birth to the couple's daughter on April 8, eight months after his death. He was 29.

1996

Croatia

1. NIKŠA ANTONINI, *SLOBODNA DALMACIJA*, CROATIA. Died in the April 3 airplane crash that claimed the lives of U.S. Commerce Secretary Ron Brown and thirty-four others. Antonini, 40, was a photographer for his Split-based daily newspaper, working out of its Zagreb office. The plane crashed during a storm en route from Tuzla to Dubrovnik.

2. NATHANIEL C. NASH, *NEW YORK TIMES*, UNITED STATES. Died April 3 in the plane crash in Croatia that killed U.S. Commerce Secretary Ron Brown and thirty-four others. He was his newspaper's Frankfurt, Germany, bureau chief and covered economics. Before his European assignment, he was chief of the Buenos Aires bureau for three years. Publisher Arthur Sulzberger Jr. said his newspaper had "lost a friend and colleague known as much for his gentleness of spirit as for his keen journalistic abilities." Nash was 44.

Text of Meeting between Secretary of State Madeleine K. Albright and Independent Media Representatives, Zagreb, Croatia, August 30, 1998 (as released by the Office of the Spokesman, U.S. Department of State)

SECRETARY ALBRIGHT: Let me begin a little bit more formally than usual. I want to thank you for giving me the opportunity to meet with you and to salute you for the work you are doing on behalf of free expression and independent journalism in Croatia. Some people believe patriotism requires conformity of viewpoints. You understand that true patriotism means love of country, not support for any particular government or ideology. You know that Croatia's standing and image in the world depend on the extent to which it welcomes the diversity of peoples, cultures, and beliefs that have long co-existed here.

The United States recognizes that this is a nation with many political voices and an active opposition. We have urged democratic reform and respect for a free media so that there is a level playing field for all. We have said that Croatia can rejoin Europe, but only as an open and democratic society. And we believe it takes a good deal more than elections to build democracy. It requires respect for the rule of law and for minority views. And it requires an independent media to keep leaders accountable.

We are proud that we have been able to support your work, through our diplomacy, through our aid programs, and through the efforts of Ambassador Montgomery. We will continue to do so. In fact, our policy on this issue was set by our first Secretary of State, Thomas Jefferson, who said that given a choice between "a government without newspapers, or newspapers without a government, I should not hesitate to prefer the latter." I want to thank you again for your efforts to give all the people of conscience in this country a voice, and most of all I want to hear from you.

Let me just say before we begin that I have been especially looking forward to this meeting, not so much as Secretary of State, but as Madeleine Albright who used to write in my academic life about the role of the press and political change. And my dissertation was about the role of the Czech press in the "Prague Spring" and I wrote a book about the Polish press during the Solidarity period, and so I have been always particularly interested in the role of the media in bringing about political change. And so meeting with all of you here is not just of interest to me as the American Secretary of State but as someone who is very, very interested in the kind of work that you are doing, and the role that you are playing in opening up Croatia. So I'd be very interested if you could tell me about Forum 21's strategy to reform the Croatian media.

QUESTION: Madam Secretary, thank you very much for your invitation and your great support for all Croatian journalists, not only for our group, for all Croatian journalists who would like to promote and defend fair and impartial media. We would also like to thank you for your support from the democratic, international community. But we still think that those problems of media must be and should be resolved within our house, only by dialogue, and the problem is that this dialogue is still to be accepted by the present authorities. This is the biggest problem.

Anyway, before I give a word to my colleague, Drazen Vukov Colic, who will describe the global media situation in Croatia, I would like to give you a small gift. This is a translation of an American book, "Freedom of Expression Handbook," that was edited by the Croatian Journalists Association, and this is the first step to develop a conscience of how media are important for all our members, and here is the program of Forum 21 in English. So, this is our small gift and it was edited also with the help of American donators.

SECRETARY ALBRIGHT: Thank you.

QUESTION: Thank you very much, Madam Secretary. We understand very well that freedom of the media is not a God given gift from the powerful to the obedient. So we are trying to seize that opportunity with both hands in every issue, every program, every article. I am going very shortly to inform you what the general public in Croatia thinks about freedom of the media. There was recently research done on that subject, and it is very indicative that the statement that "There is no democracy, full democracy, without full media freedom," is supported by 70% of the people. The second important question of "What is the level, the general state of the freedom of the media today in Croatia? Much higher and in a much better state than it was before in the former state?" and affirmative answer is only by 40% of the people. So 60% of the people are not satisfied with the state of the freedom of the media in Croatia.

There is the second important question which would partially concern our meeting too. That is the statement that the international community uses the question of the media freedom in an unfair way as a tool for unjust political pressure. Believe it or not, that statement is believed in Croatia by 32% of people. So you see, by those examples, what is the vision, in the public mind, in the public opinion. The second important question is what are the most important sources of the information on the media market.

The most important sources, of course, are the influential ones. And now we have the data which are not very encouraging for print media which are much more free than electronic media, TV and radio. So, the print media are much more free but their influence is very, very low and very limited. That shows the following: HRTV, the state-controlled television station, is regularly taken as the most important source of information by 74% percent of the population.

Dailies, which four out of six are state-controlled, but nevertheless as the main source of information, dailies are influencing only 8% of the population. And when we are talking about weeklies, which are also very important, they represent the main source of information for only 2–3% of the population. If one compares these facts, I mean the fact that information by oral communication, by conversation with friends, and family, that the main source of news oral communication is by 5%—2% more than the weeklies! So that's a general point.

I will tell you a few words about the division in the print media. It's colloquially dependent and nationally constructive, state-building media which do not exist anywhere else except in Croatia. So, the main division lines do not lie in some explicit ideological differences, but in values, in relation toward criticism of the ruling structure, in relation to most important democratic values, in relation to opening of Croatia to the world, in relation to taking up and confirming ourselves to the highest values and standards of the Western civilization. Those are the division lines. And, along those lines the polemics are going, very, very hard polemics, which are taking place almost every day between independent and so called state-controlled media. Of course, the print media are relatively more free than the electronic ones, but the state is trying to impose its will even on that freer parts of the media landscape by law suits, hundreds of them, both against journalists and newspapers, and by very limited and monopolistic distribution network for selling newspapers, and also by some kind of unjust taxes and financial pressure on the independent print media.

Let me conclude with only a few words about the Croatian Journalists' Association because I am also speaking on behalf of it. Our lady president is unfortunately absent, she is sending you her warmest and most cordial regards. The leadership of our association is very liberal, we must say, and that's very, very important. Very active in defending the freedom of the press, very open in promoting the international cooperation. Only one fact to illustrate that: Under the umbrella of the organizational network, Forum 21 was also built as part of the Journalists' Association, which is of course promoting the idea of public television, and with that I would like to conclude my remarks. Thank you very much, I was personally very encouraged by your opening statement.

SECRETARY ALBRIGHT: Thank you.

QUESTION: Thank you. I must say that Forum 21 is not a political party or political group, because we think that journalism must be separated from politics. We must deal with politics because politics deals with us, but we think that one day these two things will be finally separated.

I think that the biggest problem in Croatia is that politics still directly controls the great majority of the media, including the biggest and the most influential one which is HRT (Croatian Radio and Television). HRT is still the most influential media, the most visible, and the most controlled one. We see that the ruling party is trying to keep control over the public TV as long as possible, because six months ago Forum 21 proposed a change of the law on public broadcasting and we sent this proposal to all members of parliament, but the opposition parties were the only ones to accept our proposal, our draft, but this proposal was turned down in parliament by HDZ. We are now waiting for their new draft.

In the meantime, personnel changes at the top of HRT are not enough, because we must change the system. So, whether the new director is more liberal or less liberal than the previous one is not so important, because the system should be changed. It means above all legislation. We must change the legislation and adopt a modern broadcast law, as well as a law on private broadcasting, because these issues are connected. Also, this new law or any other law should be applied. Application of this law or any other law is very important, because our present law is not very bad, but is not being applied and that is also a problem.

The biggest problem clearly is that the office of the President of the Republic should not play the role of the editor-in-chief of all media, electronic and print. This is a very big, a very important issue. We think that the democratization of HRT, introducing the common Western standards, is essential for Croatia, because this is the most important source of information. We think that HRT needs deep and complete reform, not only by certain personalities at the top, and we as Forum 21 are ready to cooperate, but so far the ruling party has refused the dialogue. This is a very big problem.

I must stress that HRT is not the only problem. There is also the problem of small private TV and radio stations, you will hear more from my colleague, but in any case, Forum 21 will continue to fight for reform of the complete media landscape in Croatia in trying to introduce professional and democratic standards which for the moment are absent.

There is another problem also, how to reform the system, and we sent proposals. At this moment, I think that the most important issue is privatization of the third channel, and my colleague Dubravko Merlic will explain why.

QUESTION: Madam Secretary, thank you for supporting free media in Croatia. I am Dubravko Merlic, I am a member of Forum 21, but also I am an employee of HRT, with a lot of personal problems because there is no way a professional journalist can work in that house, yet.

We believe that HRT should be changed from not state-controlled but party, or to be more specific, President's office-controlled institution to public institution, and beside changes of the law, we think that the best way to improve the situation at HRT is to have competition. That's why we in Forum 21 and I can say the general public in Croatia, we believe that the third channel, the existing third channel of Croatian Television, should be privatized because that's the fastest and the cheapest way to have competition and private media.

The ruling party believes that the fourth, non-existing channel, should be given for competition for private investment. But that will be small and expensive and won't affect next parliamentary elections. Thank you.

QUESTION: Thank you. Drazen Vukov Colic also mentioned a very important problem, distribution, control of the distribution of the press. So probably Sanja Modric should explain.

QUESTION: I am very glad to meet you here in Zagreb. My name is Sanja Modric, I am assistant editor-in-chief for domestic political affairs. My newspaper is a daily newspaper, it's rather new, it has been on the market for less than five months, and since we are concerned with the circulation, we are now the second daily newspaper in Croatia, we should have a lot of money, a huge amount of money every day, because we really sell our newspaper every day in more than 80,000 copies.

But we are in trouble. This is because, it may sound bizarre, but our product is sold by—I'll tell you whom, and we just don't get our money back for this transaction. This is because the distribution in this country is really terribly monopolized. The firm which distributes printed press in Croatia has existed for tens of years, but it was privatized recently, several years ago, and the most influential man in this firm, is called Tisak, or roughly translated Print, is a man with a very strong political background in political circles, and what he does, well, everybody who comes from abroad tells us don't sell newspapers through Tisak. But in this country we don't have, we have some other distributors, but they are either very small or have a very limited regional network.

So, we are actually being blackmailed, we have to work with him and he won't give us the money back. So this is not only the problem of Jutarnji List, it is also the problem of, I don't know, Feral Tribune and Nacional and all other independent newspapers. But, we don't see any solution to this problem so far, because we don't have any other choice. People from abroad, again, would say or say very frequently, why don't publishers sue him? Well, Feral Tribune has tried that, but the problem of courts and justice in this country is that they are very, very slow. So, if you get the verdict in five years, you are under the ground.

What our publishers do is they try to bargain, they try to get at least small amounts, they wait for three months, for five months. This is one of the most serious problems of the independent print media.

SECRETARY ALBRIGHT: How do you get your paper?

QUESTION: We buy it on the market.

SECRETARY ALBRIGHT: And that's not a monopoly? That's not controlled?

QUESTION: No.

QUESTION: The government also tries to control not only the print media, but all those small private radio and TV stations. Zrinka Vrabec Mojzes is the editor-in-chief—

QUESTION: Ex-editor-in-chief. I work for one of the rare independent radio stations which managed to survive in this country. Radio 101 was founded as the first independent students' radio station during communist times, 14 years ago. Since 1995 we have had to struggle to keep our own frequency, and to keep our own independence, and we were saved thanks to the biggest demonstration which took place about two and a half years ago on the main square in Zagreb, when 120,000 people demonstrated because they did not want the state to take over our station and to have it shut down.

But we are one of the examples of how local media in this country, which are really having troubles to survive and to operate positively in the financial way. The key body which decides about the destiny of independent media in this country is the Telecommunications Council which is appointed by the parliament and, as in every democratic country, it should decide about licenses according to the quality of feasibility studies offered to the Council. However, this Council is actually formed by high-ranking politicians from the ruling party, and not by media professionals, journalists, or people who are just public personalities, and it actually does not decide about licenses, evaluating the programs which are offered, but it rather evaluates appropriateness of the existing or future owners of a certain media.

So, things look very nice on paper, they say there are more than 120 pilot radio stations in the country, and there are about 15 pilot local TV stations in the country, but in real life, more than 90% of those local media are actually controlled by the ruling party, through their owners, which are members or relatives or friends of the people from the ruling party.

What they actually do is they either deny you a license or they try to destroy you financially, or they try to make power transmitters so weak that you can't reach anybody, and this is the recipe they actually use in every other case in the country. Radio 101 was saved because it's a local radio station but it broadcasts here in Zagreb, which is the capital of Croatia and where people are brave enough to go out into the streets and demonstrate. But in small urban areas, people are still frightened, people have been threatened by different members of the ruling party, they can lose jobs, they can do very bad things to them, and this is why people are frightened to actually say something, and this is why many local independent radio stations were shut down during the past few years.

And now those which are able to broadcast, which have their legal papers, they are now facing financial problems. This is being done in a more subtle way. They say OK, you have your license, but it's almost impossible to make high-quality standard programs and to make enough money to pay people to do those programs. And all the donations which these local radio and TV stations have received are not enough. Unfortunately, they can buy new equipment, but there isn't enough money to pay everyday's programs. This is one problem. On the other hand, the minute you receive donations you are accused of being a traitor of your country, paid by agents of CIA or FBI, or whoever, it doesn't matter. It's very difficult to work for an independent media, because they know that you can't make money, you can't pay people, and, on the other hand, in public, by the state-owned media, you are accused all the time of working against your own country, of being a traitor, of doing bad things in collaboration with the bad international community and the United States, and this xenophobia is something that has been around.

QUESTION: It seems that we have a very, very sensitive government. If you try to write or publish something slightly critical, they automatically seek protection from the courts. So, Vesna Alaburic is a lawyer with caseloads of over five hundred cases.

QUESTION: Madam Secretary, besides our efforts to establish a legal framework, which would be really democratic and liberal, we have a lot of work every day with lawsuits against journalists and publishers. At this moment in this country, we are world champions in the number of law suits. We have more than five hundred cases—criminal cases and civil proceedings.

The criminal cases are against journalists who are accused for defamation and insults, and civil cases are against publishers for damages. About ninety percent of plaintiffs are public figures, mostly politicians, members of their families, and businessmen who are closely connected to the government. So, I had the opportunity to know almost all members of our political establishment, because they all sue some journalist or some publisher. I know all members of our government, maybe even the President, if he recalls being subpoenaed as a witness to one of those cases, and other businessmen and other persons.

I wouldn't bother you very much with that, but I would like to stress just three problems with that. Concerning criminal proceedings, the problem is that there is a tremendous chilling effect. If journalists are fined for publishing the truth, you can't believe it, but they could be sentenced to imprisonment because of publishing the truth. That is why the Croatian Journalist's Association, besides efforts in the last two years to have a more democratic and liberal penal code, has planned to start campaigning for the reform of penal codes. Concerning civil proceedings, the problems are extremely high amount of damages that are given to plaintiffs and can really cause the bankruptcy of independent publishers. There is probably no need to stress that, if Feral Tribune would get two verdicts for about fifty thousand dollars, then Feral Tribune would be bankrupt.

Of course, we can go to Strasbourg and the European court of human rights after all the legal steps in our country. That could mean that in five or six years we could win the case in Strasbourg, but Feral Tribune or some other independent publisher would go bankrupt in the meantime. But, these problems are concerning our judiciary. We have some very good independent judges, but in general we really can't count on an independent judiciary. That's why all these cases are extremely important and have a tremendous chilling effect, and we would like to change something concerning that. We are trying to do that by publishing this book, we are preparing another one with verdicts of the European court of human rights, to introduce European standards to our courts.

We organized a lot of panel discussions and cooperated very much with lawyers and judges from European countries and the U.S. We think that in a couple of years, we'll have a democratic legal framework and proper courts of practice as in other European countries, but the question is who will survive until then. I would just like to tell you that we really highly appreciate all the help and support that are given to us by the U.S. Government and non-government organizations, officials and activists, and that we are very glad to have U.S. Ambassador to Croatia Mr. Montgomery, because he is really our friend. He is very willing to help us whenever we need it, even he initiates it. Thank you very much.

QUESTION: How our judicial system functions in those cases can be illustrated with the case of our colleague Gordana Grbic.

QUESTION: Ms. Secretary, thank you for this opportunity. In the beginning, I would like to say something very personal. As a woman, I am very satisfied that such an important position in the U.S. administration is held by such a capable woman as you are. I am very satisfied, because in three days the Croatian Television has to abide by the court verdict and allow me to return to my previous place as a journalist on Croatian Television.

Six years ago, I was fired illegally and, until now, they had not shown any wish to do that. I will insist on providing the court's decision although currently I don't intend to go back. I'm quite satisfied with the daily newspaper Novi List, where I am working now, and I don't think that, at this moment and in these circumstances, I could do my journalist job as professionally on Croatian Television as I can in Novi List. So, I'm really happy that I don't depend on Croatian Television and that I do not have to work there and that I have a choice to do my job in Novi List.

QUESTION: And our colleague Zeljka Ogresta, one of the best and most popular TV journalists in Croatia was removed from the screen two years ago, without any explanation and she is still not working. She's just receiving her salary and is not working. She will describe her case.

QUESTION: Thank you Madam Secretary for coming. I would just like to let you know that the funny thing is that I am part of the entertainment media, but, as you know, the chief editor of the entertainment division has to be a party official. So, you can imagine how entertaining that combination is.

QUESTION: We have unofficial information that the President of the Republic does not like Zeljka's face, so she was removed. Any questions?

SECRETARY ALBRIGHT: Thank you very much for a very interesting presentation. I have many different questions.

I just met with the opposition leaders and they clearly feel that they do not have access to the official networks, etc. I think it would be very important for you all to work together, even though there should never be any collusion between the press and politicians. I think that it's very important. I think they are looking for avenues of expression and they have decided to work together as a coalition, which I think is very encouraging. So, there is a natural kind of partnership.

I have to say, listening to you, that my mind just went back a lot about the subjects that I was researching and writing about in looking at press in communist societies and many of the issues are not different, it's mostly one party's problems. It was very interesting.

For instance, the Czech press in 1968, what began to happen was that—especially people on television or radio, because it's harder to censor, would just start talking, whereas in newspapers there is a censor system, where you have to submit and there was a certain amount of time. So, clearly, when one wants to make trouble, then speaking out openly, unless they closed down all the transmitters. But, also, in terms of distribution, again, I studied a great deal how Solidarity press managed to get around a similar system, where there was a monopoly of the distribution of newspapers through the little kiosks that they have in Poland. So, they developed their own distribution system which was very rudimentary, but basically we have a different situation here, because you don't have a labor network that is on your side. It was basically all done by individuals distributing papers in their cars. So, you have, in a strange way, a system that may be more complicated, or a problem that is more complicated, because this is not a straightforward communist system and opposition that is outside of it that is trying to develop an opposition network through its media. But, many of the problems are very similar. I think that it's essential though that you're able to do the kind of work that you do, getting around it. We would like to help you, as much as possible. But, obviously, you raised the problems of outside help seems tainted.

QUESTION: Although we're grateful for every help that we receive, the problem is, as I told you, it's much easier to be a commercial radio station playing music and advertisements, because then you don't have any problems with money. The minute that you start to make a program which can influence people and which can do something about changing the political situation, you need money for this program and you can't make the money to do it. On the other side, advertising goes to the state-controlled media or they just don't pay you. This is the best way. You have lots of adverts on the air and nobody pays you.

SECRETARY ALBRIGHT: This goes to a question that I was going to ask is whether you are in a position to cover the difficult issues of refugee returns, or support for Dayton, etc.

QUESTION: We cover everything. The problem is very specifically, thinking about what is going to be with the program of Radio 101 which is listened by people who are opinion makers in this country, is can we have enough money to do what we used to do two or three years ago next autumn, because for each of those programs reporters could go to report to different places, all the programs which are done live, discussions with phone-ins, high ranking officials from all the parties on the air all the time. We need good professionals to do it, and professionals working in the local media in this country are facing the basic problem of pure survival. This is not a question of making a lot of money. It is a question of can I survive with what I earn. This is the problem with local media. At the state-owned media, you always receive your salary, no matter how low it is, but you do receive it.

SECRETARY ALBRIGHT: I know you get help from various independent aspects of our government, but do you find help from journalists from other countries—

QUESTION: Yes, we do. There is a so-called journalistic network, under the auspices of the journalistic union, our association, which is solely supported by some American and European foundations. Very often we have professors which are chosen by part domestic and part international. Journalists from around the world come to our school and it was officially proclaimed lately in the European Journalistic Union as the best journalistic workshop in all transitional countries. So, we are very well connected with our colleagues all over the world and the countries are very important in our recognition, because our lady president was elected to be the member of the executive board of the World Federation of Journalists. Jokingly, our Minister of Foreign Affairs said that the journalists have done much more in integrating Croatia into the international organization network than it was done by diplomacy itself.

QUESTION: If we can come back to the problem of Croatian Television, we believe, I think that all of us will agree that without solving that crucial problem of Croatian democracy, then you can't solve any other problem. You can't solve the problem of intolerance, ethnic, religious, and democratic tolerance. As you can see, while you have the election campaign in Bosnia, you can't even deal with problems of the Croats in Bosnia, if you don't have proper and professional TV stations. That's why we think it's the number one and top issue on the scale of democratic issues in Croatia. That's why we thank you for supporting that issue and for supporting us and our viewers and population in Croatia. It's not only that we want free media, especially free Croatian Television, it's our population that wants to have it free and impartial.

SECRETARY ALBRIGHT: I can assure you that in my discussions with President Tuđman and with others, I had this right at the top, that is that HRTV cannot operate this way. What we have done is lay out a roadmap for the government, so that it can become a part of the Euro-Atlantic institutional system and having an open and free media, especially a television that functions freely, is one of the benchmarks of what has to happen. Because we agree with you that there is no way to have an open and free system, if you don't have these things.

QUESTION: Because the problem is the third channel. The Croatian third channel is not a guarantee in itself. It's a good step ahead, but I think the most important thing is to reform the HRT, because this is something that we have and to launch a national channel is very costly and probably too much money for this market. But, we need a different approach. Therefore, the best and easiest way is to privatize the third channel and, on the other hand, we need a reform of the existing HRT, not only to remove director generals.

QUESTION: I think the key problem is in the need for mechanisms and system for decreasing influence of the leading party, because there is no guarantee that perhaps tomorrow, if a coalition government would come to power, that the situation would change, because we don't have a mechanism to help in the possibility to help independent journalists.

SECRETARY ALBRIGHT: I just hope that when you get it that you don't put garbage in, and that you don't misuse the great ability to have a free press. It does happen in countries that have a free press, that they misuse their capabilities.

QUESTION: We have to be very careful with professional ownership in the media, because there are no clear cut lines between the private ownership and the state ownership and the collective-owned newspapers and the media. Of course, you have very different situations. You have some private newspapers which are very conservative and open to the influence of the state or the government and so on. You have some kind of social ownership, which is very liberal, open and critical. So, in Croatia, you don't have the publishers association, which should be instrumental in promoting professional criteria. We have an ethics committee, but there is no way to implement decisions without consent of the publishers.

QUESTION: On the other hand, privatization is not the goal for itself, because on the other side we now have the creation of a private monopoly, cross-ownership question hasn't been resolved. We have certain figures: there are owners of TV stations, radio stations, newspapers, magazines, and this is the creation of para-state monopoly. They will probably reform HRT, but on the other side they will create a huge fortress with radio and TV stations and everything.

QUESTION: Maybe it's good to add that the bidding for this new private TV channel hasn't been opened yet, and we suppose it hasn't been opened because it's waiting for someone appropriate, with the money. So what the government does is that they try to smuggle, they always make some cosmetic changes under the pressure of the international community, and they say, look, we do have a private TV channel. But the question is who the owner is, and if the owner is one of them, maybe not really one of them, but someone under the surface, a close friend, relative, son, I don't know who, you have the same thing. And with the large audience in the country watching TV and the only source of information, the most powerful source of information, it's very hard to say to those people, look, this is controlled again. People sometimes do not recognize.

SECRETARY ALBRIGHT: That's right. What is your law about foreign ownership of—

QUESTION: 25% in each media.

QUESTION: 29% in our proposal, because we think that only in partnership with foreign investors it is possible to launch a national channel, and this is also a guarantee against manipulations of the government. If you have the 29% ownership stake, it's hard to manipulate.

QUESTION: If we have another minute, we can discuss private media. It's always a problem, people who invest money want to have some sort of editorial policy control. But, HRT is a public institution. It is being paid every month by every household. That's why that company has to be professional and independent. We can discuss whether Kutle or someone else will have this politician or not, but this is something that should be changed. That's why only part of the truth is to have private media. But this is something that is very important and believe me, everybody is aware of it.

If you can't advertise any dailies or weeklies which are not good for the government, for instance Feral Tribune can't be advertised in our company, although they want to pay. But they have been forbidden because our government doesn't want to raise their circulation through advertising. You can see that it's not only political, it's commercial, HRT is in all senses the fortress of totalitarianism in Croatia. That's why this is so important.

QUESTION: Maybe it's good to say that if you own a TV set you have to pay the fee.

QUESTION: The tragedy is that people are paying and the government, or the President's office to be more specific, is using it for its immediate propaganda.

SECRETARY ALBRIGHT: Thank you. This has been very, very informative, and I just want to assure you as I have that this is number one talking point in terms of—as we talk about the importance of democratization in Croatia, and that it is not real unless there is access and HRT is capable of being able to broadcast different opinions.

I hope very much that the coalition takes this up as one of their major platform issues, because they can be the beneficiaries of it, but I do think there has to be some way that they defend you and you defend them, because it is part of the same problem.

Thank you all very much, I enjoyed this very much. Thank you.

For Further Reading

Alleyne, Mark D. *News Revolution: Political and Economic Decisions about Global Information*. New York: St. Martin's Press, 1997.

Baker, Randall. *Summer in the Balkans: Laughter and Tears after Communism*. West Hartford, Conn.: Kumarian Press, 1994.

Becker, Ted, and Christa Daryl Slaton. *The Future of Teledemocracy*. Westport, Conn.: Praeger, 2000.

Bert, Wayne. *The Reluctant Superpower: United States' Policy in Bosnia, 1991–95*. New York: St. Martin's Press, 1997.

Blanchard, Margaret A. *Exporting the First Amendment: The Press-Government Crusade of 1945–1952*. New York: Longman, 1986.

Blau, George E. *Invasion Balkans!: The German Campaign in the Balkans, Spring 1941*. Shippensburg, Pa.: Burd Street Press, 1997.

Blumler, Jay, and Michael Gurevitch. *The Crisis of Public Communication*. New York: Routledge, 1995.

Carter, F. W., and H. T. Norris, eds. *The Changing Shape of the Balkans*. Boulder, Colo.: Westview Press, 1996.

Cliffe, Lionel, Maureen Ramsay, and Dave Bartlett. *The Politics of Lying: Implications for Democracy*. New York: St. Martin's Press, 2000.

Dahlgren, Peter, and Colin Sparks, eds. *Communication and Citizenship: Journalism and the Public Sphere in the New Media Age*. London and New York: Routledge, 1991.

Danopoulos, Constantine P., and Kostas G. Messas, eds. *Crises in the Balkans: Views from the Participants*. Boulder, Colo.: Westview Press, 1997.

Dawisha, Karen, and Bruce Parrott, eds. *Politics, Power, and the Struggle for Democracy in South-East Europe*. New York: Cambridge University Press, 1997.

Denton, Robert E., Jr., ed. *The 1996 Presidential Campaign: A Communication Perspective*. Westport, Conn.: Praeger, 1998.

Fromkin, David. *Kosovo Crossing: American Ideals Meet Reality on the Balkan Battlefields*. New York: Free Press, 1999.

Gaunt, Philip. *Making the Newsmakers: International Handbook on Journalism Training*. Westport, Conn.: Greenwood Press, 1992.

Gerasimos, Augustinos, ed. *Diverse Paths to Modernity in Southeastern Europe: Essays in National Development*. New York: Greenwood Press, 1991.

Gleason, Gregory. *Federalism and Nationalism: The Struggle for Republican Rights in the USSR*. Boulder, Colo.: Westview Press, 1990.

Glenny, Misha. *The Balkans: Nationalism, War, and the Great Powers, 1804–1999*. New York: Viking, 2000.

Goldstein, Robert Justin, ed. *The War for the Public Mind: Political Censorship in Nineteenth-century Europe*. Westport, Conn.: Praeger, 2000.

Grünbaum, Irene. *Escape through the Balkans: The Autobiography of Irene Grünbaum*. Lincoln: University of Nebraska Press, 1996.

Hereth, Michael. *Alexis de Tocqueville: Threats to Freedom in Democracy*. Durham, N.C.: Duke University Press, 1986.

Jankovic, Branimir M. *The Balkans in International Relations*. Basingstoke, Eng.: Macmillan, 1988.

Jelavich, Barbara. *Russia's Balkan Entanglements, 1806–1914*. New York: Cambridge University Press, 1991.

Kaplan, Robert. *Balkan Ghosts: A Journey through History*. New York: St. Martin's Press, 1993.

Kendall, Kathleen E. *Communication in the Presidential Primaries: Candidates and the Media, 1912–2000*. Westport, Conn.: Praeger, 2000.

Kitromilides, Paschalis. *Enlightenment, Nationalism and Orthodoxy: Studies in the Culture and Political Thought of South-eastern Europe*. Brookfield, Vt.: Variorum, 1994.

Kostis, Kostas P., ed. *Modern Banking in the Balkans and West-European Capital in the Nineteenth and Twentieth Centuries*. Aldershot, Eng.: Brookfield, 1999.

Lanao, Jario E. *Freedom of the Press and the Law: Laws that Affect Journalism in the Americas*. Miami, Fla.: Inter American Press Association, 1999.

Larrabee, F. Stephen. *The Volatile Powder Keg: Balkan Security after the Cold War*. Washington, D.C.: American University Press, 1994.

Lichtenberg, Judith, ed. *Democracy and the Mass Media: A Collection of Essays*. New York: Cambridge University Press, 1990.

Liotta, P. H. *The Wreckage Reconsidered: Five Oxymorons from Balkan Deconstruction*. Lanham, Md.: Lexington Books, 1999.

McCombs, Maxwell, Donald L. Shaw, and David Weaver, eds. *Communication and Democracy: Exploring the Intellectual Frontiers in Agenda-setting Theory*. Mahwah, N.J.: Lawrence Erlbaum Associates, 1997.

Mestrovic, Stjepan G., Slaven Letica, and Miroslav Goreta. *Habits of the Balkan Heart: Social Character and the Fall of Communism*. College Station: Texas A&M University Press, 1993.

Mouzelis, Nicos P. *Politics in the Semi-periphery: Early Parliamentarianism and Late Industrialisation in the Balkans and Latin America*. Basingstoke, Eng.: Macmillan, 1986.

Moy, Patricia, and Michael Pfau. *With Malice toward All?: The Media and Public Confidence in Democratic Institutions.* Westport, Conn.: Praeger, 2000.

Neuman, Russell W., Marion R. Just, and Ann N. Crigler. *Common Knowledge: News and the Construction of Political Meaning.* Chicago: University of Chicago Press, 1992.

Norris, H. T. *Islam in the Balkans: Religion and Society between Europe and the Arab World.* Columbia: University of South Carolina Press, 1993.

Omrcanin, Ivo. *Holocaust of Croatians.* Washington, D.C.: Samizdat, 1986.

O'Neil, Patrick H., ed. *Communicating Democracy: The Media and Political Transitions.* Boulder, Colo.: Lynne Rienner, 1998.

Palairet, M. R. *The Balkan Economies 1800–1914: Evolution without Development.* New York: Cambridge University Press, 1997.

Pavlowitch, Stevan K. *A History of the Balkans, 1804–1945.* New York: Longman, 1999.

Pilger, John. *Hidden Agendas.* New York: New Press, 1998.

Ponder, Stephen. *Managing the Press: Origins of the Media Presidency, 1897–1933.* New York: St. Martin's Press, 1999.

Poulton, Hugh. *The Balkans: Minorities and States in Conflict.* London: Minority Rights Group, 1993.

Poulton, Hugh, and Suha Taji-Faroukl, eds. *Muslim Identity and the Balkan State.* New York: New York University Press in association with the Islamic Council, 1997.

Pridham, Geoffrey, and Tom Gallagher, eds. *Experimenting with Democracy: Regime Change in the Balkans.* New York: Routledge, 2000.

Reeves, Geoffrey W. *Communications and the "Third World."* New York: Routledge, 1993.

Sabol, Zeljko, ed. *Croatian Parliament.* Zagreb: Parliament of the Republic of Croatia: Nakladni zavod Globus: Skolska knjiga, 1995.

Shoup, Paul S., ed. *Problems of Balkan Security: Southeastern Europe in the 1990s.* Washington, D.C.: Wilson Center Press, 1990.

Sikiric, Andelko, ed. *Principal State Acts* [Collection of the English Translations of the Principal State Acts of the Republic of Croatia]. Zagreb: Parliament of the Republic of Croatia, 1993.

Stahl, Paul H., ed. *Name and Social Structure: Examples from Southeast Europe.* Boulder, Colo.: East European Monographs, 1998.

Stempel, Guido H., III, and Jacqueline Nash Gifford, eds. *Historical Dictionary of Political Communication in the United States.* Westport, Conn.: Greenwood Press, 1999.

Stoianovich, Traian. *Between East and West: The Balkan and Mediterranean Worlds.* New Rochelle, N.Y.: A. D. Caratzas, 1992.

———. *Balkan Worlds: The First and Last Europe.* Armonk, N.Y.: M. E. Sharpe, 1994.

Stuckey, Mary E. *The Theory and Practice of Political Communication Research.* Albany: State University of New York Press, 1996.

Tanter, Raymond, and John Psarouthakis. *Balancing in the Balkans.* New York: St. Martin's Press, 1999.

Thompson, Mark. *Forging War: The Media in Serbia, Croatia, Bosnia and Hercegovina.* Luton, Eng.: University of Luton Press, 1999.

Todorova, Mariia Nikolaeva. *Imagining the Balkans.* New York: Oxford University Press, 1997.

Tsipis, Kosta, ed. *Common Security Regimes in the Balkans*. Boulder, Colo.: East European Monographs, 1996.

U.S. Congress. House Committee on International Relations. The U.S. Role in Kosovo. 106th Cong., 1st sess., February 10, 1999. Washington, D.C.: Government Printing Office, 1999.

————. Hearing on the Balkans: What are U.S. Interest and the Goals of U.S. Engagement? 106th Cong., 1st sess., August 4, 1999. Washington, D.C.: Government Printing Office, 2000.

Watts, Duncan. *Political Communication Today*. New York: Manchester University Press; New York: Distributed by St. Martin's Press, 1997.

Weaver, James H., Michael T. Rock, and Kenneth Kusterer. *Achieving Broad-based Sustainable Development: Governance, Environment, and Growth*. West Hartford, Conn.: Kumarian Press, 1997.

Woodhull, Nancy J., and Robert W. Snyder, eds. *Journalists in Peril*. New Brunswick, N.J.: Transaction Publishers, 1998.

Young, Peter R., ed. *Defence and the Media in Time of Limited War*. Portland, Or.: Frank Cass, 1992.

Zarkovic Bookman, Milica. *Economic Decline and Nationalism in the Balkans*. New York: St. Martin's Press, 1994.

Zlatar, Zdenko. *Our Kingdom Come: The Counter-Reformation, the Republic of Dubrovnik, and the Liberation of the Balkan Slavs*. Boulder, Colo.: East European Monographs; New York: Distributed by Columbia University Press, 1992.

Index

About the Authors

STJEPAN MALOVIĆ is Professor of Journalism at the University of Zagreb and educational director of the Croatian Press Association. A practicing journalist since 1968, Malović reported on domestic and foreign affairs during the years of Communism, through the war and transition period, and into the current era of press reform in Croatia. The author of two earlier books, Malović was Editor-in-Chief of *Vecernji list*, the largest daily newspaper in Croatia.

GARY W. SELNOW is Professor of Communication at San Francisco State University and director of World Internet Resources for Education and Development (WiRED), a non-profit corporation that brings the Internet to war-torn regions. Selnow is the author/co-author of six earlier books, including *Society's Impact on Television* and *High Tech Campaigns*. *Electronic Whistle-Stops*, his latest book about the use of the Internet in American politics, was published by Praeger in 1998.